Cariboo Trips & Trails

Cariboo Trips & Trails

A guide to British Columbia's Cariboo Gold Rush Country

Murphy Shewchuk

Fitzhenry & Whiteside

Fitzhenry and Whiteside Limited
195 Allstate Parkway
Markham, Ontario L3R 4T8

In the United States:
311 Washington Street,
Brighton, Massachusetts 02135

www.fitzhenry.ca   godwit@fitzhenry.ca

Fitzhenry & Whiteside acknowledges with thanks the Canada Council for the Arts, and the Ontario Arts Council for their support of our publishing program. We acknowledge the financial support of the Government of Canada through the Book Publishing Industry Development Program (BPIDP) for our publishing activities.

 Canada Council Conseil des Arts
for the Arts du Canada

 ONTARIO ARTS COUNCIL
CONSEIL DES ARTS DE L'ONTARIO

Library and Archives Canada Cataloguing in Publication
Shewchuk, Murphy
Cariboo trips & trails : a guide to British Columbia's Cariboo Gold
Rush country / Murphy Shewchuk.
Includes index.
ISBN 978-1-55455-031-9
1. Trails—British Columbia—Cariboo Region—Guidebooks.
2. Trails—British Columbia—Chilcotin River Region—Guidebooks.
3. Cariboo Region (B.C.)—Guidebooks. 4. Chilcotin River Region
(B.C.)—Guidebooks. I. Title. II. Title: Cariboo trips and trails.
FC3845.C3A3 2008   917.11'75045   C2008-900266-0

United States Cataloguing-in-Publication Data
Shewchuk, Murphy.
Cariboo trips & trails : a guide to British Columbia's Cariboo Gold Rush country / Murphy Shewchuk.
[340] p. : photos., maps ; cm.
Includes bibliographical references and index.
Summary: A guide book of the Cariboo-Chilcotin region of British Columbia.
ISBN: 978-1-55455-031-9 (pbk.)
1. Trails—British Columbia—Cariboo Region—Guidebooks. 2. Trails—British Columbia—Chilcotin River. 3. Region—
Guidebooks. 3. Cariboo Region (B.C.)—Guidebooks. 4. Chilcotin River Region (B.C.)—Guidebooks. I. Cariboo trips and
trails. II. Title.
917.175/045 dc22 F1089.C3.S549 2008

Cover and interior design by Kerry Plumley
Cover image by Murphy Shewchuck
All images courtesy of Murphy Shewchuck unless otherwise credited
Printed and bound in Canada

1 3 5 7 9 10 8 6 4 2

Dedication

To Katharine

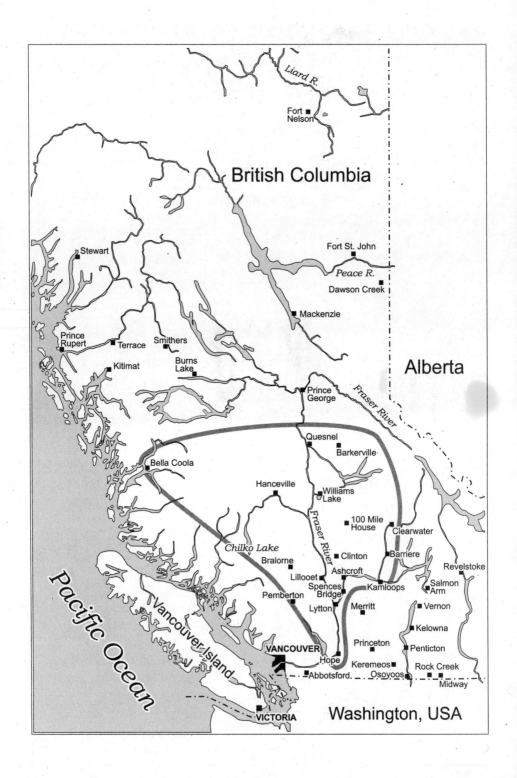

CONTENTS

List of Maps   Page xi
Introduction   Page xiii
Checklist for Camping   Page xvii
Acknowledgments   Pabe xix
Topographic Maps   Page xxi
Abbreviations Used   Page xxiii
Symbols Used   Page xxiv

The Fraser Canyon Route:
The Wagon Road to the Cariboo

Chapter 1   Trans-Canada Highway: Hope to Lytton   Page 5
             The Alexandra Bridges   Page 10
             Hell's Gate Fishways   Page 15
             SS *Skuzzy*   Page 16
Chapter 2   Lytton to Lillooet via Highway 12   Page 19
Chapter 3   Lillooet to Lytton via the West Bank of the Fraser   Page 29
             Earlscourt Farm   Page 37
Chapter 4   Exploring the Fraser River Trail:
             Lillooet to Williams Lake   Page 41
Chapter 5   The Marble Canyon Route:
             Highway 99 — Lillooet to Hat Creek House   Page 55

The Thompson River Route: Sagebrush, Bunchgrass, and Rattlesnakes

Chapter 6	The Thompson River Road: Exploring Beyond	
	the Asphalt Ribbon	Page 65
	The Skihist Park Trail	Page 69
	The Great Landslide	Page 76
	Widow Smith of Spence's Bridge	Page 78
	Ashcroft Opera House	Page 81
	Walhachin: Garden of Eden	Page 84
	Hoodoos on the Thompson	Page 88
Chapter 7	Whitewater Weekend: Rafting the Thompson	
	and Fraser Rivers	Page 93
Chapter 8	Hat Creek Loop: A Scarce Natural Treasure	Page 101
Chapter 9	Deadman-Vidette Road: Red Cliffs and	
	Blue Lakes	Page 113
Chapter 10	Red Lake Road: (Tranquille – Criss Creek Road)	
	Kamloops – Red Lake – Savona	Page 124

Cariboo Roadhouses: The "Waggon" Road to Barkerville

Chapter 11	Highway 97: The Cariboo Road	
	Cache Creek to Quesnel	Page 141
Chapter 12	Highway 26: The Barkerville Road	
	Quesnel to Barkerville	Page 164
Chapter 13	Southwest Cariboo Loop: Clinton – Kelly Lake	
	– Big Bar – Clinton	Page 175

Chapter 14   Green Lake Loop: 70 Mile House to 100 Mile House
via Green Lake, Lone Butte, and Horse Lake   Page 187

Chapter 15   West Bonaparte Loop: 70 Mile House –
Bonaparte Lake – Loon Lake – 20 Mile House   Page 195

Chapter 16   Bridge Lake Road (Highway 24):
93 Mile House – Bridge Lake – Little Fort   Page 204

Chapter 17   Moose Valley Canoe Route: An Alternative
to Bowron Lake Provincial Park   Page 212

Chapter 18   East Cariboo Loop: 100 Mile House – Horsefly –
Likely – McLeese Lake   Page 221

Chapter 19   Backroad to Barkerville:
150 Mile House – Likely – Barkerville   Page 236

Chapter 20   Cariboo Lake Country Backroad: Clearwater to
100 Mile House   Page 249

West of the Fraser River: The South Chilcotin Connection

Chapter 21   Bridge River Gold:
Lillooet – Gold Bridge – Bralorne   Page 261

Chapter 22   Coast Mountains Circle Tour: Lillooet –
Pemberton – Gold Bridge – Lillooet   Page 279

The Chilcotin Plateau:
The Connection to the Pacific

Chapter 23   Chilcotin Country Highway 20: Williams Lake
             to Bella Coola   Page 294
Chapter 24   The Dome Trail   Page 303
Chapter 25   Ts'il?os Provincial Park:
             Exploring Chilko Lake Country   Page 308

Wells Gray Provincial Park: Wilderness,
Waterfalls, and Volcanoes

Chapter 26   Wells Gray Provincial Park West:
             100 Mile House to Mahood Lake   Page 323
Chapter 27   Wells Gray Provincial Park East:
             Clearwater to Clearwater Lake   Page 333
Chapter 28   Trophy Mountain Trail   Page 345
Chapter 29   Sticta Falls Trail   Page 349
Chapter 30   Clearwater River Road and Mahood River Trial   Page 352
Chapter 31   A Jewel in a Snowy Setting: Creating the Landscape Page 359
Chapter 32   The Interior Salish First Nations Peoples:
             The First Known Human Inhabitants   Page 362
Chapter 33   Fur and Gold: Before the Rush   Page 369
Chapter 34   Cattle Ranches   Page 373
Chapter 35   Rockhound Paradise   Page 375
Chapter 36   Gems and Minerals   Page 382
Chapter 37   Making Your GPS Work for You!
             GPS Basics and More   Page 384

             Information Sources   Page 392
             About the Author   Page 399
             Bibliography   Page 401
             Index   Page 404

List of Maps

British Columbia   Page vi

Hope-Lytton   Page 6

Lytton-Lillooet   Page 20

Lytton-Lillooet Loop   Page 28

Lillooet-Williams Lake   Page 40

Lillooet-Hat Creek   Page 56

Spences Bridge-Kamloops   Page 66

Hat Creek   Page 102

Deadman-Vidette Road   Page 114

Red Lake Road   Page 125

Williams Lake-Barkerville   Page 166

Southwest Cariboo   Page 174

Green Lake   Page 186

Southeast Cariboo   Page 196

Moose Valley   Page 213

East Cariboo Loop   Page 220

Clearwater-100 Mile House   Page 250

Bridge River   Page 262

Williams Lake-Bella Coola   Page 295

The Dome Trail   Page 303

Chilko Lake   Page 309

Mahood Lake   Page 324

Clearwater-Wells Gray   Page 332

Trophy Mountain   Page 346

Sticta Falls Trail   Page 351

Mahood River   Page 353

Introduction

The first thing you will note as you scan through this book is that it isn't just about that nebulous, hard to define British Columbia Interior region called the Cariboo. With 2008 marking the 150th anniversary of the start of the 1858 Fraser River gold rush (which then became the 1860s Cariboo gold rush), it would be difficult to write a book about the region without expanding the boundaries to take in the Fraser Canyon as far south as Hope. Equally difficult to ignore are the parts of British Columbia west of the Fraser River known as the Bridge River Country and the Chilcotin.

The eastern boundary of the Cariboo is also difficult to define. Barkerville was the world-famous culmination of the Cariboo gold rush, but the mountain ranges to the east and south are part of Wells Gray Provincial Park, which is also accessible from Clearwater on Yellowhead Highway 5 and the North Thompson Valley. While the northern boundary of the Cariboo Regional District is north of Quesnel, a trip up Highway 97 soon shows that the grasslands plateau, so much a dominant feature of the Cariboo, has given way to the timber-clad hills of the Prince George region.

A closer study of this book will also reveal that it isn't just about backroads and trails. It is a guide to a selection of highways, secondary roads, backroads, and even a few trails that wind through the Thompson-Cariboo region. It is also an attempt to answer a few of the questions that come up as you explore this spectacular region.

What shaped the Cariboo and created the unusual land forms and landmarks? Who came here first and who lives here now? When was the region first explored by Europeans? Where does this road lead? Why did it go there? And, probably as important, can I follow the road today?

I can't answer all the questions, nor can I cover more than a sample of the tens of thousands of kilometres of roads and trails throughout the region. However, I do hope that I can give you enough information to spark your curiosity and help you discover the riches that continue to attract people to the Cariboo.

Simon Fraser, an explorer of the nineteenth century fur trade era, "discovered" Lytton (or *Tlkumtcin*, as the First Nations peoples knew it) in 1808 while searching for an economical trade route to the Pacific Ocean. "Discovered" is a word that frequently appears in our written history, but the Interior Salish and Athapaskan

First Nations peoples "discovered" this land as much as 10,000 years before European sailors and fur traders "discovered" it. Some anthropologists suggest that Lytton may be the oldest continuously inhabited settlement in North America.

Lifestyles Changed

While the First Nations peoples lived with the land, changing it little over the centuries, the fur trade "monoculture" prompted a significant, though slow, change in their life patterns. The discovery of gold and the subsequent swarm of prospectors, packers, merchants, and various hangers-on drastically speeded up the change as they explored every river and creek from Chilliwack to Prince George. The newcomers brought tools and clothing and guns and, in later years, alcohol and disease that decimated many First Nations villages.

The influx of people also changed the land to suit their ranching and transportation needs. Timber was cut for homes, fences, and corrals; cleared for fields and roads; and burned for heating fuel and steam to drive the sternwheelers and the mills. The

Gold can be credited (or blamed) with the rapid development of the BC Interior in the 1860s.

grasslands were ploughed or overgrazed, altering the wildlife patterns forever.

All this is part of the Cariboo history, but history can be important to the backroads explorer. Knowing where the roads were going and why they went there can make today's exploring that much more enjoyable.

The Cariboo is Fragile

As a note of caution, the dry grasslands of the Cariboo are fragile and should be treated with respect. Please drive only on established roadways; the spring runoff or a sudden rainstorm can turn a hillside tire rut into a major gully, destroying the delicate rangeland.

Most important of all, recognize that this land is someone's home. Be a good guest. Do not leave refuse behind. Stow it where containers are provided or take it out with you. A discarded bottle could start a fire in the hot sun, or a discarded can could create a trap for wildlife.

Trail Etiquette

Trails are often traversed by hooves, feet, and wheels, so to avoid conflict, danger, and damage, use common sense, communication, and courtesy. Trail protocol suggests that the most mobile yields the right of way, but there are exceptions to this rule. Ideally, cyclists yield to everyone, and hikers yield to horses. A loaded string of horses going uphill always has the right of way, and a cyclist climbing steeply will appreciate the same courtesy.

Hikers: If you encounter horse riders, your group should step off to the same side of the trail, the lower side if possible, allowing two to three metres for them to pass. If you come up on horses from behind, greet the riders before you pass so they're aware you're there. Otherwise, you might startle either the animal or rider.

Mountain Bikers: Always anticipate a horse or hiker around a blind curve. Prevent the possible sudden, unexpected encounter from a bike's quick and silent approach. Yield to hikers and equestrians. Get off the bike and move to the lower side of the trail to let horses pass. When approaching from behind, speak so they know you're there. Learn to minimize damage to trails with techniques such as riding and not sliding, and cycle on designated trails. Bicycle tires easily damage meadows. Stay off trails when they're wet and muddy. Otherwise, they'll become pathways for water erosion.

Horse Riders: Use an experienced, steady mount, and give clear directions to other trail users on how you would like them to stand clear. In steep, rough country, downhill traffic yields to uphill travellers, but use common sense. Whoever can pull off easiest should. Avoid soft and muddy trails. Warn others of wire, potholes, and boggy areas. Above all, respect private property, and "No Trespassing" signs, and leave gates as you found them.

IMPORTANT NOTICE

The backroads and/or trails described in this book are not patrolled or supervised. Cellular phone coverage may be marginal or non-existent. Always carry appropriate emergency supplies and maps. A compass and/or GPS will also be helpful. If using electronic equipment, be sure to have fresh and spare batteries.

Although every effort has been made to provide accurate information, road and trail conditions in this region are constantly changing. Consequently, neither the author nor the publisher can guarantee the continuing accuracy of this information.

We look forward to corrections and comments on ways that you think this book can be improved. Please write to the author care of the publisher at the address listed in the front of the book.

GPS References

I have included Global Positioning System (GPS) latitude and longitude references for many points of interest in this book. The information has been taken directly from field data files generated by a variety of Garmin GPS receivers. In general, these references have been checked using OziExplorer, Garmin MapSource, and Google Earth and should be accurate to within 15 metres. However, errors of up to 100 metres are possible as are errors in data entry (mine and yours). Tree cover, satellite configuration, and equipment settings may also contribute to differences in readings. The GPS references should help in locating such places as backroad and trail junctions, but should not be relied on to replace maps, a compass, and good "bush" sense.

A hand held GPS, particularly one equipped with or capable of accepting topographical maps, is a useful tool for any backcountry explorer. Note that many of the "street" GPS units do not have the topographical detail necessary for backcountry exploring.

Checklist for Camping

Backcountry camping can be a wonderful experience. However, it is often too easy to forget essential pieces of equipment until you are in the wilderness — then, it is just too embarrassing to admit that you are rubbing two sticks together because you forgot the matches.

The following list of frequently used camping items (in alphabetical order) was provided by Jim Reid of the Coleman Camping Company. Use it when planning your next trip, and then adapt it to your own needs.

You may want to keep track of those pieces of equipment that you had and didn't need, or needed and didn't have. This will help you on your future trips. Good camping.

- ❏ Air mattress
- ❏ Blankets
- ❏ Camera and film or memory cards
- ❏ Coffee pot
- ❏ Compass and/or GPS
- ❏ Cooking utensils
- ❏ Cooler
- ❏ Dishpan and pot scrubbers
- ❏ Eating utensils
- ❏ First aid kit
- ❏ Flares/Mirror
- ❏ Flashlight and spare batteries
- ❏ Folding chairs or camp stools
- ❏ Folding stands for cooler or stove
- ❏ Fuel
- ❏ Ground cloth
- ❏ Hand axe
- ❏ Ice or ice substitutes
- ❏ Insect repellent
- ❏ Knife
- ❏ Lantern and mantles
- ❏ Lighter – disposable butane
- ❏ Maps
- ❏ Matches and waterproof holder
- ❏ Pad and pen or pencil
- ❏ Plastic zipper bags
- ❏ Prescription medicine
- ❏ Radiant heater (cold weather)
- ❏ Rope, cord or wire
- ❏ Shovel – small folding type
- ❏ Sleeping bags
- ❏ Snakebite Kit
- ❏ Soap - biodegradable
- ❏ Stove
- ❏ Sunglasses
- ❏ Suntan oil or lotion
- ❏ Tablecloth
- ❏ Tent and poles
- ❏ Tent stakes
- ❏ Toilet paper
- ❏ Toiletries
- ❏ Tool kit, hammer and nails
- ❏ Towels – paper and bath
- ❏ Trash bags
- ❏ Water containers
- ❏ Water purification tablets

Acknowledgments

British Columbia's Cariboo-Chilcotin region has fascinated me since I was a teenager growing up in the gold mining communities of Pioneer and Bralorne, over 100 kilometres west of Lillooet. The mines offered a far different lifestyle and the Coast Mountains were a drastically different terrain from the Saskatchewan farm that was my home until I was 12 years old.

In the 1950s, Pioneer was a community of 200 to 300 people at an elevation of 1,220 metres in a deep V-shaped valley. Gold drew people to this wilderness community. The mine supplied most of the employment and owned most of the houses and facilities. TV and daytime radio reception was non-existent. With the support of the mining company, the community built its own recreation facilities, such as a curling rink, hockey rink, and softball field. Our home was in "Top Townsite" on a natural bench on the mountainside. Our backyard was 2,595-metre-high Mount Fergusson. Our playground was a vast network of mining roads and trails — some nearly a century old — that extended up the Cadwallader Creek valley and into the surrounding mountains.

Without TV to distract us, my school chums (Alfie Madsen, Lloyd Smith, Fred Baumbach, Danny Miller, Bobby Macpherson and others) and I made our own entertainment. As these were the days when "quality parental supervision" had yet to be invented, this included exploring the mountain trails, building tree forts, fishing in the streams and lakes, skiing on the slopes, and generally testing ourselves and our environment. Despite a few close calls and more than a few bruises, we learned to appreciate the land and what it had to offer. We also learned that "Nature doesn't give a damn" about us and that we were the only ones responsible for our survival.

After high school, we went on to make our livings in a variety of ways and places. My work took me across the country, but eventually brought me back — for a couple of years — to the Bridge River Valley. It was during the early 1970s that I met Margaret "Ma" Murray, the feisty editor of the Bridge River – *Lillooet News* and began writing outdoor material for her paper. After a move to Kamloops, I developed an outdoor column for the *Kamloops Daily Sentinel* and this branched out to articles for Art Downs' *BC Outdoors* magazine and a host of other magazines and books.

The mountains and my friends helped foster my appreciation for the outdoors, and my editors influenced how I presented my views about my surroundings. My readers have also encouraged me with suggestions and feedback. However, my greatest appreciation goes to the museum curators, historians, and fellow writers who have been free with their information and advice over the past half century. The list is long, but those near the top are Mary Balf, formerly of the Kamloops Museum; Renee Chipman, formerly of the Lillooet Museum; Dorothy Dodge of Lytton; Pat Lean, formerly of Merritt; Peggy Patenaude of 153 Mile House; plus a host of protectors of history at such "exotic" places as Clinton, 100 Mile House, Horsefly, Likely, Quesnel Forks, and Barkerville.

While the history of the region is important, the geography is of equal value. For backroads maps and information, I wish to thank the staff at the BC Ministry of Forests and the BC Ministry of Tourism, Sport and the Arts.

I would especially like to thank my wife, Katharine, for her hours of note-taking and expert advice on the flora and fauna of the region.

Murphy Shewchuk

Topographic Maps

The following 1:50,000 topographic maps are referred to in this book.

100 Mile House, BC 92 P/11.
Alkali Lake, BC 92 O/16.
Ashcroft, BC 92 I/11.
Beaver Creek, BC 93 A/5
Big Bar Creek, BC 92 O/1.
Birkenhead Lake, BC 92 J/10.
Boston Bar, BC 92 H/14.
Bralorne, BC 92 J/15.
Bridge Lake, BC 92 P/7.
Bridge River, BC 92 J/16.
Cache Creek, BC 92 I/14.
Canim Lake, BC 92 P/15.
Cariboo Lake, BC 93 A/14.
Cherry Creek, BC 92 I/10.
Chu Chua Creek, BC 92 P/8.
Clearwater, BC 92 P/9.
Clinton, BC 92 P/4.
Criss Creek, BC 92 P/2.
Deka Lake, BC 92 P/10.
Dog Creek, BC 92 O/9.
Drummond Lake, BC 93 B/2.
Duffey Lake, BC 92 J/8.
Empire Valley, BC 92 O/8.
Green Lake, BC 92 P/6.
Gustafsen Lake, BC 92 P/12.
Hanceville, BC 92 O/14.
Hope, BC 92 H/6.
Hydraulic, BC 93 A/12.

Jesmond, BC 92 P/5.
Kamloops, BC 92 I/9.
Lac La Hache, BC 92 P/14.
Lillooet, BC 92 I/12.
Loon Lake, BC 92 P/3.
Lytton, BC 92 I/14.
MacKay River, BC 92 A/7.
Mahood Lake, BC 92 P/16.
McKinley Creek, BC 93 A/2.
Mitchell Lake, BC 93 A/15.
Murtle Lake, BC 83 D/4.
North Creek, BC 92 J/11.
Pavilion, BC 92 I/13.
Pemberton, BC 92 J/7.
Riske Creek, BC 92 O/15.
Scuzzy Mountain, BC 92 H/13.
Shalalth, BC 92 J/9.
Soda Creek, BC 93 B/8.
Spanish Lake, BC 93 A/11.
Spectacle Lakes, BC 93 H/3.
Spences Bridge, BC 92 I/6.
Spuzzum, BC 92 H/11.
Stein River, BC 92 I/5.
Tranquille River, BC 92 I/15.
Vavenby, BC 82 M/12.
Wells, BC 93 H/4.
West Raft River, BC 82 M/13.
Williams Lake, BC 93 B/1.

The paper maps may be available from major book stores.

They are also available on CD-ROM from:
Spectrum Digital Imaging Ltd.
#3 - 3990 Marguerite Street
Vancouver, BC V6J 4G1
Tel: (778) 327-9752 Fax: (866) 524-2865
E-mail: spectrumdigital@shaw.ca
Website: http://www.mapsdigital.com/

At the time of writing, Spectrum Digital Imaging's following DVD-ROM contained all the required maps and more: Cat. 6001 B.C. South of Latitude 55 (740 Maps)

There are also a variety of other map sources available through book stores or on the Internet.

GPS Maps

The Garmin MapSource Topo Canada CD-ROM contains the maps for the region. These maps can be viewed on your computer or uploaded into the newer Garmin GPS units. I use a Garmin GPSmap 76CSx and find it extremely helpful in tracking my travels as well as determining my location when exploring.

In addition to the traditional paper maps, digital maps of the Cariboo area are available from a variety of sources.

Backroad Mapbooks

Mussio Ventures Ltd. publishes a series of mapbooks in both digital and bound paper formats. These maps can be helpful when following the descriptions in this book. If you are considering the CD-ROM versions, the Thompson Okanagan CD covers the southern portion and the Cariboo Chilcotin Coast CD covers the north and west parts of the region. The digital version uses Memory-Map Navigator. In this program, waypoint data can be entered using the Overlay -> Create New -> Mark function. Additional information is available from www.backroadmapbooks.com and www.memory-map.com .

Google Earth Satellite Images

As we go to press, the Google Earth satellite maps (http://earth.google.com/) for the rural areas do not present enough detail to differentiate the trails from the surrounding countryside, but they do present an exciting way to view the terrain and gain some perspective before embarking on an exploration trip. Google's "Placemark" tool can be used to enter the Latitude and Longitude information presented here to mark important landmarks and trail junctions.

Abbreviations Used

B & B	bed and breakfast
cm	centimetre
CPR	Canadian Pacific Railway
elev.	elevation
FOSS	Friends of the South Slopes
FS	Forest Service
FSR	Fire Service Road
GNR	Great Northern Railway
GPS	Global Positioning System
ha	hectare
hwy	highway
JS	authored by Judie Steeves
km	kilometre
KVR	Kettle Valley Railway
LRMP	Land and Resource Management Plan
m	metre
MS	authored by Murphy Shewchuk
rd	road
RV	recreational vehicle
stn	station
TCT	Trans Canada Trail
topo	topographic or topographic map

Symbols Used

📷 Photography Opportunities   🛏 Accommodations

🦌 Wildlife Viewing   🍴 Meal Service

🐦 Bird Watching   ⛽ Fuel

🌼 Wildflowers   📞 Public Telephone

🚶 Interpretive Trail   ➕ First Aid Station

🔭 Point of Interest   **H** Hospital

👥 Viewpoint   **M** Museum

🌲 Picnic Site   ✈ Airport

⛺ Open Picnic Shelter   **?** Information Centre

🏠 Enclosed Picnic Shelter   ⚓ Marina

🛖 Sleeping Shelter   🏊 Swimming Beach

⛺ Wilderness Campsite   🎣 Angling

🚐 RV Park   ❄ Ice Fishing

🏕 Campground   🚤 Boat Launch

🔥 Campfire Ring   🛶 Canoe Portage

🚽 RV Sani-Station   🚣 Canoeing & Kayaking

🚻 Public Washrooms   ⛵ Sailing

📻 Amphitheatre   🚤 Motor Boating

Windsurfing

 Hiking Trail

 Rock Climbing Route

 Golf Course

 Rockhounding

 Shooting Sports

 Horse Riding

 Bicycle Trail

 Mountain Bicycle Trail

 Motorcycle Trail

 Four-Wheel-Drive Road

 Winter Sports

 Alpine Ski Hill

 Nordic Ski Trail

 Snowshoe Trail

 Sledding Hill

 Ice Skating

 Snowmobile Trail

 Chairlift

 Gondola Lift

 Cave

 Tunnel

 Recycling

 Radio Observatory

 Wheelchair Access

 Parking

The Fraser Canyon Route: The Wagon Road to the Cariboo

Prehistoric Highway

Although archaeologists such as David and Mary Jo Sanger suggest that First Nations peoples have been living in the Fraser Canyon region for at least 6,000 and as many as 9,000 years, it wasn't until two centuries ago that Simon Fraser and his party of 24 men became the first Europeans to traverse the canyon "highway."

"I have been for a long period among the Rocky Mountains," Simon Fraser wrote in June 1808 while in the vicinity of Hell's Gate Rapids, "but have never seen anything to equal this country, for I cannot find words to describe our situation at times. We had to pass where no human being should venture."

After reaching the Pacific on July 2, 1808, Fraser retraced his steps along the spiderweb of trails and ladders on the canyon walls. Fraser's report was so damning that it was 16 years before anyone bothered to re-examine the Fraser Canyon route. In December 1824, James McMillan explored the canyon, hoping to establish a fur brigade route from the coast to the interior, but his assessment was equally negative. In 1828, Hudson's Bay Company (HBC) Governor George Simpson and his crew ran the canyon with canoes, but the ride was so challenging that Simpson decided that the river "… cannot under any circumstances be attempted by loaded craft …"

The fur traders again attempted to use the lower Fraser Canyon as part of the brigade route in 1846-47, but were no more successful and decided on an overland route from the Nicola Valley to Tulameen, and over the Cascade Mountains to Hope. The HBC Brigade Trail between Tulameen and Hope remained the prime route of commerce from 1848 to 1860.

The Fraser River Gold Rush

Word of the discovery of gold in what is now British Columbia leaked out a decade later, and the spring of 1858 saw a swarm of gold seekers invade the fur trader's domain. On March 23, 1858, the first big strike was made on a sandbar about 16 kilometres north of Hope. Hill's Bar relinquished $2 million in gold before the end of the season. As the summer ended, paddlewheel steamboats were plying the river as far north as Yale, where the cliffs and rapids blocked further reasonable transportation.

A mule trail was attempted, but transport was limited until a wagon road was blasted out of the Fraser Canyon walls and Joseph Trutch's Alexandra Bridge was completed in September 1863. The gold seekers swarmed north into the Cariboo, leaving behind worked-over gravel bars and First Nations communities in disarray.

When the Cariboo's "easy pickings" were exhausted, the miners and those who stripped them of their new-found wealth moved on to the Columbia River and the Kootenays and, later, to the Cassiar and the Klondike. Some even shipped out to New Zealand and Australia.

Twin Steel Ribbons

Nearly two decades later, on May 15, 1880, the first blast of No. 1 tunnel, just

A stop-of-interest plaque at Jackass Mountain, 20 kilometres south of Lytton.

A Canadian Pacific Railway bridge across the Fraser River near Cicso (Siska), approximately six kilometres south of Lytton.

north of Yale, marked the beginning of Canadian Pacific Railway (CPR) construction in the canyon — and the beginning of the demise of the Cariboo Wagon Road. The horse-drawn wagons of the B.C. Express Company that had carried freight to the goldfields were now carrying supplies for the railway workers — and charging $10 a ton to work themselves out of business.

By the spring of 1884, despite all manner of natural and man-made obstacles, including an earthquake and the deaths of countless workers, the railway was completed through the Fraser Canyon. The Chinese labourers, the bridge builders, and the track layers pressed on up the Thompson River to Ashcroft and eastward to Savona and Kamloops. In October 1885, contractor Andrew Onderdonk paid off his army of workers at Yale, and the ensuing party marked the end of the Fraser Canyon's railway boom.

Five years after the contract to build the Canadian Pacific Railway was signed, the initial construction of the railway was completed. On November 7, 1885, a group of railway executives and workers watched as Donald Smith, an enthusiastic advocate and financial supporter of the CPR, hammered in the last spike at Craigellachie, British Columbia.

Floods Finish off the Wagon Road

The Fraser River was man's constant nemesis. It didn't play favourites, taking out the railway and the wagon road at frequent intervals. In 1876, floods washed out parts of the wagon road. In 1882, the river exceeded the previous high-water mark, damaging both railway and roadway. In 1894, the river launched an all-out assault on the intruders. Every bridge along the wagon road was washed out. Trutch's Alexandra Bridge, normally 30 metres above the river, was so severely damaged that it was never repaired. While construction crews rebuilt the railway and most of the wagon road, the gap remained at Alexandra until A.L. Carruthers' bridge was opened 32 years later.

The Trans-Canada Highway

The present highway system was approved by the *Trans-Canada Highway Act* of 1948, with construction commencing in 1950. Travellers in the Fraser Canyon in the 1950s may remember the constant delays and detours as mountains were moved to turn a rocky wagon trail into a two-lane highway. While the Trans-Canada Highway was officially opened in 1962, the current Alexandra Bridge wasn't opened until a year later.

The present highway remains primarily a two-lane route. Although rock bolts have replaced cedar roots, the highway still clings to the canyon walls in much the same manner as the ladders that carried Simon Fraser and his men.

Enjoy the scenery, but remember that daydreaming can be deadly.

CHAPTER 1

Trans-Canada Highway: Hope to Lytton

STATISTICS

	Map see page 6
Distance:	110 km, Hope to Lytton.
Travel Time:	Two to three hours.
Condition:	Paved highway.
Season:	Open year-round.
Topo Maps:	Hope, BC 92 H/6.
(1:50,000)	Spuzzum, BC 92 H/11.
	Boston Bar, BC 92 H/14.
	Scuzzy Mountain, BC 92 H/13.
	Lytton, BC 92 I/4.
Communities:	Hope, Yale, Boston Bar, and Lytton.

The Hope Visitor Information Centre at 919 Water Avenue, just off the Trans-Canada Highway in the southeast corner of the downtown area, is a good place to start any trip up the Fraser Canyon and the Trans-Canada Highway. The welcoming staff can fill you in on the recreation opportunities in the immediate area as well as the attractions along the canyon route north to Lytton.

As an aside, when you are finished exploring British Columbia's Cariboo region, you can return to Hope and set out northeast on Coquihalla Highway 5 or east on Crowsnest Highway 3 to explore the Coquihalla, Coldwater and Nicola, or Okanagan-Similkameen regions. *Coquihalla Trips & Trails* and *Okanagan Trips & Trails* can be your guide books to further adventure.

Hope is a good location to fill up the fuel tank before embarking on your north-ward journey. It is also a good place to stock up the grub box and, should you want a cup of coffee and a muffin before hitting the road, one of our favourite stops is the Blue Moose Coffee House, located on Wallace Street, across from the town hall and a beautiful park.

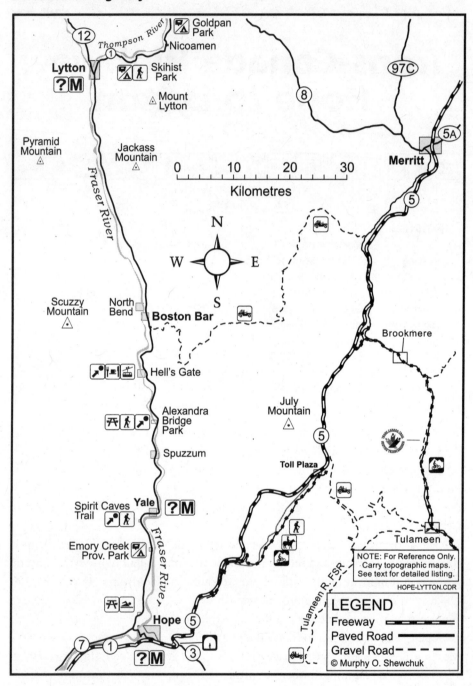

12

Thompson River

1

Goldpan Park

Nicoamen

Lytton

?M

Skihist Park

Mount Lytton

97C

8

5A

Merritt

Pyramid Mountain

Jackass Mountain

0   10   20   30

Kilometres

5

N

W   E

S

Scuzzy Mountain

North Bend

Boston Bar

Brookmere

Hell's Gate

July Mountain

5

Alexandra Bridge Park

Spuzzum

Toll Plaza

Spirit Caves Trail

Yale

?M

Tulameen

Emory Creek Prov. Park

Fraser River

NOTE: For Reference Only. Carry topographic maps. See text for detailed listing.

HOPE-LYTTON.CDR

Hope

5

7   1

?M

3

Tulameen R. FSR

LEGEND

Freeway

Paved Road

Gravel Road

© Murphy O. Shewchuk

Lake of the Woods

The Trans-Canada Highway follows the Fraser northwestward before crossing the river and heading north. Your first possible diversion is the junction with Highway 7, but if your destination is still the Cariboo and points north, stay on Highway 1 as it climbs away from the river. If you picked up some goodies in Hope and are looking for a pleasant picnic site, there is one at Schkam Lake (Lake of the Woods), approximately 5 kilometres from Hope.

American Creek, near km 8, is one of the many Fraser Canyon landmarks that got its name during the 1858 gold rush. Emory Creek and the nearby Emory Creek Provincial Park (km 18) also take their names from the gold rush period. The 34-unit campground is located on what was a gold rush shack town in 1858 and a railway construction town from 1879 to 1885. During the heyday of CPR construction, it boasted its own newspaper, a brewery, nine saloons, and a sawmill.

Spirit Caves Trail

Watch for the Spirit Caves trailhead on the west side of the highway just south of Gordon Creek (km 21.5) and across the highway from the Pioneer Cemetery. Allow three to four hours for the round trip to the "caves" — actually some serious man-size cracks in a jumble of boulders. The trail is fairly steep in places with numerous switchbacks and viewpoints of Yale and the Fraser River. It is a five-kilometre round trip with an elevation gain of 500

Yale from the Spirit Caves Trail. Use extreme caution at the viewpoints.

metres. Carry lunch and plenty of water. Watch out for the slugs and check yourself for ticks after the hike.

Yale

Like Emory Creek, the community of Yale has seen its fortunes boom and bust. Unlike Emory Creek, Yale still has a wide variety of amenities, including a restaurant or two, garage services, and a fine museum and historic interpretive site. The first of seven Fraser Canyon highway tunnels is on the eastern outskirts of Yale.

Yale has been the gateway to the Fraser Canyon for as many as one hundred centuries.

Archaeologists have found indications that the Pacific Ocean may have lapped at Yale's doorstep as the land began to rebound from the last ice age. They have also found indications of First Nations communities in the area as long ago as 9,000 years before the present (BP).

By the time fur trade explorer Simon Fraser ventured down the canyon to the vicinity of Yale, on June 28, 1808, the Native peoples had established Yale as the head of navigation for their canoes and the start of the cliff-hanging trail up the canyon to Camchin, now Lytton. While the Native peoples used the canyon trail as a trade route, the fur traders didn't consider it viable, even after attempts in 1828, 1848, and 1849.

Fort Yale (named after James Murray Yale) was built in 1848 by Ovid Allard to serve the fur brigades, but it was closed when the brigades abandoned the canyon in favour of a route to Hope via the Nicola Valley and Tulameen.

Boom and Bust

In 1858, half a century after Simon Fraser explored the area, news leaked out that gold had been found in the Fraser and its tributaries, and Yale again became the head of navigation. The Cariboo gold rush prompted the building of a wagon road to replace the cliff-hanging trails. With the Native canoes replaced by paddlewheel steamers for downriver navigation, Yale boomed. At its peak it boasted an area population of 30,000, an Anglican Church, a schoolhouse, a jail, and a number of stores, hotels, and blacksmith shops.

When the gold rush waned, Yale withered until the 1880s and construction of the Canadian Pacific Railway brought another boom. After the last spike at Craigellachie in 1885, Yale languished until Canadian Northern Railway con-

Alexandra Bridges

Spuzzum, at km 43, once supported a restaurant and service station. However, little remains today to indicate that this settlement was once an important stop for travellers on their way to the goldfields.

The smooth arch of the Alexandra Bridge (km 44) marks the third bridge to cross the river at this point. A pullout at the southwest end of the bridge sports a monument to the Royal Engineers who played a major part in the development of British Columbia's road and trail system during the gold rush period.

struction in 1911. A minor boom followed in the 1950s with the construction of the Trans-Canada Highway.

A Pleasant Place to Live

While the boom town days are gone and may never return, Yale is still a "pleasant place to live and a pleasant place to visit." Take a couple of hours out of your schedule and visit the museum and the Church of St. John the Divine, said to be the oldest church in BC still standing on its original site. While at the museum, ask the friendly staff to point out the other fascinating community landmarks.

Yale's Church of St. John the Divine, said to be the oldest church in BC still standing on its original site

The Alexandra Bridges

Whether driving the Trans-Canada Highway between Yale and Boston Bar or rafting through the Fraser Canyon, you can't help noticing the graceful curving arch of the Alexandra Bridge. It is noteworthy that three bridges crossing the Fraser River at this location north of Spuzzum have been named after Princess Alexandra.

First Bridge Opened in 1863

Joseph W. Trutch built the first bridge during the Cariboo gold rush as part of the contracts he held for construction of the Cariboo Wagon Road through the Fraser Canyon. Trutch hired a San Francisco engineer, A.S. Halledie, early in 1863. By September of the same year, the bridge had been designed, constructed, load tested, and opened to traffic.

Trutch's bridge (officially named the Alexandra Bridge in honour of the then Princess of Wales) spanned 82 metres. It bridged the entire width of the Fraser River at the narrowest point below Hell's Gate. Halledie used an ingenious scheme to prevent the flexing that was so common on bridges of that era. Early reports say that he was so successful that four horses drawing a wagon loaded with three tons produced no more than one-half inch deflection.

The bridge felt the traffic of thousands of gold seekers, mules, horses, cattle, and possibly even a few camels before the completion of the Canadian Pacific Railway in 1885 made the canyon road obsolete.

Flood of 1894 Swept Deck Away

Though no longer maintained, the first bridge continued to carry local traffic until the great flood of 1894. During the freshet of that year, the water rose 27 metres at the bridge site. The rushing torrent reached the bridge deck and swept much of it away. Despite the damage, travellers used it as a footbridge until the cables were cut in 1912.

The closure of the wagon road and the Alexandra Bridge left British Columbia without a road connection to the coast and, in the early 1920s, the government decided to rebuild both.

The Provincial Department of Public Works, then in charge of public highways, undertook the design of the second Alexandra Bridge. This task became the responsibility of the Provincial Bridge Engineer, A.L. Carruthers. The second bridge, like its predecessor, is also a suspension bridge. Carruthers began design work in early 1925. By August 1926, the construction crews had finished and load tested the bridge.

Despite the inadequacy of the canyon highway for the rapidly improving automobile, it remained in service until the early 1960s.

Third Bridge Opened in 1963

The third and present Alexandra Bridge is located a few hundred metres downstream from the original site. Here, the river is considerably wider, resulting in a span of 245 metres compared with 85 metres of the second bridge.

With the completion of the present bridge in 1963, Mr. Carruthers' bridge, like Trutch's bridge before it, became obsolete. Thanks to the representations of a few interested individuals, the old bridge has not been demolished. The government has built a picnic site on the Trans-Canada Highway, just north of the present bridge, and the second bridge can easily be reached on foot. Also in the area are traces of the old Cariboo Wagon Road and an old Fur Brigade Trail that once linked the Interior to the Coast via the Nicola and Coldwater valleys.

Provincial Park Established in 1984

Thanks to the efforts of the public and the Historic Sites Branch of the Provincial Parks Department, the bridge was designated a historic site in 1974. Fifty-five-hectare Alexandra Bridge Provincial Park was established at the site in 1984. There is an access trail to the old bridge from the west side of the highway near the northeast end of the present bridge.

A.L. Carruthers' 1926 Alexandra Bridge is the central feature of a BC provincial park.

The distinctive arch of the Alexandra Bridge as viewed from a whitewater raft on the Fraser River.

There is also a small picnic site near the north end of the bridge. A trail follows parts of the pre-1963 "highway" down to the 1926 Alexandra Bridge. Remnants of the original Cariboo Wagon Road can be found upstream of the 1926 bridge.

Hell's Gate Airtram

After winding through a series of tunnels north of Alexandra, the Trans-Canada Highway takes you past a parking lot carved out of the mountain (km 55) and the upper terminal of the Hell's Gate Airtram. Unlike many aerial tramways, this one is designed to

Katharine hikes the trail to Alexandra Bridge.

A monument to the skills of the Royal Engineers stands at the southwest end of the Alexandra Bridge.

carry its payload down to its destination on the rocks just above the Fraser River high-water mark.

Capable of carrying over 500 passengers per hour, the dual cabin tram takes little over two minutes to descend 157 metres. The lower observation deck is home to a fisheries display, a fudge factory, a trading post and gift shop, and a variety of eateries. There is also a suspension bridge across the river and a trail back up to the highway, should you decide get a little exercise on the way back up.

The Hell's Gate Airtram can take you down to an observation deck just above the Fraser River.

Anderson River and Boston Bar

The highway continues north up the canyon to Boston Bar, where there is a variety of services, including RV parks, food and fuel supplies, a hotel, and various coffee shops. There is also a campground near the Anderson River (km 62.5).

These place names reflect two different eras in British Columbia history. The Anderson River gets its name from Alexander Caulfield Anderson (1814–1884), a Hudson's Bay Company fur trader who was instrumental in finding a supply route from the Interior to the Coast. A.C. Anderson explored various routes, including one from Lillooet west along what is now Anderson and Seton Lakes as well as a route over the Cascade Mountains from the Nicola Valley to Spuzzum. The latter route followed Uztilius Creek and a section of the Anderson River.

Hell's Gate Fishways

The Hell's Gate gorge has been a challenge to passage since man (and fish) first moved up the canyon after the last ice age. The spawning sockeye managed to shoot the rapids despite the impediments of man, accidental or otherwise, until 1913, when Great Northern Railway construction caused a rockslide that blocked part of the Fraser River.

More than 31 million sockeye were harvested from the 1913 run, a catch total that has never been repeated. But when the remaining spawners reached Hell's Gate, they ran into an almost impenetrable obstacle. All but the hardiest fish were blocked by the slides that narrowed the already-narrow channel and created a 5-metre-high waterfall. By 1915, the removal of 45,000 cubic metres of rock from the channel had eased the problem, but the 33-metre-wide Hell's Gate gorge still remained one of the toughest obstacles on the river.

The migrating salmon have since been aided in their passage through Hell's Gate by specially designed fishways, the first of which was built in 1946 at a cost of $1 million. The design and construction of the fishway was complicated by the fact that Hell's Gate carries the water from 220,000 square kilometres of British Columbia — about one-quarter of the province — and the river levels can fluctuate as much as 5 metres in a day.

The first fishway proved successful, and more were added in 1947, 1951, 1965, and 1966.

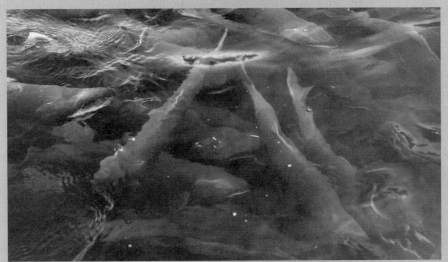

Sockeye salmon that have successfully faced the challenge of Hell's Gate spawn in the Adams River, near Chase, BC.

Neither of these routes proved viable, and Anderson finally settled on a route that traversed the Cascade Mountains in a nearly direct route from Tulameen to Hope.

According to the Akriggs in *1001 British Columbia Place Names*, Boston Bar gets its name from the Native peoples' term for the American prospectors during the 1858 gold rush. The "Boston Men" disliked the Native peoples and fought them whenever they met. The trouble culminated in the so-called "Battle of Boston Bar" on August 14, 1858. The *San Francisco Bulletin* reported that the fight "lasted three hours, and resulted in the complete rout of the savages. Seven of the Indians were known to have been killed, and a number wounded ... About 150 white men were in the fight."

SS *Skuzzy*

A daring railway builder and contractor, Andrew Onderdonk always worked in an effort to increase efficiency and reduce costs. One such venture was the building of the paddlewheel steamer SS *Skuzzy* at Spuzzum in May 1882. According to Art Downs in *Paddlewheels on the Frontier*, Onderdonk intended to sail the *Skuzzy* upriver through Hell's Gate to Boston Bar and transport supplies by boat from Lytton to Boston Bar.

The challenge was awesome. Veteran skipper Ausbury Insley swung the *Skuzzy* into the relentless current on May 17. He gradually worked the *Skuzzy* upstream through the Black Canyon and then into the constriction called Hell's Gate. The steamer fought the roaring water again and again, but the battle was futile.

Four months later, when the river had dropped considerably, the *Skuzzy*, now under Captain S.R. Smith, again swung into the silt-laden current. For 10 days she assaulted the rapids, but each attempt failed.

Then, in a final desperate move, Andrew Onderdonk ordered ring bolts drilled into rock walls and 125 Chinese labourers stationed along the rim. With the labourers pulling on ropes, steam capstans vibrating, and the paddlewheel churning, the *Skuzzy* crested the rapids. All of this was observed by cheering spectators who had laid their wagers and were transported daily from Yale via five railroad cars. Odds against the little steamboat reached as high as one hundred to one.

After serving faithfully on the Fraser River, she was moved to the Shuswap Lake system to continue her work serving the railway construction crews. If the SS *Skuzzy* had had a mind, she would surely have realized that the "iron horse" she was serving was determined to take away her reason for existing.

Boston Bar to Lytton

Although not quite as nasty as the section between Yale and Boston Bar, the road north to Lytton was still a challenge for road and railway builders. The benches above the river provided some respite from the sheer rock faces, but there were exceptions such as Jackass Mountain.

The Jackass Mountain section is still a long climb with some challenging turns at the top. A stop-of-interest plaque at a viewpoint commemorates the loss of a loaded mule, but there were others deaths and near misses during wagon road and railway construction. One story to come out of 1950s highway construction involved a line of vehicles waiting for a break in the construction. Apparently, a large boulder rolled down the mountainside and landed in the back seat of a car. According to reports at the time, no one was injured, and the contractor paid off the shaken driver and sent him on his way.

Longest Continuously Inhabited Community

Lytton's claim to fame, though unenviable, is as Canada's hot spot, with recorded temperatures as high as 44.4°C. (On June 3, 2007, it set a record for that date of 37.8°C.)

Another claim to fame that remains unsubstantiated is as Canada's longest continuously inhabited community, with numbers in excess of 7,000 years being reported. According to the Introduction in *Thompson Ethnobotany*, "The earliest documented evidence of human occupation of the southern Interior is about 9,000 B.P., near Yale . . . Further inland, two sites have been dated at 8,600 B.P. — one at the east side of the Thompson River just south of Spences Bridge, and one near Kamloops . . . The Lochnore-Nesikep locality between Lytton and Lillooet apparently extends back to about 6,000 years B.P."

While it may take further research to verify the "longest continuously inhabited" claim, it is fair to say that people have been meandering through the area for as many as 9,000 years. Simon Fraser reported visiting a large Native camp above the Stein River on Saturday, June 18, 1808. The next day he reached a village of 400 people at the mouth of the Thompson River and another village of 1,200, where Lytton is now standing. And, notes Fraser, ". . . I had to shake hands with all of them."

Options Abound

The junction of the Trans-Canada Highway (Highway 1) and Highway 12 presents a variety of choices. You can continue northeast on the Trans-Canada Highway to Spences Bridge, Cache Creek, or Kamloops and find lots of opportunities to explore. You can also take Highway 12 northwest to Lillooet where you again have more decisions to make. Do you go southwest to Pemberton, west to the Bridge River Valley, or north to the Cariboo?

Most of the options are laid out on the following pages.

GPS References for major points of interest
Ref: WGS 84 - Lat/Lon hddd.ddddd
Allow +/-100 metres due to data conversions

Wpt	Km	Description	Latitude	Longitude	Elev.
FC01	0	Jct Highway 1 and Hwy 3 Hope Info Centre	N49.37670	W121.44223	47 m
FC02	1.7	Fraser River Bridge	N49.38650	W121.45114	54 m
FC03	5.5	Lake of the Woods	N49.41018	W121.44459	167 m
FC04	17.0	Emory Creek	N49.50840	W121.41708	59 m
FC05	21.7	Spirit Caves trailhead	N49.54623	W121.43999	71 m
FC06	24.0	Yale traffic light	N49.56313	W121.43127	77 m
FC07	25.3	Yale Tunnel	N49.56291	W121.41519	85 m
FC08	29.5	Saddle Rock Tunnel	N49.59016	W121.40832	94 m
FC09	35.8	Sailor Bar Tunnel	N49.63673	W121.40221	98 m
FC10	44.0	Alexandra Bridge	N49.70096	W121.41036	140 m
FC11	46.0	Alexandra Lodge	N49.71878	W121.42041	124 m
FC12	47.6	Alexandra Tunnel	N49.73048	W121.43058	193 m
FC13	52.5	Ferrabee Tunnel	N49.76403	W121.43240	323 m
FC14	54.6	Hell's Gate Airtram	N49.78054	W121.44422	268 m
FC15	57.5	China Bar Tunnel	N49.80284	W121.45591	187 m
FC16	62.5	Anderson Creek Campground	N49.83461	W121.43150	151 m
FC17	66.0	Boston Bar	N49.86463	W121.44170	159 m
FC18	90.5	Jackass Mountain	N50.06917	W121.54560	286 m
FC19	94.5	Kanaka Bar	N50.10444	W121.55805	273 m
FC20	100.0	Siska (Cisco)	N50.14760	W121.57284	226 m
FC21	109.0	Jct with Hwy 12 to Lytton	N50.22329	W121.57644	258 m
FC22	110.0	Downtown Lytton	N50.23113	W121.58185	198 m

CHAPTER 2

Lytton to Lillooet via Highway 12

STATISTICS

Maps see page 20.

Distance:	65 km, Lytton to Lillooet via Highway 12.
Travel time:	One hour.
Condition:	Paved Lytton to Lillooet (Hwy 12).
Season:	Highway 12 maintained year-round.
Topo Maps:	Lytton, BC 92 I/14.
(1:50,000)	Stein River, BC 92 I/5.
	Lillooet, BC 92 I/12.
Communities:	Lytton, Lillooet, and Cache Creek

The junction of Highways 1 and 12 at the southern access to Lytton (255 kilometres northeast of Vancouver) is an excellent reference point in a circle tour that takes in one of the most spectacular and historically significant areas in the BC Interior. (The junction is also a good place to check your fuel, tires, and so on since service is limited for the next 65 kilometres.)

In addition to achieving fame (or notoriety) as Canada's hot spot several times each year, Lytton has another claim to fame. Some historians suggest that this community at the junction of the Thompson and Fraser rivers has had the longest continuing inhabitation of any in the BC Interior.

At 500 people, the population of the Lytton area today is not significant. In fact, it is less than half what it was when Simon Fraser made his historic trek down the Fraser River in 1808. The Thompson Native peoples, part of the broadly dispersed Interior Salish nation, had a major community on the benches above the river confluence. Disease, introduced by the European traders and gold seekers, was a major factor in reducing this thriving Native community.

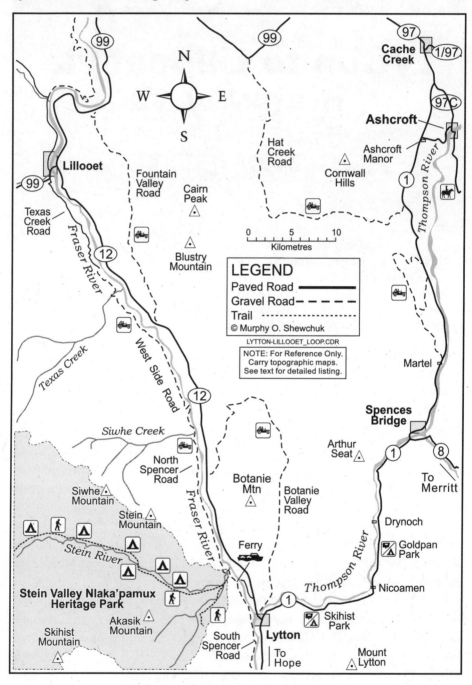

Cache Creek

97

1/97

99

99

Ashcroft

97C

Ashcroft Manor

Thompson River

Lillooet

Hat Creek Road

Cornwall Hills

99

Fountain Valley Road

Cairn Peak

Texas Creek Road

Fraser River

12

Blustry Mountain

LEGEND
Paved Road
Gravel Road
Trail
© Murphy O. Shewchuk

LYTTON-LILLOOET_LOOP.CDR

NOTE: For Reference Only. Carry topographic maps. See text for detailed listing.

0   5   10
Kilometres

West Side Road

12

Martel

Texas Creek

Siwhe Creek

Spences Bridge

North Spencer Road

Arthur Seat

1

8

To Merritt

Siwhe Mountain

Botanie Mtn

Botanie Valley Road

Stein Mountain

Fraser River

Drynoch

Stein River

Goldpan Park

Stein Valley Nlaka'pamux Heritage Park

Ferry

Nicoamen

Thompson River

Akasik Mountain

Skihist Mountain

South Spencer Road

Skihist Park

1

Lytton

To Hope

Mount Lytton

The clear green Thompson disappears into the Fraser River at Lytton.

Canadian Pacific Railway

With the junction of Highways 1 and 12 as km 0, the Canadian Pacific Railway underpass at km 0.6 is the first significant landmark. Lytton was the northern boundary of one of the most challenging sections of railway construction in the world. Andrew Onderdonk, the best of the nineteenth century railway builders, took up the challenge of the Fraser Canyon. After four years and many lost lives, trains rolled through Lytton in the spring of 1884. The last spike, driven at Craigellachie near Revelstoke, in November 1885, marked the completion of the CPR line across Canada.

Downtown Lytton (km 1.2) offers restaurant services, groceries, and an excellent tourist information centre and museum.

Watch for the Lillooet signs near the north end of Lytton's "main drag," then turn left and down the hill toward the bridge across the Thompson River. The CPR wasn't the only railway to play a part in Lytton's history. On October 19, 1909, BC Premier Richard McBride signed a contract for the construction of the Canadian Northern Pacific Railway from Yellowhead Pass to Vancouver via

Horses on the benchland high above the Fraser River, halfway between Lytton and Lillooet.

Kamloops. The railway was completed in 1915, but the sinking economy and First World War forced the Canadian government to take it over. After a name change, the Canadian National Railway (CNR) was subsequently extended across Canada.

The CNR bridge and a new highway bridge cross the Thompson River (km 1.7) near its mouth. Far below, the green Thompson disappears into the perpetually muddy Fraser River.

Botanie Valley

The Botanie Valley Road (to the right at km 2.2) offers the first of many back road alternate routes to Highway 12. A 43-kilometre-long summer road winds up

Botanie Creek to Botanie Lake, where it swings around the north slope of Botanie Mountain before following Izman Creek southwest to Highway 12 at km 20.3. Good lake fishing, abundant wildflowers, and a few challenging mud holes make the trip worthwhile even if it is double the distance and takes quadruple the time.

Lytton Ferry

Lytton Ferry Road, at km 2.4, is worth noting. If you survive (I mean complete) the loop, this could be your return route to Highway 12. A two-car reaction ferry provides access to the west side of the Fraser River. The ferry is tethered to cables suspended across the Fraser River. By means of the motor and cable controls, the operator angles the twin hulls so that the ferry reacts to the river current and is pushed from one side of the river to the other.

Access to the Stein Valley wilderness hiking trails is only a short drive north of the ferry slip on the west side of the river, and a dry weather road continues north to Lillooet. Winter ice and high water in the spring often force ferry closures, so check with the Ministry of Highways before planning a trip up the west side.

If you look toward the Fraser near km 4.6, you may catch a glimpse of St.

This current-powered ferry provides access to the west side of the Fraser River at Lytton.

George's School, one of the last church-run Native residential schools to close its doors. On the uphill side, fire-scarred pine and fir line Highway 12. With the summer heat come forest fires that clear away the undergrowth. In late April and early May, arrowleaf balsamroot paint the slopes with dabs of yellow while Saskatoon bushes provide splashes of snow-white blossoms. After winding along the benchland well back from the river for 10 kilometres, Highway 12 descends to the foot of an outcropping of red rock, a short distance above the Fraser. Pay attention to the "Slow" signs — there isn't much room for mistakes.

Laluwissin Creek Road

Well-used Laluwissin Creek Forest Road, halfway between the km 20 signpost and Izman Creek (km 20.7), climbs into the lake-studded valley north of Botanie Mountain. This is one exit to the previously mentioned Botanie Valley Road.

For the next 20 kilometres, black shade-cloth-covered ginseng fields, hayfields, and wooden barn buildings provide a contrast to a rugged mountain backdrop reminiscent of scenes in the Swiss Alps. Many of the benches on both sides of the Fraser grow three or four crops of hay each year beneath the man-made rainbows of irrigation sprinklers. Ginseng, in contrast, is a crop that takes three or four years to mature. Outside the range of the sprinklers, sagebrush and rabbit bush survive on the dry slopes.

Fountain Valley Road

Fountain Valley Road (km 39.5) marks the south end of another interesting detour. A 28-kilometre-long backroad winds up through the Fountain Valley and back to the Fraser Canyon and Highway 99 about 14 kilometres northeast of Lillooet. There are Forest Service recreation sites at Kwotlenemo (Fountain) Lake that provide a welcome respite from the summer heat of the canyon.

For nearly a century, the Big Slide area (km 44.6) was considered the most treacherous piece of road in BC. It kept all but the most foolhardy drivers out of (or in) Lillooet. Improvements to this section of the highway began in 1967, and although still one lane, it is now paved. However, a quick glance at the talus slopes and the Fraser River far below will provide ample reason to respect the 30 km/h speed limit.

Bridge of the 23 Camels

The Lytton-Lillooet Loop leaves Highway 12 at the junction with Highway 99 near km 62. It's just a short jaunt west to the Fraser River and the Bridge of the 23 Camels. The bridge across the Fraser River near here was also the site of a ferry that crossed the river in the late 1850s and early 1860s. It may have been the true Mile 0 of the first road to the Cariboo. An inscription on a cairn near the west end of the bridge illustrates one facet of that colourful period:

THE BRIDGE OF THE 23 CAMELS

So named to commemorate British Columbia's first — and last —experience with camels, 23 of which were imported in 1862 by John Callbreath of Seton Portage to pack supplies from Lillooet to the Upper Cariboo. The experiment failed when the Bactrian Camels were found to frighten horses, domestic stock and even humans. They were turned loose and most were never seen again. A few survived and the last died in 1905 after many years as a ranch pet.

The Bridge of the 23 Camels was officially dedicated by the Honorable William R. Bennett, Premier of BC, September 22, 1980.

Plaque at the west end of the Bridge of the 23 Camels.

Lytton to Lillooet via Highway 12

Lillooet

A junction at the west end of the bridge is the reference point for the return trip to Lytton via the west side of the Fraser River. Before heading south, you may wish to detour into town to stock up on supplies and visit the local museum. Located in a former Anglican church near Lillooet's official Mile 0 Cairn, the museum contains a wealth of information and artifacts dealing with the history of the area. The Native peoples, gold seekers, settlers, and railroaders are well represented. There is also a special display focused on Margaret "Ma" Murray, a newspapering lady whose sharp wit and caustic tongue brought worldwide attention to Lillooet and British Columbia.

This junction is also a departure point for the Bridge River Valley and the historic quartz gold mines set in the heart of the Coast Range Mountains. (See the Bridge River Gold chapter for details.) You can also follow Highway 99 (Duffey Lake Road) west and south to Pemberton, Whistler, and Squamish. (See the Coast Mountains Circle Tour chapter for details.)

If you are looking for a place to camp, there is a serviced campground near the junction of Cayoosh Creek and the Fraser River, just south of the Bridge of the 23 Camels.

Note: See the *Information Sources* chapter at the end of the book for contact information for the services mentioned here.

GPS References for major points of interest
Ref: WGS 84 - Lat/Lon hddd.ddddd
Allow +/-100 metres due to data conversions

Wpt	Km	Description	Latitude	Longitude
LL01	0	Jct Hwy 1 and Hwy 12	N50.22443	W121.57758
LL02	1.5	Downtown Lytton	N50.23392	W121.58080
LL03	2.1	Botanie Creek Rd	N50.24103	W121.58058
LL04	2.5	Lytton Ferry Rd and Hwy 12	N50.24224	W121.58215
LL05	20.3	Laluwissin Creek FS Rd	N50.37978	W121.66661
LL06	39.5	Fountain Valley Rd	N50.53011	W121.75170
LL07	44.7	Big Slide	N50.56198	W121.80227
LL08	61.8	Jct Hwy 99	N50.68476	W121.91899
LL09	62.5	Bridge of the 23 Camels	N50.68414	W121.92806
LL10	64.5	Lillooet Mile 0 Cairn	N50.69126	W121.93754

Lillooet and the Fraser River as viewed from Highway 99, northeast of Lillooet.

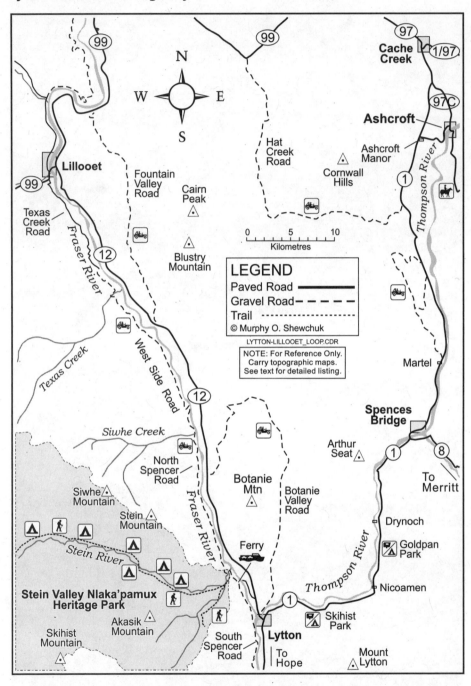

CHAPTER 3

Lillooet to Lytton via the West Bank of the Fraser

STATISTICS

	Map see page 28.
Distance:	70 km, Lillooet to Lytton via Texas Creek Road.
Travel time:	Two to three hours.
Condition:	Mostly gravel Lillooet to Lytton (west side).
Season:	Best in dry weather.
Topo Maps:	Lillooet, BC 92 I/12.
(1:50,000)	Stein River, BC 92 I/5.
	Lytton, BC 92 I/14.
Communities:	Lytton, Lillooet, and Cache Creek.

Don't Forget to Visit Lillooet

A junction at the west end of the bridge is the reference point for the return trip to Lytton via the west side of the Fraser River. Before heading south, you may wish to detour into town to stock up on supplies and visit the local museum. Located in a former Anglican church near Lillooet's official Mile 0 Cairn, the museum contains a wealth of information and artifacts dealing with the history of the area. The Native peoples, gold seekers, settlers, and railroaders are well represented. There is also a special display focused on Margaret "Ma" Murray, a newspapering lady whose sharp wit and caustic tongue brought world-wide attention to Lillooet and British Columbia.

This junction is also a departure point for the Bridge River Valley and the historic quartz gold mines set in the heart of the Coast Range Mountains. (See the Bridge River Gold chapter for details.) You can also follow Highway 99 (Duffey Lake Road) west and south to Pemberton, Whistler, and Squamish.

If you are looking for a place to camp, there is a serviced campground near the junction of Cayoosh Creek and the Fraser River, just south of the Bridge of the 23 Camels.

With the junction near the west end of the Bridge of the 23 Camels as Km 0,

· head south across the Cayoosh Creek bridge (km 0.1). Take the left fork to Texas Creek Road (km 0.5) and begin the steady climb away from the Fraser River and Cayoosh Creek.

Seton Lake Option

Before heading south toward Lytton, you may wish to detour west to Seton Lake. It's less than five kilometres, and the attractions include boating, swimming, salmon spawning channels, a BC Hydro recreation site with tent and vehicle campsites, and a spectacular view of Seton Lake from a short distance up Duffey Lake Road.

Margaret "Ma" Murray (1888-1982), the editor of the Bridge River – Lillooet News, attracted admirers and enemies with her forthrightness and salty language.
© 1977 Murphy Shewchuk.

Meanwhile, back on Texas Creek Road, you'll soon cross Seton Canal (km 0.9). Just in case you were wondering, this canal feeds a small hydroelectric plant on the shores of the Fraser, just downstream from the mouth of Cayoosh Creek. From a water flow perspective, the Seton generating station is the final phase of the Bridge River power system. Built in the 1950s and 60s, the system was British Columbia's first major hydroelectric development. It includes a dam and generating plant near Gold Bridge, a major dam on the Bridge River near Mission Mountain, and two large power plants on the shores of Seton Lake at Shalalth. In total, the system develops approximately 500 million watts of energy.

Seton Lake gets its beautiful green colour from the glacial silt carried down the Bridge River and through the tunnels and penstocks to the hydroelectric plant on the lakeshore at Shalalth.

Texas Creek Road

The Texas Creek Road continues south, winding through the benches and along the hillside high above the Fraser. This is an agriculturally diverse area. Sheep ranches, orchards, and small holdings make use of the limited arable land and water from nearby streams. The long growing season and hot, dry climate once served as the base for a large market gardening industry. Flowers were grown for perfume, and fruit and vegetables were supplied to the lower mainland.

Purvis Road near km 12 marked the turnoff to the home and orchard of an old friend of mine. Ron Purvis, who has passed away, was a frequent contributor to *BC Outdoors* magazine in the 1960s and 1970s with a rockhounding column. His book, *Treasure Hunting in British Columbia*, published in 1971, was the rockhound's bible for nearly a decade. Before retiring to his orchard, Ron Purvis had served as Boys' Supervisor at St. George's Indian Residential School at Lytton. Purvis taught rockhounding and gem-cutting classes (where I met him) and supervised a variety of other projects during his "retirement."

Lillooet to Lytton via the West Bank of the Fraser

A narrow road along the north side of Texas Creek leads up into the spectacular Coast Range Mountains.

The pavement begins to thin as you get farther south, and by the time you reach Texas Creek (km 19) you're on dusty gravel. Just before the bridge, a Forest Service road heads up Texas and Skimath creeks into the Coast Mountains. This road provides "at your own risk" access to some of the wildest and most scenic mountain terrain in southwestern BC. According to BC Parks, the bridges on the Texas Creek Forest Service Road to about the km 10 mark have been rated for maximum 10-ton vehicle travel. However, there are a couple of very narrow, rough locations in that stretch of road that are not recommended for vehicle traffic. The bridge over Molybdenite Creek at the km 10 mark is an ATV/foot bridge only.

A Stein River Park trailhead is located at approximately the km 23 mark of the road. Here the jagged ridges and alpine vales of the Coast Mountains reach elevations of over 2,500 metres. In addition to serious backroading, there are backcountry bushwhacking trails that link the headwaters of Texas Creek with Cottonwood Creek, an important tributary of the Stein.

If you're not into serious alpine exploring, there is a pleasant rest stop with tables and a toilet at the Texas Creek Bridge. Beyond the bridge, the vast expanse of black provides shade for ginseng gardens. According to some sources, ginseng takes three to four years to mature, and in the process, it takes certain minerals out of the soil that make it difficult to grow a second ginseng crop in the same location. After the ginseng is harvested, the shade cloth and the network of anchors and cables holding it up are removed, and the fields returned to alfalfa or hay.

Road Narrows Significantly

The road down the west side of the Fraser narrows significantly near km 25. The next 30 kilometres are not for the faint-hearted or ill-equipped. Although we had no difficulty taking our truck and camper through to Lytton in September 2006, there are numerous locations where passing an oncoming vehicle means backing up to the nearest wide spot. Large RVs and vehicles pulling trailers should definitely not use this route. Mud and loose sand or gravel can make some of the hills particularly disconcerting. Check your tires and your nitro pills — if either are questionable, head back to Lillooet.

Now that I've got the disclaimer over with, the fun begins. The road cuts through open stands of fir and ponderosa pine, with a carpet of wildflowers or berries beneath them. The yellow sunflower-like blossoms of the arrowleaf balsamroot *(Balsamorhiza sagittata)* present a short but intense show in April and early May. The dozen or so different varieties of Saskatoons send forth their white blossoms before the leaves emerge, and lilacs gone wild mark wherever there was a settlement.

Saskatoon bushes show their white blossoms long before most other wildflowers.

Boulders Piled by Chinese Miners

If you can find a safe place to pull over to enjoy the view of the Fraser River some two hundred to three hundred metres below you, you may catch a glimpse of piles of boulders near the river flats. These were hand-moved by hundreds of Chinese miners in search of gold-bearing sand that had been overlooked by the initial onslaught in the Fraser River gold rush of 1858. No one really knows how much gold was recovered, but there are strong suspicions that coffins sent back to China contained a significant amount of jade and gold along with the bodies of the poor departed Chinese miners.

North Spencer Road

Although there are a few ranches or farms along this route, the largest settlement is at 18 Mile, near km 38. This is also the point where Texas Creek Road becomes North Spencer Road. Askom Mountain, at 2,800 metres, forms a striking backdrop to this wide alluvial bench. Below the road, a short distance north, is a little Native cemetery, the final resting place for many members of the Adams clan.

Although the road appears to slowly improve as you continue south, it's all relative. Most city drivers will still consider it to be little more than a tortuous goat path

The Fraser Canyon from the west side of the Fraser near 18 Mile.

— reminiscent of the original Cariboo Wagon Road in the lower Fraser Canyon. Undulating roller-coaster runs through the trees are interspersed with creek-crossings on one-lane bridges, switchback descents over pure sand, and the not-infrequent glimpse several hundred metres straight down to the muddy Fraser.

The Stein River has been an important part of the life of the Nlaka'pamux people for more than 7,000 years.

If you look across the Fraser near km 50, you should see the north entrance to the Botanie Valley Loop mentioned in the Lytton to Lillooet section. Along this section you should also see the stark difference between the creek-bottom vegetation and the open semi-desert slopes. The road switchbacks through conglomerate bluffs, across short side valleys filled with cedar, alder, and vine maple, and back out onto slopes that barely support sagebrush and cactus. Where water can be diverted, the sandy benches are fertile. Many of them are still being cultivated using horse-drawn equipment and ancient farm tractors.

Stein River

The first glimpse of "modern" civilization is the new Stein subdivision near km 60. The road then descends to the Stein River a short distance farther south, and continues along the benchland for another six kilometres through Earlscourt Farm to the Lytton reaction ferry. Watch for a sign marking the side road to the start of the Stein Heritage Trail.

Earlscourt Farm

Farm buildings on the west side of the Fraser River, about four kilometres south of the Stein River and two kilometres north of the Lytton Ferry, mark the site of a once-great mansion.

According to Dorothy Dodge, curator of the Lytton Museum, Thomas G. Earl (1829–1921) settled on the land in 1860. He built a thriving fruit farm and shipped apples to the Royal Agriculture & Industrial Society show in London, England. His apples were well-received and he became the first person in British Columbia to ship apples commercially.

30,000 Boxes of Apples

Mr. Earl sold the farm to R.V. Winch of Vancouver in 1912. Mr. Winch named the farm Earlscourt, and continued to build up the orchard. R.V. Winch's son, Harry, greatly enlarged the operation. According to a letter from Victor Spencer (son of Col. Victor Spencer), "At one time the property produced 30,000 boxes of apples and the C.N.R. built a rail siding at Winch Spur so as to let off the boxcars to be loaded with apples. These apples all went East and then to England."

R.V. Winch also built a fine mansion on the property. He gave the mansion to his daughter, Isabella Gertrude Winch, when she married Col. Victor Spencer. Col. Spencer later bought the farm and gradually turned the aging orchard into hayfield.

During the Second World War, Col. Spencer decided he wanted new Hereford bulls for his ranch. In 1943, he went to Herefordshire, England, and bought several bulls. After a three-month quarantine in Quebec, they arrived to replenish the award-winning Earlscourt Farm herd.

Mansion Burned in 1993

Dr. and Mrs. Raymond Mundall purchased the property in 1962. The Mundalls returned to the United States where Raymond Mundall worked as a doctor. They subsequently spent 11 years in Belize, Central America, doing missionary work and establishing a fifteen-bed hospital. The Mundalls retired to Canada in February 1991 and lived in the mansion until it burned in March 1993.

According to a *Lillooet News* report at the time of the fire, the Mundalls said "... the house covered approximately 18,000 square feet and the 30 foot by 30 foot living room was just right for family visits ... The last family gathering, held at Christmas [1992], saw approximately 45 people sitting down for dinner."

Dr. Raymond Mundall died in August 1997 and Mrs. Mundall married Bryce Newell several years later. The Newells plus sons Daniel and Merritt Mundall and their respective families still live on Earlscourt Farm.

Lillooet to Lytton via the West Bank of the Fraser

Stein Valley Nlaka'pamux Heritage Provincial Park was officially established in 1995 to protect approximately 107,191 hectares of the Stein Watershed and is jointly managed by the Lytton First Nation and BC Parks. The name "Stein" comes from the Nlaka'pamux word *stagyn*, which means "hidden place," referring to the fact that the valley and the extent of the watershed is not very noticeable from the Stein River's mouth on the Fraser River. The valley has been extremely important to the Nlaka'pamux people for thousands of years, both spiritually and for sustenance. Part of the heritage value is the large number of pictographs still visible today in various parts of the valley, ranging in size from single symbols to one of the largest pictograph sites in Canada.

There isn't space here to expand on the Stein trail system, but there are several good books on the market that do present detailed information.

South Spencer Road

A side road climbs to the right about half a kilometre before the reaction ferry (km 67). This well-used Forest Service road continues south along the benches to North Bend and Boston Bar where a relatively new bridge has replaced the aerial ferry that was once the main access to North Bend and the west side of the Fraser.

Lytton Ferry

If Lytton is your destination, take the two-car ferry across the Fraser and continue two kilometres south into the village, completing a circle tour that should give you something to talk about for a year or two.

Note: See the *Information Sources* chapter at the end of the book for contact information on most of the services mentioned here.

GPS References for major points of interest
Ref: WGS 84 - Lat/Lon hddd.ddddd
Allow +/-100 metres due to data conversions

Wpt	Km	Description	Latitude	Longitude
LL11	0	Jct Hwy 99 and Rd 40	N50.68095	W121.93374
LL12	0.6	Texas Creek Rd	N50.67612	W121.93267
LL13	1.0	Seton Canal	N50.67230	W121.93050
LL14	12.3	Pavement ends	N50.59496	W121.86343
LL15	18.4	Texas Creek	N50.56051	W121.82753
LL16	23.4	Log house and church	N50.53142	W121.78590
LL17	25.4	McPhee Creek	N50.52056	W121.76887
LL18	28.0	End of maintained public road	N50.50572	W121.74397
LL19	34.5	Views of Fraser Canyon	N50.45584	W121.71072
LL20	35.6	Intipam Creek	N50.44713	W121.70694
LL21	36.8	Jct North Spencer Rd	N50.44647	W121.70033
LL22	40.2	Siwhe Creek	N50.42581	W121.69194
LL23	44.1	Nikwoi Creek	N50.40037	W121.68991
LL24	47.0	Inkoiko Creek	N50.37842	W121.68588
LL25	48.7	Viewpoint	N50.36739	W121.68338
LL26	55.4	Nepuchin Creek	N50.31833	W121.65891
LL27	59.0	Stein Village	N50.28944	W121.64241
LL28	60.5	Stein River	N50.28572	W121.63353
LL29	61.6	Stein Trail Rd	N50.27852	W121.62701
LL30	64.7	Earlscourt Farm	N50.25712	W121.60606
LL31	65.7	Jct South Spencer Rd	N50.25006	W121.59840

Exploring the Fraser River Trail

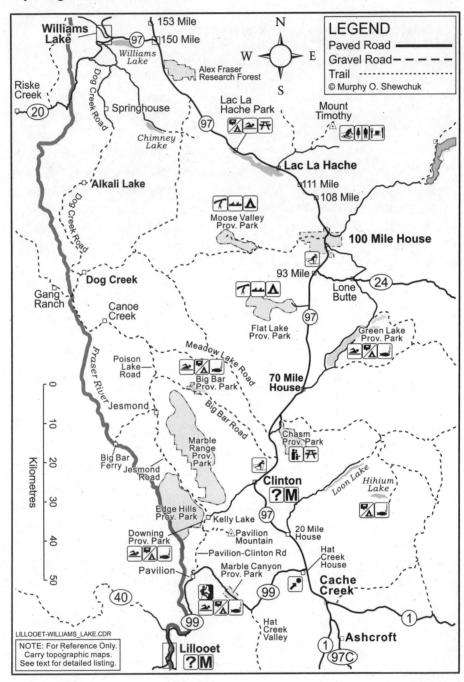

LEGEND
Paved Road
Gravel Road
Trail
© Murphy O. Shewchuk

N
W — E
S

Williams Lake
153 Mile
150 Mile
97
Williams Lake
Alex Fraser Research Forest
Riske Creek
20
Springhouse
Dog Creek Road
Chimney Lake
Lac La Hache Park
97
Mount Timothy
Alkali Lake
Lac La Hache
111 Mile
108 Mile
Moose Valley Prov. Park
100 Mile House
Dog Creek
93 Mile
24
Lone Butte
Gang Ranch
Canoe Creek
Flat Lake Prov. Park
97
Green Lake Prov. Park
Meadow Lake Road
70 Mile House
Fraser River
Poison Lake Road
Big Bar Prov. Park
Jesmond
Big Bar Road
Chasm Prov. Park
Marble Range Prov. Park
Loon Lake
Hihium Lake
Big Bar Ferry
Jesmond Road
Clinton
? M
Kilometres
0
10
20
30
40
50
Edge Hills Prov. Park
Kelly Lake
97
20 Mile House
Downing Prov. Park
Pavilion Mountain
Pavilion-Clinton Rd
Hat Creek House
Cache Creek
Marble Canyon Prov. Park
Pavilion
99
1
40
99
Hat Creek Valley
Ashcroft
1
97C

LILLOOET-WILLIAMS_LAKE.CDR

NOTE: For Reference Only.
Carry topographic maps.
See text for detailed listing.

Lillooet
? M

CHAPTER 4

Exploring the Fraser River Trail: Lillooet to Williams Lake

STATISTICS

	Map see page 40.
Distance:	240 km, Lillooet to Williams Lake.
Travel Time:	Four to six hours.
Elevation Gain:	1,240 metres.
Condition:	Mostly gravel, with some paved sections.
Season:	The Pavilion–Clinton section may be closed in winter.
Topo Maps:	Lillooet, BC 92 I/12.
(1:50,000)	Pavilion, BC 92 I/13.
	Clinton, BC 92 P/4.
	Jesmond, BC 92 P/5.
	Empire Valley, BC 92 O/8.
	Dog Creek, BC 92 O/9.
	Alkali Lake, BC 92 O/16.
	Williams Lake, BC 93 B/1.
Communities:	Lillooet, Clinton, 100 Mile House, and Williams Lake.

A little-known back road parallels British Columbia's Fraser River from Lillooet to Williams Lake, passing through a rough and scenic portion of the Cariboo that time seems to have left behind. Portions of this 240-kilometre road have been paved, while on other parts, the improvements have been limited to straightening a few corners and widening it enough to permit safe passage of modern motorized vehicles. Otherwise, the river trail, as it is also known, has changed little in the past century.

This is dry country sagebrush, scrub pine, and bunchgrass seem to be all that thrive on the lower benches. At higher elevations, lodgepole pine, aspen, and willow populate the wetter slopes and glacier-carved hollows. But even in the heaviest forest area, there is still bunchgrass, and nowhere does the timber growth compare to the giants of the Pacific rain forest a mountain range to the west.

Exploring the Fraser River Trail

This is cattle country — and has been for a century and a half. It is said that Col. Palmer drove the first cattle herd into this area in 1858, planning to sell beef to the hungry Argonauts participating in the Fraser River gold rush. He sold some of his mixed herd of Texas Longhorns, milk cows, and Shorthorns to pioneer settlers along the way, helping to establish the nucleus of some of British Columbia's most famous ranches. Because even "scrub" stock sold for as much as $125 a head, Col. Palmer's cattle drive was only the first of many into the gold country.

Today, the unpredictable Texas Longhorns have gone the way of all mean and nasty critters and instead, calm, white-faced Herefords forage on the bunchgrass of the Cariboo.

Lillooet, a quiet village on the west bank of the Fraser River, 325 kilometres from Vancouver and 65 kilometres north of Lytton and the Trans-Canada Highway, was the starting point of the original trail to the goldfields of the Fraser and Cariboo. In order to avoid the treacherous lower Fraser Canyon, the miners traveled from Victoria by boat and by boat and foot to Harrison Lake. Then, alternately by the same methods along a route that included Lillooet Lake, Anderson Lake, and Seton Lake before again reaching the Fraser River at Lillooet. Lillooet was a boom town in the late 1850s and early 1860s, boasting a population of 16,000 hardy souls and all the amenities of civilization, including a brewery.

Today, Lillooet is noted for jade, sunshine, sagebrush and, for some, the late Margaret "Ma" Murray, once the fiery editor of the *Bridge River - Lillooet News*.

Mile 0

The Mile 0 Cairn, symbolically marking the start of the first Cariboo trail, is located in the heart of the village and across the street from the Lillooet Museum. Housed in the former St. Mary's Anglican Church, the museum opened in May 1969 and has since gained a widespread reputation as one of the better small museums in the province. A worthwhile stop for anyone planning to follow the gold rush trail, the museum's collection of ranch machinery, homesteading implements, pioneer kitchen utensils, and Native artifacts can help establish the mood for the trip to come.

No visit to Lillooet is complete without a visit to the notorious Hanging Tree. Stories have filtered down through the years of gold rush murderers being hanged from the strong branches of this gnarled pine. Serious historians, however, doubt that British Columbia's first Chief Justice, Matthew Baillie Begbie (The Hanging Judge) would have allowed the recipient of so harsh a sentence to suffer his fate without at least the luxury of a proper scaffold.

Parsonville, on the east side of the Fraser River, near the east end of the Bridge of the 23 Camels, was originally a ferry slip and the actual location of the first Mile 0. From here the original trail twisted its way northeast, climbing up to the benchland high above the muddy Fraser. Today, Highway 99 follows much the same route as far as Pavilion. Ranch names such as 15 Mile, 17 Mile, and 19 Mile reflect the locations of the mile markers established in 1862 by Sgt. John McMurphy and the Royal Engineers.

Pioneer Flour Mill

The Pavilion General Store, located at 21 Mile, was a wayside roadhouse and also the location of the first flour mill in the area. Originally built in 1872 as a water-

Lillooet's Hanging Tree. © *1976 Murphy Shewchuk*

powered mill to grind local grain, it continued in operation until 1909. Prior to its destruction by fire in 2000, a cowbell hung over the door to the general store, sounding a resonant note each time the door opened — a sound that undoubtedly brought back memories to many a farm boy.

Holy Trinity Catholic Church stands in the heart of the Pavilion Native community. It serves as a landmark for the road that follows the original river trail over Pavilion Mountain. Although similar to many Native churches built at the turn of

The Fraser River viewed from Highway 99 near 15 Mile.

the last century, its one outstanding feature is the delicate woodwork of its elegant spire.

For the next five kilometres, the rough and dusty road switchbacks up the mountain, offering a panoramic view of the ranchland across the Fraser River and the Fraser Canyon far below. Overhead, 500-kilovolt lines carry Peace River power to British Columbia's Lower Mainland. In May, the hillsides are ablaze with the yellow sunflower-like blossoms of the arrowleaf balsamroot, once used by the Native peoples for food and medicine. In late June and early July, clumps of prickly pear cactus show their delicate orange and yellow-green blossoms to the sun for a few hours after a rain shower. In October, it is the aspen and willow that grow in the infrequent creek beds that paint stripes of red, yellow, and gold.

Carson Ranch

On the flat top of the mountain is the domain of the Diamond S Ranch. Still known by many old-timers as the Carson Ranch, it was established by Robert Carson in 1867. Born in Edinburgh in 1841, Carson led a colourful life before settling down to ranching on the mountaintop. As a young lad he came to British Columbia by a circuitous route. His journey included a stop in Ohio, a close brush with death in a wagon train attack in Colorado, stops in California and Idaho, and a trip through the Okanagan. Robert Carson made his stake as a packer on the goldfield trails. After setting up his ranch, he expanded his operation by selling hay

The alpine meadows of Pavilion Mountain are a wildflower paradise in early summer.

and feed to the BX teamsters hauling freight over the wagon road. His wife put their children through school selling butter as far away as Williams Lake.

Eventually, Carson's ranch was taken over by his son-in-law, a member of the pioneer Bryson family. It was later sold to Col. Victor Spencer and then to Vancouver businessman J.E. Termuende.

Pavilion Mountain Side Trip

For about eight kilometres, the road passes through open ranchland, offering an excellent view of the snow-capped Coast Range to the west and the high hills surrounding the Hat Creek Valley to the south. Then a junction to the left on a sharp downhill turn marks the start of a 9.6-kilometre winding gravel road to the summit of Pavilion Mountain. This road gradually climbs east along the ridge, gaining 650 metres before reaching the 2,090-metre summit. This road is infrequently maintained and is likely to be free of snow only from early July to mid-September. Despite these challenges, the panorama views from the alpine meadows can be worth the trip. Note that the meadows are delicate. Please stay on the established roads.

Cliffside Road

Meanwhile, back at the junction to Pavilion Mountain summit, after a short dash through the timber, Pavilion-Clinton Road twists down a narrow cliffside track to Kelly Lake, dropping almost six hundred metres in less than six kilometres. While the road up from Pavilion is no place for the weak-hearted, the descent to Kelly Lake is certainly no place for those with weak brakes. Caution is especially necessary on weekdays as this can sometimes be a busy road for logging trucks.

Downing Provincial Park, on the east end of Kelly Lake, offers a welcome respite at the end of a hot, dusty day. The favourite haunt of local fishermen, it is equipped with picnic tables set in the meadow among the willows and ample room to park a recreational vehicle or set up a tent.

Note: The Pavilion-Clinton Road is usually only passable from May to October. In the off-season or during wet weather, this leg of the river trail can be bypassed by continuing east on Highway 99 from Pavilion to Hat Creek House

Loading horses onto the Big Bar Ferry prior to a ride into the French Bar Creek area.

(11 kilometres north of Cache Creek) and then north on Highway 97 to Clinton. From Clinton, it is a 20-kilometre drive west to Kelly Lake and the next leg of the trail of gold and cattle.

Kelly Lake Ranch

The weather-beaten buildings of the Kelly Lake Ranch, originally established by Edward Kelly in 1866, serve as a landmark for the junction of Clinton and Jesmond roads. The route is now north along Jesmond Road through a narrow, timbered valley bordered on the east by colourful limestone cliffs of the Marble Range.

Several small homesteads or ranchettes border the start of the road north. Twenty-five kilometres north of the junction is the Circle H Mountain Lodge. According to one source, the ranch was first surveyed and registered to the Hallers of Big Bar Creek in the 1890s. In more recent years, the lodge has served as a guest ranch and base for cross-country skiing.

Big Bar Ferry

A few kilometres beyond the Jesmond Post Office (easily missed on the east side of the road) is the junction to the Big Bar Ferry. The Big Bar reaction ferry (powered by the strong river current) has been in operation since 1894 and serves several ranches and homesteads on the west side of the Fraser. The well-equipped four-wheeler, travelling with another similarly equipped venturesome spirit can cross the Fraser on the reaction ferry and return to Lillooet via the West Pavilion Forest Service Road.

Red Dog Saloon

North of the junction to the ferry, the ranch trail dips into a hollow that carries Big Bar Creek. Also nestled in the hollow are the distinctive green buildings of the OK Ranch.

Joseph Haller, the first settler in this location, was born in Pittsburgh, Pennsylvania, in 1825 and came to British Columbia via Sacramento in July of 1858. He worked in the mines of the Fraser and Cariboo for two years before buying a dozen donkeys and going into the packing business. In 1862, Haller established "a house for travelers and a store with grub" on Big Bar Creek. His winter supplies included 8,000 pounds of flour and "90 gallons schnapps of different kinds." Known locally as the "Red Dog Saloon," Haller's was a popular stopping place for miners and packers.

Harry Marriott, pioneer rancher and author of *Cariboo Cowboy*, along with

George Harrison, consolidated several smaller ranches to form the well-known OK Ranch.

Big Bar Lake Provincial Park

A detour east at a junction a short distance beyond the OK Ranch leads 12 kilometres to five-kilometre-long Big Bar Lake. Equipped with a provincial campsite, picnic site, and boat launch, it is another of the Cariboo's many popular fishing holes.

North of the junction, the river trail (now called Poison Lake Road) continues north through the scrub timber parkland, occasionally passing under the 500-kilovolt power lines. After winding through about 11 kilometres of questionable terrain, it joins the more travelled Meadow Lake Road that links the river trail with Highway 97 at 59 Mile, approximately 20 kilometres north of Clinton.

From here, the road continues northward, gradually swinging west as it passes picturesque abandoned log cabins and a narrow pass cut through limestone mountains.

Irrigation ditches carry water to the hayfields. Outside the range of the irrigation, prickly pear cactus, bunchgrass, and sagebrush thrive.

The Fraser River at the Gang Ranch Bridge.

Canoe Creek Valley

The broad, irrigated hayfields of the Canoe Creek valley come as somewhat of a surprise after many kilometres of narrow valleys and dry country. The colourful Roman Catholic Church at the Canoe Creek Native community, built in 1900, was recently repainted, creating a bright landmark visible for some distance.

BC Cattle Company

Also a visible landmark is the two-story tan-coloured ranch house of the BC Cattle Company. In the autumn, the windrows of hay follow the contours of the benchland all the way to the cliffs overlooking the Fraser River. Across the muddy river stretches the almost limitless cattle country of the Gang Ranch. Down below, jutting out of the water where the river disappears around a corner on its southward journey, can be seen Pulpit Rock, a favourite landmark of the river rafters who drift by each summer.

Gang Ranch

The Fraser River trail follows the contours of the canyon and side gullies down to a bridge strung across the Fraser River — the main access to the world-famous Gang Ranch. With an area of 2,330 square kilometres, the Gang Ranch is almost half the size of the province of Prince Edward Island. This ranch was established in 1883 by Thaddeus Harper. He and his brother Jerome came to British Columbia in the early days of the gold rush, driving cattle up from the United States. Jerome Harper's JH brand is one of the oldest still in use in British Columbia.

From the junction to the Gang Ranch Bridge, the road climbs up the wall of the east side of the canyon in a seemingly endless series of hairpin turns, each offering a view more spectacular than the last. Then the zigzagging ceases and the road winds northward, sometimes passing beneath wine-red lava cliffs deposited countless centuries ago.

Dog Creek

Almost without warning, the dusty river trail begins to descend, and through openings in the timbers, lush green fields can be seen far below. A sheltered oasis in the desert, Dog Creek seems incongruous after traversing so much dry country. The high valley walls break the winds while the creek provides water, and mild winter weather often allows cattle to graze the fields in January, a sharp contrast to the ranchland up on the plateau.

One of the earliest settlers at Dog Creek is said to be a French nobleman named Comte de Versepeuch (or Versepuche). One story suggests that the Count, being a practical man, traded off his elegant tricornered hat and an elaborate blue satin jacket (from the court of Louis XVI) to Chief Alexis for a tidy band of sturdy horses. Versepeuch set up a waterwheel to power a whipsaw and built himself a substantial house. He also put his mechanical talent to work to help Samuel Leander Charles Brown build the first flour mill established by private enterprise in mainland British Columbia. It ground its first wheat in 1861, and a number of years later was moved to the Empire Valley.

Approximately 11 kilometres north is the weathered remnants of the Dog Creek RCAF station, which served as western Canada's second line of defence in case of attack from the Japanese in World War II.

Alkali Lake

Now the road swings away from the Fraser, angling northeast into the plateau country. The Cariboo region, with its numerous ponds, sloughs, and lakes, has

A picturesque barn alongside Dog Creek Road at Alkali Lake Ranch.

the most concentrated waterfowl nesting habitat in British Columbia. One of the richest of these is Alkali Lake. Also known as the Reidemann Wildlife Sanctuary, the lake is closed to hunting, trapping, and the discharge of firearms.

A detailed water bird survey was carried out in the spring of 1991 that recorded 30 species on the lake between mid-March and mid-June. The most common species were American widgeon, Canada goose, American coot, mallard, lesser scaup, and northern pintail. The study also recorded hooded mergansers, tundra swans, and American white pelicans. Of the more than 12,400 birds counted, other noteworthy species included American bittern, bald eagle, and ring-necked pheasant.

A short distance beyond marshy Alkali Lake, the distinctive red buildings of Alkali Lake Ranch come into view. Pre-empted in March of 1861, Alkali Lake claims to be the oldest ranch in British Columbia. It, too, served as a roadhouse for travellers on the river trail during the first years of the gold rush.

The Native village a short distance north of the ranch headquarters has apparently seen new growth in recent years. A school, store, and log homes bear testimony to a revival in self-reliance for the Native community.

Springhouse

Halfway between Alkali Lake and Williams Lake (50 kilometres to the north) lies the community of Springhouse. An airstrip and floatplane base here are the first significant signs of modern civilization since leaving Lillooet.

A short distance later, the rail fence and signpost of the Springhouse Trails Ranch beckons with the chance to pass the night at a modern guest ranch and campsite. There is a hot shower to soak off the dust of a day in the saddle and a sauna to ease the aches and pains of a vacation well spent. The Springhouse dining room has gained a widespread reputation for good food and friendly service.

Williams Lake Stampede

Situated off the old fur brigade trail, the tiny settlement that formed the basis for Williams Lake served as a supply centre for the miners following the river trail north. When the Cariboo Wagon Road was constructed, it is said that a quarrel between the contractor and a local settler resulted in the settlement being bypassed. The valley slumbered until the twin steel rails of the Pacific Great Eastern Railway (now the British Columbia Railway/Canadian National Railway) snaked northward. With the arrival of the railway, Williams Lake became a major supply centre and stockyard, earning such nicknames as "Cowtown" and "Willie's Puddle" from the neighbouring cowboys. Today, upwards of 40,000 head of cattle pass through its auction yards each year and British Columbia's premier rodeo, the Williams Lake Stampede, usually held on the July 1st weekend, is known across the continent.

For most holiday travellers, Williams Lake and the junction of the river road with Highway 97 is the end of the backroad adventure. But for the miners of the early 1860s, the river road continued north another 25 kilometres to where it again met the Fraser River. Above the treacherous canyon, steamboats docked at Soda Creek and loaded men and equipment for the remainder of the journey to Quesnel and the gateway to the rich placer claims of the Cariboo creeks.

Today, though a modern highway carries traffic through the Cariboo country at a breathtaking speed, there still are those who like to slip into the past and mosey along the Fraser River trail.

Note: See the *Information Sources* chapter at the end of the book for contact information on the services mentioned here.

GPS References for major points of interest
Ref: WGS 84 - Lat/Lon hddd.ddddd
Allow +/-100 metres due to data conversions

Wpt	Km	Description	Latitude	Longitude	Elev.
W01		Mile 0 Cairn — Lillooet	N50.69177	W121.93712	250 m
W02	0	0 km – Hwy 12 and Hwy 99	N50.68571	W121.91999	217 m
W03	14.0	Jct Fountain Valley Rd	N50.74238	W121.86476	384 m
W04	16.5	Spectacular views	N50.75134	W121.84413	311 m
W05	32.0	Pavilion store	N50.87159	W121.83157	664 m
W06	33.0	0 km — Pavilion-Clinton Rd	N50.88088	W121.82900	709 m
W07	46.3	46.3 km — Diamond S Ranch Gate	N50.95955	W121.79740	1,364 m
W08	48.5	Start 14% down	N50.96919	W121.78020	1,540 m
W09	49.7 (0)	Jct to Pavilion Mountain	N50.98001	W121.77838	1,440 m
W10	(9.6)	Summit – Pavilion Mountain	N50.97395	W121.68448	2,065 m
W11	53.4	Jct Pear Lake Rd	N50.99360	W121.79093	1,085 m
W12	55.6	Downing Provincial Park	N51.01058	W121.77904	1,089 m
W13	56.4	Jct Jesmond Rd	N51.01286	W121.76974	1,102 m
W14	66.9	Jct High Bar Rd	N51.07952	W121.85873	1,432 m
W15	79.0	Circle H Ranch	N51.16010	W121.93595	1,357 m
W16	92.3	Jesmond Post Office	N51.25679	W121.95374	1,168 m
W17	93.6	Jct Big Bar Ferry	N51.26667	W121.96271	1,148 m
W18	98.2	Big Bar Guest Ranch	N51.30225	W121.98338	1,036 m
W19	102.6	Jct Poison Lake Rd and Big Bar Lake Rd	N51.33588	W121.97127	1,048 m
W20	112.2	Jct Meadow Lake Rd	N51.41321	W121.97960	994 m
W21	127.9	Canoe Creek Indian Reserve	N51.47095	W122.15028	787 m
W22	128.7	BC Cattle Company	N51.47027	W122.16013	760 m
W23	145.9	Jct to Gang Ranch	N51.52677	W122.27866	414 m
W24	155	Jct to Upper Dog Creek	N51.58138	W122.23767	662 m
W25	166	Dog Creek Airport	N51.63121	W122.24512	1,030 m
W26	188	Alkali Lake Ranch	N51.78729	W122.24757	657 m
W27	214	Springhouse Airport	N51.95600	W122.14324	972 m
W28	216	Springhouse Trails Ranch	N51.98341	W122.15001	917 m
W29	228	Jct Chimney Valley Rd	N52.05871	W122.11302	740 m
W30	237	Jct Highway 20 – Williams Lake	N52.11178	W122.15051	672 m

The Marble Canyon Route

The striking limestone ridges and precipices of the Marble Canyon have attracted climbers from all over North America.

CHAPTER 5

The Marble Canyon Route: Highway 99 — Lillooet to Hat Creek House

STATISTICS

	Maps see pages 40 and 56.
Distance:	75 km, Lillooet to Highway 97 at Hat Creek.
Travel Time:	One to two hours.
Elevation Gain:	630 metres.
Condition:	Paved highway.
Season:	Open year-round.
Topo Maps:	Lillooet, BC 92 I/12.
(1:50,000)	Pavilion, BC 92 I/13.
	Cache Creek, BC 92 I/14.
Communities:	Lillooet, Clinton, and Cache Creek.

The first part of this route is described in the *Lillooet to Williams Lake* chapter. It covers the 33-kilometre section from Lillooet to the Pavilion First Nations community and the junction of the Pavilion-Clinton Road.

This short description will help with a few of the highlights to be found along Highway 99 between Pavilion and Hat Creek House at the junction of Highway 99 and Cariboo Highway 97.

Pavilion-Clinton Road

Holy Trinity Catholic Church, 33 kilometres northeast of the junction of Highways 12 and 99 at Lillooet, stands in the heart of the Pavilion Native community. It serves as a landmark for the road that follows the original Fraser River trail over Pavilion Mountain. As described in the previous chapter, the Pavilion Mountain road was the more direct route to the goldfields, but it was and still is only passable during the summer months.

Marble Canyon Road follows Highway 99 to Highway 97 at Hat Creek House (Carquille on some maps). Note that some old maps show this as Highway 12, an extension of the highway from Lytton to Lillooet. This was a much longer route,

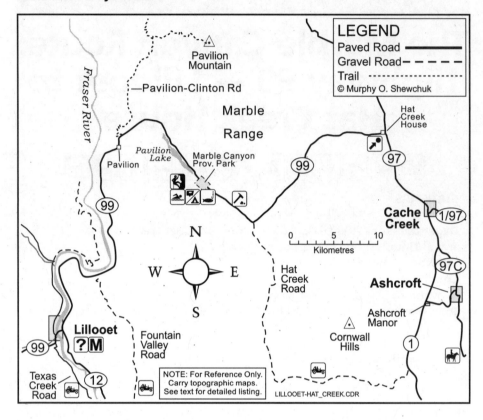

heading south and then east before meeting the Cariboo Wagon Road near Hat Creek House. But with an elevation at the pass of 850 metres, compared to 1580 metres at the highpoint on the Pavilion Mountain route, it definitely had a longer season and much easier grades.

Pavilion Lake: Glimpses of an Ancient Sea Floor

Pavilion Lake, near km 40, has attracted international attention because of underwater growths that might be related to ancient dendritic reef structures and thereby yield some clues to the origin of ancient stromatolites. An underwater video filmed by a sport diver has prompted a research project by Simon Fraser University's Underwater Research Lab and a team of NASA Ames Research Center scientists. Work started in 1997 and has grown to include scientists from the University of British Columbia, McMaster University, and other universities around the world.

The microbialites, as they have been named, that grow along the walls of the lake are not the only feature of interest. There is a collection of interconnected

While Pavilion Lake has been an important destination for First Nations peoples for centuries, it has recently attracted the attention of scientists because of life forms that are even older than humans.

mounds on a submerged ridge in the centre of the lake that has intrigued the scientists. More information on the Pavilion Lake Research Project is available from the University of British Columbia website at http://supercritical.civil.ubc.ca/~pavilion/index.php and the Simon Fraser University website at http://www.ensc.sfu.ca/research/url/pav/index.html.

Sky Blue Waters Resort

The first cabins at Sky Blue Waters Resort were built in 1934, although I suspect that "resort" wasn't part of the name back then. When I first visited the place in the late 1950s, it was a fishing camp on beautiful Pavilion Lake as well as an ideally located lunch stop on the long drive from the Bridge River Valley to Kamloops.

The Marble Canyon Route

Although highway improvements have meant that the road no longer winds through the middle of the resort, neither the fishing nor the lake has changed much in the past half-century. If you are looking for a break from the city, Sky Blue Waters Resort offers seven "rustic" cabins ("rustic" means central toilets and showers) plus four waterfront tenting areas.

The resort is currently normally open from the Victoria Day weekend to Thanksgiving, but with the increased interest in ice fishing and ice climbing, the Ts'kw'aylaxw First Nation is considering winterizing the cabins to extend the season.

Marble Canyon Cliffs

There is a trail that leads up to the Marble Canyon cliffs at km 44.7 near the east end of Pavilion Lake. The initial trail winds through pine and juniper, providing access to the base of the cliffs and a better view of the surrounding countryside. This is just one of the routes to the base of what has become known as the "Cinderella of BC rock," because of its still relatively undiscovered beauty.

I'm not a rock climber. I can't pass judgment on these beautiful crags, but I will quote a few sentences from the introduction to the 37 pages of description that Lyle Knight has in *Central BC Rocks*: "The setting is outstanding with towering walls of clean limestone rising majestically above the jeweled lakes in the valley floor . . . The climbing is of moderate difficulty and quality with the majority of the route being in the 5.7 to 5.10 range . . . Marble Canyon has meant many things to many people for many years."

Ice climbing has recently become a popular sport, and Marble Canyon has one of the best and most easily accessed icefalls in the region.

Marble Canyon Provincial Park Campground

Unlike the majority of well-spaced, treed BC Parks campgrounds, the 30-unit Marble Canyon "high-density" campground does not accept reservations. The roadside park was established in 1956 and expanded to take in Pavilion Lake and some of the limestone cliffs in 2001. It operates on a first-come, first-served basis and can fill up early on summer weekends.

Graymont Limestone Quarry

The Graymont Lime Plant, at km 50.5, produces a range of lime and limestone products, including high calcium quicklime and screened limestone. Lime is produced in two rotary preheater kilns with a combined annual production capacity of 235,000 tonnes.

Roger Porter and a visitor ride the Barnard's Express stagecoach at Hat Creek House.

Hat Creek Road

A junction to the south at km 54 marks the start of a gravel backroad that could take you south and east to the Trans-Canada Highway south of Ashcroft. The section from the south end of the Hat Creek Valley via Oregon Jack Creek to Highway 1 should not be attempted with a motorhome or a vehicle pulling a trailer. Signs at the southeast end suggest that a 4x4 be the mode of transportation at the best of times. See the *Hat Creek Loop* chapter for details.

Hat Creek House ·

Hat Creek House, initially a 1860s roadhouse and restaurant and later a working cattle ranch, has become an historic attraction complete with interpretive guides, a restaurant, and a campground. The historic site is located just south of Highway 99 at km 73.5, less than a kilometre from Highway 97.

The roadhouse has been preserved in much the same condition as it was when it catered to stagecoach traffic. The barns are still there and you may have an opportunity to ride in (or on) a stagecoach drawn by a team of horses. There is also a First Nations pithouse or kikuli in a glade near the creek.

Note: See the *Information Sources* chapter at the end of the book for contact information on the services mentioned here.

GPS References for major points of interest
Ref: WGS 84 - Lat/Lon hddd.ddddd
Allow +/-100 metres due to data conversions

Wpt	Km	Description	Latitude	Longitude	Elev.
W01		Mile 0 Cairn – Lillooet	N50.69177	W121.93712	250 m
W02	0	0 km – Hwy 12 and Hwy 99	N50.68571	W121.91999	217 m
W03	14.0	Jct Fountain Valley Rd	N50.74238	W121.86476	384 m
W04	16.5	Spectacular Views	N50.75134	W121.84413	311 m
W05	32.0	Pavilion store	N50.87159	W121.83157	664 m
W06	33.0	Jct Pavilion-Clinton Rd	N50.88088	W121.82900	709 m
W07	40.0	Pavilion Lake west end	N50.88149	W121.82745	805 m
W08	42.5	Sky Blue Waters Resort	N50.86180	W121.72788	805 m
W09	44.7	Marble Canyon Cliffs Trail	N50.84814	W121.70959	805 m
W10	46.0	Crown Lake	N50.83862	W121.69971	812 m
W11	47.0	Marble Canyon Park Campground	N50.83303	W121.70959	812 m
W12	50.5	Graymont Lime Plant	N50.81359	W121.64885	830 m
W13	54.0	Hat Creek Road Jct	N50.79647	W121.61055	823 m
W14	73.5	Hat Creek House historic site	N50.88706	W121.41041	490 m
W15	74.2	Jct Hwy 99 and Hwy 97	N50.88777	W121.40041	495 m

The Thompson River Route: Sagebrush, Bunchgrass, and Rattlesnakes

Lytton, at the junction of the Thompson and Fraser rivers, marks a major division in geography and how that geography influenced the people who followed the retreating glaciers northward.

The muddy Fraser River flows down from the north, passing through steep-walled canyons carved through the glacial silt and debris left behind a hundred

Wildlife were important to the survival of the Thompson Salish people.

centuries ago. The summer winds funnel up the canyon, creating a blast-furnace effect that, coupled with an average annual precipitation in the 30 to 35 centimetre range, does little to support the forests found on the west side of the Coast Range Mountains.

Temperatures that often exceed 40°C support little more than hardy ponderosa pine, bunchgrass, and sagebrush. Saskatoon bushes and arrowleaf balsamroot present their sunflower-like blossoms to the bumblebees in April and May. Prickly pear cactus follow in June.

These plants, as well as a

wide variety of other dry land plants and shrubs, served the Thompson First Nations peoples. They also hunted wildlife in the timbered side valleys, but an important staple in their diet was the sockeye salmon that migrated up both rivers in the summer and fall. These were caught by gaff or dip net and dried on open-air racks.

Wagon Road North

The Thompson River, cleaned of its glacial silt by several large lake systems, flows in from the northeast. Though a rough and tumble river on the last 20 kilometres of its run to the Fraser, the Thompson canyons aren't quite as steep-walled and imposing.

The Thompson Salish people traded (and occasionally battled) with the Halkomelem to the south as well as the Lillooet people to the west. The Thompson Salish influence extended north the Ashcroft area and east to Nicola Lake.

When the fur traders arrived in the early 1800s, they developed trading posts in Kamloops and in the south Okanagan, and used the First Nations trade routes to take the furs to the Pacific and bring back trade goods, first via the Columbia River and later via the lower Fraser River. Pack horses were the prime transportation from Kamloops to the coast, with the fall brigades said to reach as many as 200 horses and 50 men.

The 1858 gold rush — prompted by the discovery of gold in the Nicoamen River, 17 kilometres northeast of Lytton nearly a decade earlier — proved the inadequacies of the fur brigade trails. The resulting 1860s wagon road up the Fraser Canyon left the Fraser at Lytton and followed the Thompson River upstream to Ashcroft and Cache Creek. Cache Creek became the junction for the road heading north to Clinton and the "real" Cariboo. It was also the departure point for the road heading east to Kamloops Lake. Savona, at the west end of Kamloops Lake, became the departure point for water transportation to Kamloops and the Shuswap Lake system.

Railways and Highways

As in the Fraser Canyon, the wagon road up the Thompson served the miners and their suppliers for two decades before carrying supplies for the railway builders. The Canadian Pacific Railway and, later, the Canadian Northern Pacific Railway, followed the Thompson River upstream to Kamloops where the Canadian Pacific Railway continued east to Calgary via Rogers Pass. The Canadian Northern Pacific Railway headed north to Tête Jaune Cache and Edmonton via the North

The Thompson River near Martel, north of Spences Bridge.

Thompson River and Yellowhead Pass.

The railways took the freight traffic off the wagon road, relegating it to secondary status for half a century until the automobile promoted the reconstruction of the road system and the Trans-Canada Highway.

New Gateway to the Cariboo

While the railways managed to cling to the Fraser and Thompson canyons, politics, economics, and an elevation difference of nearly 600 metres in the 50 kilometres to Clinton has meant that a railway was never built into the Cariboo from Ashcroft. As noted in the Cache Creek to Barkerville chapter, when the CPR was completed, Ashcroft became the new gateway to the Cariboo.

As noted in the following chapters, the Trans-Canada Highway has also become the gateway to a host of recreational opportunities.

The Thompson River Road: Exploring Beyond the Asphalt Ribbon

STATISTICS

	Map see page 66.
Distance:	85 km, Lytton to Cache Creek.
	85 km, Cache Creek to Kamloops.
Travel Time:	Minimum two hours.
Condition:	Paved two to four lane highway.
Season:	Open year-round.
Topo Maps:	Lytton, BC 92 I/14.
(1:50,000)	Stein River, BC 92 I/5.
	Spences Bridge, BC 92 I/6.
	Ashcroft, BC 92 I/11.
	Cache Creek, BC 92 I/14.
	Tranquille River, BC 92 I/15.
	Cherry Creek, BC 92 I/10.
	Kamloops, BC 92 I/9.
Communities:	Lytton, Spences Bridge, Ashcroft, Cache Creek, Savona, and Kamloops.

An asphalt ribbon follows the Thompson River, first clinging precariously to the cliffs of the canyon carved through the northern reaches of the Cascade Mountains, then snaking along the edge of the wild whitewater. On an August afternoon, the shimmering pavement resembles a scene from *Lawrence of Arabia*. It can be compared to a drive through hell, except that hell is probably cooler. In mid-January, the scene might be from *Never Cry Wolf*, grey pavement, grey sagebrush, and grey hills competing with a grey sky to emulate a tundra landscape.

If the Trans-Canada Highway between Lytton and Kamloops has any redeeming features, few people slow down long enough to look for them.

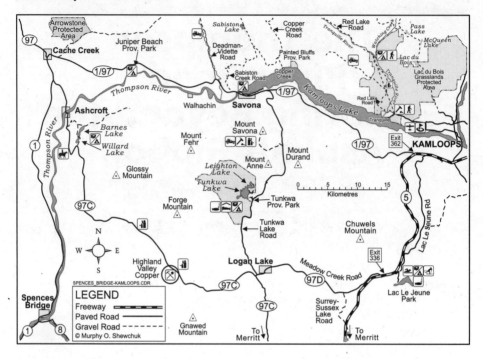

However, you'll discover that there is colour and life along the Thompson River Road if you take time to leave the yellow centreline.

No Backroad, but . . .

History has been tattered by the black and yellow asphalt ribbon, but the remnants of ancient Indian trails and the famed Cariboo Waggon Road have not been erased. The 165-kilometre drive from Lytton to Kamloops offers dozens of opportunities to slip away from the speeding traffic and discover a part of British Columbia that has intrigued humans for a hundred centuries. You'll discover that a two-hour drive can turn into a two-day adventure and provide a whole new perspective of what the BC Interior has to offer.

Oldest Continuously Inhabited Settlement in North America

The clear, green Thompson River seems to fight for its life as it hugs the east shore of the Fraser River at Lytton. It has just bounced through dozens of whitewater rapids and passed under one of British Columbia's newest bridges, and now it is about to lose its identity in the perpetually muddy Fraser. It doesn't take much imagination to link the fate of the Thompson to the community that clings to the benchland above.

Known as "Tlkumtcin" by the natives and bastardized to "Camchin" and "Kumsheen" by the European traders and settlers, Lytton has been an important village in the Thompson Salish Nation for 7,000 years or more. In late summer and autumn the two rivers that flow past the village teem with salmon, a staple food of the First Nations peoples.

When fur trade explorer Simon Fraser and his voyageurs visited the village on the morning of Sunday, June 19, 1808, there were four hundred Natives living here. Across the Fraser River was another village of about 1,200 and, wrote Fraser in his journals, ". . . I had to shake hands with all of them." The next morning, after trading for dried salmon, Fraser named the river flowing in from the east after his good friend and fellow explorer, David Thompson.

For the next half-century, Kumsheen was little more than an occasional stop on the fur trade circuit. Then, gold was discovered a short distance up the Thompson River and all hell broke loose. On November 11, 1858, only a few months into the Fraser River gold rush, Governor James Douglas named the settlement after Sir Edward Bulwer-Lytton, Secretary of State for the Colonies.

Bulwer-Lytton (1803–73) is remembered today chiefly as a novelist and dramatist. In recent years, the English Department at San Jose State University has held a Bulwer-Lytton Fiction Contest for the wordiest opening of a novel, in keeping with Bulwer-Lytton's notorious "It was a dark and stormy night . . ."

Riding a Roller Coaster in a Washing Machine

The treacherous Thompson River undoubtedly claimed countless lives over the centuries. Bark canoes and fire-carved dugouts were no match for the standing waves that could upend even the best Native boatman. It has taken rubber rafts and plastic kayaks to tame the "Jaws of Death." And it has taken whitewater rafting enthusiasts such as Bernie Fandrich to turn what was once a death-defying feat into a summer industry.

Bernie began rafting the Thompson River 1973 — I think it was 1975 that I had my first "ride" with him and Tom Brown, then a retired BC Lions football quarterback. For the first decade or two, Bernie based his operation out of a warehouse in downtown Lytton. Then, realizing that there was more to rafting than just rafting, Bernie, his family, and staff began building a world-class rafting resort on a picturesque bench high above the Thompson River about six kilometres northeast of Lytton. (See the *Whitewater Rafting* chapter for more information.)

Walk the Cariboo Waggon Road

Skihist Provincial Park, a few minutes north of the Kumsheen resort, is deceptive.

Part of the original Cariboo Waggon Road winds through Skihist Provincial Park.

Few casual highway travellers realize the extent of the 33-hectare park hidden by scattered ponderosa pines. The landscaped rest stop alongside the highway is only a small portion of the park. A winding road extends up the mountain to 58 campsites hidden among the trees.

And in the coolness of the morning, you can take a three-hour hike on a loop trail that winds even farther up the mountainside. Good boots and a full water bottle are essential, but otherwise it's a relatively easy trail. The payoff is the opportunity to add a few upland birds to your life-list and take some excellent photos of the Thompson Canyon, complete with two railways and the previously mentioned ribbon of asphalt. If you do the loop in a clockwise direction, your final hundred steps will be along the original 1860s Cariboo Waggon Road.

Skihist Provincial Park Trail

STATISTICS

Map see page 70.
Distance:	6 to 8 km, depending on viewpoint trips.
Travel Time:	Three to five hours.
Condition:	Narrow mountain trail.
Season:	May through September.
Topo Maps:	Hope, BC 92 H/6.
(1:50,000)	Stein River, BC 92 I/5.
	Lytton, BC 92 I/4.
	Prospect Creek, BC 92 I/3.
Communities:	Lytton and Spences Bridge.

Mountainside Park

Skihist Provincial Park is built on the side of Mount Lytton, approximately 7.7 kilometres northeast of Lytton. There is a picnic area on the north side of the highway, set on a bench between the highway and the Thompson River. A trail along the edge of the bank presents some spectacular views of the weather-worn Scarped Range, an extension of the North Cascade Mountains. Below and across the river run the tracks of the Canadian Pacific and Canadian National railways.

The 58-site campground is located in a ponderosa pine forest on the south side of the highway, up and away from the traffic noise.

Skihist Trails

There is a network of trails to several viewpoints on the south side of the park. Parking is not available at the upper trailhead, but there is room to squeeze a vehicle or two off the road at the lower trailhead near campsite 20.

In my opinion, this is a better place to park because the return part of the loop trail will bring you back down to your vehicle without any extra climbing.

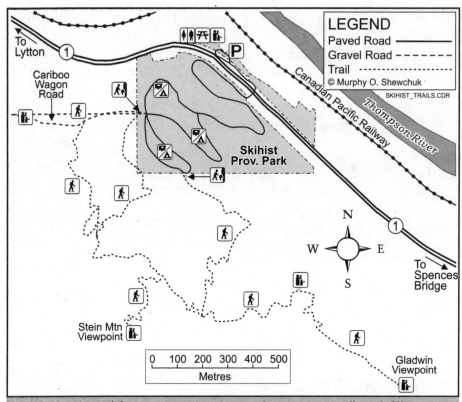

After parking (if you are not staying at the campground) and filling your water bottle, take the three-hundred-metre walk to the upper trailhead near campsite 29. There is a general trailhead sign and a map post near the start of the trail. Keep left to follow the foot trail and not the old road. It is a kilometre south and up to the first junction, where you have an option of going left (southeast) about 1.2 kilometres to Gladwin Lookout, where you'll have a spectacular view of the Thompson Canyon, the Trans-Canada Highway, two railway tracks, and the scarred mountains to the north.

Bench Trail

After a break at the Gladwin Lookout, retrace your steps to the junction and follow the sign for the trail to the west. It is fairly flat for the first six hundred metres, with a side trip south and up to the Stein Mountain Lookout Point. Note that this is not Stein Mountain, but a viewpoint on the side of Mount Lytton that presents an excellent opportunity to photograph the Coast Range peaks to the west of the Fraser Canyon.

Katharine hikes up the Skihist Park trail to Gladwin Lookout.

Cariboo Waggon Road

Then the Skihist loop trail begin a switchback descent to the old Cariboo Waggon Road. A junction to the left (west) a short distance down the switchback trail offers you the opportunity to take a longer, more scenic route to the old road. Once on the wagon road, if you still have any energy left, you can walk west for another three hundred metres for more views of the Thompson Canyon.

Go Prepared

While the Skihist trails aren't particularly demanding, they are not wheelchair accessible and should not be attempted without good footwear and plenty of drinking water. Bug repellent and bear spray may also be a useful part of your kit. Allow the better part of a day if you plan to visit Gladwin Lookout, and Stein Lookout and do the full circle. Because this can be some of the driest and hottest country in British Columbia, plan to get an early start and dress accordingly.

"Mad dogs . . ."

Remember, Noël Coward had it right: "Mad dogs and Englishmen go out in the midday sun . . ."

Anita Gilderdale and Sheila Dinsdale stop for a break at the Gladwin Viewpoint.

The Thompson Canyon from Gladwin Lookout. Note the southbound CN freight train in the lower centre, a northbound CN freight in the centre, the Trans-Canada Highway in the top centre, and a road to a private ranch in the upper right. And the river runs through it all.

Winding Road

The Trans-Canada Highway drops down to river level at a railway underpass near km 13 (with the south entrance to Lytton as km 0). The snake-like set of curves gouged out of the cliff has probably taken as many lives as the roaring river below. If this is your first trip up the Thompson Canyon, pay close attention to the "Slow" signs and the oncoming traffic.

If the water is low, you should be able to recognize the distinctive "Frog" that divides the river near km 16.5, creating the first major rapids on the rafting trip from Spences Bridge to Lytton.

Nicoamen River Gold

The spectacular waterfalls to your right a few seconds past the "Frog" marks an important bit of British Columbia history that few people know about.

Hudson's Bay Company Chief Trader Donald McLean, noted for his cruelty and his notorious sons, the McLean Boys, is believed to have purchased the first significant amounts of gold found in the Interior. The information is sketchy and sometimes conflicting, but a number of historical clues suggest that the Native peoples who sold him the gold found it in the Nicoamen River as early as 1852. A shipment of gold sent to the mint in San Francisco prompted the 1858 gold rush. However, Hill's Bar, on the Fraser River near Yale, proved to be rich and diverted the gold seekers before they reached the Thompson River.

The Mountain Blocked the River

A stop-of-interest sign on the southern outskirts of Spences Bridge marks a century-old disaster:

A Great Landslide
Suddenly on the afternoon of August 13, 1905, the lower side of the mountain slid away. Rumbling across the valley in seconds, the slide buried alive five Indians and dammed the Thompson River for over four hours. The trapped waters swept over the nearby Indian village drowning thirteen persons.

If you take a close look at Murray Falls, across the Thompson from the stop-of-interest sign, you may notice a tunnel and the remnants of a flume that was tacked to the rock face. From the 1880s to the 1940s, this flume carried water to prize apple orchards at Spences Bridge.

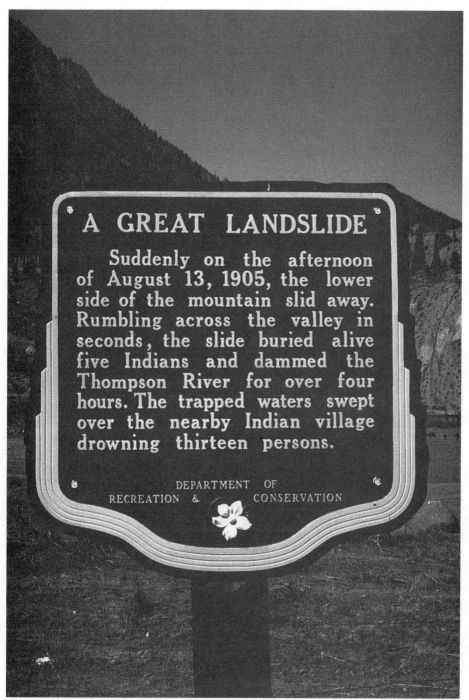

A GREAT LANDSLIDE

Suddenly on the afternoon of August 13, 1905, the lower side of the mountain slid away. Rumbling across the valley in seconds, the slide buried alive five Indians and dammed the Thompson River for over four hours. The trapped waters swept over the nearby Indian village drowning thirteen persons.

DEPARTMENT OF
RECREATION & CONSERVATION

Stop-of-interest sign at Spences Bridge.

The Great Landslide

The August 18, 1905, issue of *The Nicola Herald* describes the landslide in greater detail:

> At 2:30 p.m. last Sunday the inhabitants of Spences Bridge were startled to see a large land slide coming down the mountain on the north side of the (Thompson) river . . . directly opposite the Indian rancherie.
>
> The slide descended to the river with great velocity and swept the water and debris on the poor, unfortunate Indians. Many ran for their lives, others in their houses were swept away . . . without a moment's warning.
>
> . . . nothing now remains but debris and rocks. The new church was the most substantial building, but it was . . . reduced to kindling wood.
>
> Immediately the slide descended, a mighty wave, ten to fifteen feet high, started up the river . . . sweeping for over two miles and flooding the buildings on the river bottom. The river was completely dammed for a couple of hours and rose over twenty feet . . . before it found an outlet.
>
> The work of rescue was commenced immediately and twelve maimed and injured men, women and children were picked up and placed in the temporary hospital . . . Fifteen are killed and thirteen injured all belonging to the Indian population.

A story in the following issue of *The Nicola Herald*, dated August 31, 1905, presented a reason behind the slide. CPR consulting engineer, H. J. Cambie, had a strong opinion on the matter:

> . . . the clays of this dry and arid part of the province which have been deprived by excessive evaporation during many centuries of nearly all their

The clay benches on the slopes of Arthur Seat Mountain slid into the Thompson River on August 13, 1905.

moisture, will take up about 60 per cent of their own weight of water without changing their shape, but if a trifle more is added, they lose all cohesion and spread out quite flat.

"No doubt this is what happened to a bench about 300 feet above the Thompson River, which the Indians had been irrigating for months past, and saturating with water. Portions of the same field slid in a similar manner in 1883 and in 1899 . . .

Nicola Detour

The Highway 8 junction, just north of the landslide sign, presents an opportunity to detour off the Trans-Canada Highway. Steelhead fishermen camp near the river just north of the old bridge across the Thompson River. If you are interested in a longer drive and some serious high-country fishing, you could take Highway 8 and explore Pimainus or Chataway Lakes. However, if you are really interested in exploring the backroads of the Nicola, consider purchasing a copy of *Coquihalla Trips & Trails* by Murphy Shewchuk.

Widow Smith of Spence's Bridge

Newlywed Jessie Ann Smith left Scotland in February 1884 and travelled with her orchardist husband, John, to the British Columbia community of Spence's Bridge. Thirty-year-old Jessie Ann's strict Presbyterian upbringing and her training as a teacher, musician, and banker did little to prepare her for the exciting life she was about to lead as a pioneer in British Columbia's fledgling ranching and fruit industry.

Her story, a love story with a historical twist, begins with her childhood in Scotland and follows her by ship across the Atlantic and by rail across the United States to the west coast of British Columbia. Her introduction to Canada includes a work train trip up the Fraser Canyon on the still-under-construction Canadian Pacific Railway. After an

A silver cup presented to Mrs. Jesse Ann Smith by the Vancouver Exhibition Association "For Commercial Fruit Grown East of the Cascades — Spences Bridge B.C. 1914."

attempt on her husband's life, they left Spence's Bridge for a harsh decade of

Thomas Spence's Bridge

The settlement was first known as Cook's Ferry, a reference to Mortimer Cook who, in the 1860s, ran a ferry across the Thompson River to serve travellers on their way to the Cariboo goldfields. While the goldfields have lost their lustre, the Inn at Spences Bridge, the Log Cabin Pub, and Acacia Grove R.V. Park & Cabins present opportunities to partake in local hospitality.

If you take the time to explore the village between the existing "old" one-lane bridge and the newer highway bridge, you may notice the footings of still another bridge. Thomas Spence built the first bridge here in 1865, and to recover his costs he was permitted to charge a toll.

homesteading in an upland valley south of Merritt. In 1897, after the death of John Smith's former employer, the family returned to rebuild the Spence's Bridge orchard.

John Smith died in 1905, the delayed result of a Granite Creek mining accident. Jessie Ann Smith and her children continued working the Spence's Bridge orchard and their Grimes Golden apples won top honours in shows in Canada, the United States, and England. King Edward VII sought the apples of the "Widow Smith of Spence's Bridge" at a London horticultural show in 1909, prompting a local versifier to pen the following:

> The King? Ay, ay — no less than he,
> None other than His Majesty;
> His car already comes to stand
> At Islington's exhibit grand,
> Ingenuous to a high degree —
> "I've come," he says most graciously,
> "Those luscious Golden Grimes to see
> Of Widow Smith's from fair B.C."
> With dainty taste and polished mien
> He deems them fitting for the Queen.
> Forthwith he executes command
> That they be sent to Buckingham.

With the aid of three of her granddaughters, Jessie Ann Smith began writing her life story in the mid-1930s. Her granddaughter Audrey Ward helped complete the book and *Widow Smith of Spence's Bridge* was first published by Sonotek Publishing Ltd. in 1989.

The Ashcroft Manor Roadhouse once served gold seekers on the way to the Cariboo.

Stops & Detours

After crossing the flats, the highway climbs steadily north of Spences Bridge, passing several roadside orchards, fruit stands, and a campground on its way up to the benchlands high above the river. On a hot day you may discover that a basket of fruit or a jug of soft apple cider is ample reason to pull off for a stop.

You may also discover that a detour up Venables Valley Road can take you off the beaten track into a hidden vale. If you managed to spot the first turn-off (to your right) before you passed it, your backroad jaunt will bring you back to the highway a few kilometres farther north. A side road to the right (east) near the north end of Venables Valley Road leads to the old Basque Ranch. Basque also had its 15 minutes of fame as the site of the last spike in the Canadian Northern Pacific Railway, a predecessor to the Canadian National Railway.

If you are really into detours, Hat Creek Road, near km 28.5, offers an even longer and more exciting detour. If you take this backroad, described in the *Hat Creek Loop* chapter, you could come out at Highway 97, 11 kilometres north of Cache Creek.

Fox Hunters

Brothers Clement Francis and Henry Pennant Cornwall built the Ashcroft Manor and a roadhouse to serve the gold rush traffic in 1862. By 1868 it was

Ashcroft Opera House

Although a disastrous fire recently destroyed part of the village core, Ashcroft is still well worth a detour off the burning blacktop. The Ashcroft Museum is one of the finest in the region and the recently refurbished Ashcroft Opera House at 401 Brink Street has been attracting big-name acts to a small-town venue.

The Barra MacNeils on stage at the Ashcroft Opera House.

Built in 1889 as an opera house and operated by McGillivray and Veasey, it featured such travelling opera companies as the Royal Lilliputian Opera Company from Australia and the Pollard Opera Company. (Reserved seats $1.00; general admission 75¢.) It was later operated as a theatre by Fred Peters, with Lew Cummings playing the music to accompany the silent films. After several incarnations, including a short life as Frank's New & Used, present owner and impresario Martin Comtois has revived the building as an "opera house." Although the "operas" are few and far between, a recent year's lineup of jazz, blues, country, cabaret, and acoustic guitar performances numbered over 70 and included Cape Breton's famous Barra MacNeils for a three-night stand.

If you are interested in a pleasant outdoor stroll through time, Ashcroft's Heritage Place Park is well worth the visit. You'll find a railway caboose, mine cars, a replica of a waterwheel used to drive a pioneer flour mill, and other historical items. Picnic tables and welcome shade also make this a pleasant place to relax.

A replica of the historic Harper's Mill waterwheel at Ashcroft Heritage Place.

running smoothly and they had time to pursue their favourite sport — fox hunting. Unfortunately, they couldn't find any foxes and had to set their imported hounds after the wily and elusive coyote. However, rumours are that a coyote runs faster than the little red fox, and the hounds and horses got plenty of exercise — but seldom a coyote.

The Ashcroft Manor house was destroyed by fire in 1943, but the roadhouse survives as an interesting arts and crafts shop. Behind the roadhouse, hidden by the trees, is the Ashcroft Manor Teahouse. A side road near Ashcroft Manor winds down to the village of Ashcroft, returning to Highway 1 about six kilometres north of the Manor.

Cache Creek Junction

The name has evoked various wild and woolly stories about Cariboo stage robbers hiding their loot, and of Donald McLean caching gold in the nearby hills before leaving for the Chilcotin War — and ultimately his death. However, the name appears on fur trader Samuel Black's 1835 map long before gold was discovered. Indeed, it probably originated when the location was used as a collection point for furs destined for Thompson's River Post (Kamloops).

While furs aren't on the menu, Cache Creek has a wide variety of services to cater to today's travelling public.

Highway 97 winds up into the Cariboo and points farther north, while the Trans-Canada Highway climbs eastward up onto the benches high above the Thompson River.

Ghost Along the River

A stop-of-interest plaque tells part of the story:

Ghost of Walhachin

Here bloomed a "Garden of Eden"! The sagebrush desert changed to orchards through imagination and industry of English settlers during 1907–14. Then the men left to fight — and die — for King and country. A storm ripped out the vital irrigation flume. Now only ghosts of flume, trees, and homes remain to mock this once thriving settlement.

"Ghost of Walhachin" stop-of-interest sign near the Trans-Canada Highway.

Walhachin: Garden of Eden

In January 1908, Charles E. Barnes, an American civil engineer, formed the British Columbia Horticultural Estates Limited and set about acquiring land a few miles west of Savona. Some 1,800 hectares (4,500 acres) in all, bisected by the Thompson River and the Canadian Pacific Railway, became part of the dream.

A townsite, including neat little four-room houses, a general store, a packing house, and a hotel was soon built on the south side of the river.

The dream began to move with determination. The land was divided into five- and ten-acre blocks sold for $350 an acre planted with young fruit trees, $50 less without, with an irrigation water rate of $4 per acre per year. The irrigation water was carried by 27 kilometres of flume and ditch from Deadman River because, although the Thompson River was only a few hundred feet below the cultivated benchland, it was then too expensive to pump the vast amounts of water needed.

Barnes advertised this "Garden of Eden" in British newspapers and about 70 young Englishmen were wooed by this promotional material. They came to settle the land and work on the construction of the complex irrigation system. While the fruit trees were growing to maturity, market gardening was practiced, and the hot summer sun encouraged good crops of corn, tomatoes, onions, and even tobacco.

In the fall of 1913, the first carload of Jonathan apples was shipped to market. In August of the following year, England declared war on Germany, and one month later 40 of Walhachin's finest enlisted. Before long the total included the entire eligible male population.

Left alone at Walhachin, the wives and the older men tried to carry on, but they faced the heartbreaking and endless task of repairing hastily built flumes and ditches, and watching the often-dry orchards burn in the sun.

Many of them soon realized the hopelessness of their situation and, giving up all they invested, returned to their homes and relatives in England. Only a few stayed on to live at Walhachin.

Little more than traces of the garden rows and the occasional live tree mark the passing of man. Rotting flumes amid the sagebrush show that Barnes' followers had toiled while they was here, but little else indicates that this was once a "Garden of Eden."

A century-old apple tree at Walhachin.

Deadman-Vidette Road

According to sketchy records of the North West Fur Company, the valley acquired the basis for its name about 1815, when Monsieur Charette, a clerk or senior labourer temporarily in charge of the post at Kamloops, met an untimely death near here. As the story goes, Charette was travelling through the area with a Native companion when an argument developed over where they should camp. A knife in the hands of Charette's companion ended the discussion.

If you are still looking for more detours, you can head north on Deadman-Vidette Road and enjoy spectacular "moonscape" scenery, half a dozen fine fishing lakes, and a beautiful waterfall. Check out the *Deadman-Vidette Road* chapter for details.

Sabiston Creek Road

Just beyond the crest of the hill overlooking Kamloops Lake, a gravel road leads off to the north and loops through the hills and mountains to Copper Creek, Red Lake, and then back down via the Tranquille Valley to Kamloops at the east end of Kamloops Lake. See the *Red Lake Road* chapter for additional information.

Savona, Once a Steamboat Port...

After traversing the arid benchland for nearly 35 kilometres, the Trans-Canada Highway drops back down to the Thompson River at the west end of Kamloops Lake.

Francois Saveneux settled on the south shore of the foot of Kamloops Lake in 1858. He ran the first cable ferry across "Boute du Lac," serving the American miners who were then swarming into the country in search of Cariboo gold. It seems to have been a profitable venture, run in conjunction with the Hudson's Bay Company wharf and warehouse on the north shore. Saveneux died in 1862, but his wife continued to run Savona's Ferry for a few more years. In 1870, the government took over the ferry operation.

In the meantime, the new wave of miners heading to the Columbia River prompted the construction of the first steamboat to ply Kamloops Lake. The SS *Marten* was built at Chase from whip-sawed lumber and floated down to Savona's Ferry where it was fitted with machinery brought up the new wagon road from Cache Creek. The "Big Bend" gold rush didn't last long and the SS *Marten* was soon reduced to towing logs and lumber.

An interesting side note is that in early May 1875, after a lapse of nine years, the *Marten* carried a load of freight from Kamloops 193 kilometres up the North Thompson River. An amazing feat, even by today's standards.

During the Canadian Pacific Railway construction in the mid-1880s, the CPR built the 41-metre-long stern-wheeler SS *Skuzzy* to carry freight for rail crews. The *Skuzzy* quickly worked itself and the port of Savona's Ferry out of business. As a side note, the *Skuzzy* holds a unique place in Canadian history as the only steamboat to traverse the fearsome Hell's Gate rapids on the Fraser River — upstream.

During the railway construction, the name of the community was changed to Van Horne, after one of the CPR dignitaries. However, the dusty settlement lacked sufficient "dignity" and by 1910 the name reverted to Savona.

Incidentally, just in case you are wondering about the pronunciation, in 1880 the Marquis of Lorne, on official tour as Governor General, was warned to accent the first syllable and to pronounce it "Sav-a-na" rather than "Sa-vone-ah."

Steelhead Provincial Park

If you are looking for a place to camp before heading into the high-country (or after having been snowed out on the May long weekend), consider Steelhead Provincial Park at the foot of Kamloops Lake near where Savona's Ferry is likely to have been. There are 40 campsites at the park, some with tent pads, as well as

Kamloops Lake from Steelhead Provincial Park at Savona.

Hoodoos on the Thompson

Interested in photographing the carved stone columns of ancient civilizations but can't afford a trip to Greece or Rome? Well, fret not. British Columbia has a wealth of colourful and intriguing stone and clay columns – often called hoodoos – and some of the most interesting stand in the Thompson valley.

A trip along the scenic Trans-Canada Highway from Lytton to Chase, with the occasional detour, will give you the opportunity to capture on film more sculpted works than any holiday in Europe.

Carved by Nature

The only difference here is, instead of a human artisan working the raw material, nature is the sculptor; instead of the traditional chisel and mallet smashing the intractable marble or granite block, cliffs of stone or clay are worked by the force of wind, rain, and frost.

Using materials deposited 10,000 years ago by melting glaciers, the drier climate has become the artist. Summer winds, winter frosts, and the occasional rain storm — the area has less than 25 centimetres of

This incredible hoodoo rock formation is located in the Deadman Valley, approximately 18 kilometres north of the Trans-Canada Highway.

annual precipitation — continually carve the cliffs, creating a multitude of pinnacles and columns that excite the imagination of anyone who has ever made castles in the sand.

Scattered Throughout the Valley

There are many similar examples of nature's artistry scattered throughout the valley. The Thompson River from Savona to Lytton passes through a deep canyon with cliffs that have also been artistically chiselled by nature. Here, the colours are breathtaking, varying from deep red through gold, orange, brown, and cream to slate black. A trip down the river on a kayak or whitewater raft or a journey on one of the many side roads will reveal picturesque columns not visible from the highway.

Deadman Valley, northwest of Savona, has probably the highest concentration of hoodoos and multi-coloured rock formations in the region.

Balancing Rock

The cliffs along the shores of Kamloops Lake are carved, in many places, into a maze of multi-coloured pinnacles. Possibly the most photographed hoodoo of all stands on a hillside east of Savona. Thousands of picture postcards have been sold showing this 20-metre stone-capped spire. Known locally as the Balancing Rock, it resembles an eighteenth century soldier with a tri-cornered cocked hat.

The balancing rock is less than a half-hour's walk from the highway, if you are interested in taking a closer look. Park your vehicle off the roadway opposite the skeet range, 5.5 kilometres east of Savona, and follow the pair of tire tracks down toward the lake, gradually angling eastward.

You will soon spot the stone-capped column on the north side of a gully that angles across the slope in the direction of Kamloops, at the east end of the lake. A fairly good trail leads right down toward the stone soldier. With a bit of effort, you can work yourself into a good picture-taking position. You'll need to experiment with a variety of lenses and positions to adequately capture the immensity of this impressive monument to nature's power.

South Thompson River

Although outside the scope of this book, the backroad along the north side of the South Thompson River, between Kamloops and Chase, passes along the bottom of cliffs that play host to hundreds of the photogenic clay columns.

The wind and rain has created these awesome sculptures, and the dry climate has helped preserve them.

Whatever you do, watch your footing and keep your distance. A slip can result in severe gravel rash, or worse, it could bring down these fragile reminders of the semi-desert climate. Treat them with respect so that others may also be able to look at them.

a picnic area with an excellent view down the lake. The heritage buildings should interest the kids and provide a bit of shade on a hot day.

If you are looking for fuel, food, or a campground, Savona has them all. If you are looking for more detours, consider Tunkwa Lake Road at the east end of the village. It will take you south through one of BC's newest parks, a route covered in *Coquihalla Trips & Trails*.

Balancing Rock Trail

Another of nature's dry country oddities, a large balancing rock, is located on the slopes of a gully below the highway approximately five kilometres east of Tunkwa Lake Road. A gate near the crest of the hill marks the start of a trail down to the balancing rock and a group of wind-carved clay hoodoos.

Kamloops Lake Viewpoint

Beyond Savona, the highway climbs up the mountainside, offering an excellent panorama of Kamloops Lake and Kamloops from a viewpoint just east of the crest. A stop-of-interest sign adds a bit to the historical information of the area.

Steamboat Saga

Smooth rivers and great lakes once were the highways of travel. On them plied stately paddle-wheelers, helping exploration and settlement of the Interior. They speeded gold-seekers bound for the "Big Bend" rush of 1864–65. They freighted grain from the Okanagan. They were vital in the building of the CPR — and doomed by the railway they helped to build.

Rock Climbing

The rock bluffs below the viewpoint are a favourite of local climbers. Lyle Knight describes the series of crags known as "The Beach" in his book *Central BC Rock*: "The access is easy and public, the views are spectacular. And the climbing is shaded for most of the day."

Yellowhead Highway 5 South

In the final approach to Kamloops, the Trans-Canada Highway links up with Highway 5 (a.k.a. Coquihalla Highway 5 Phase 2), the freeway link to the Nicola Valley and points southwest. If your origin or ultimate destination is BC's Lower Mainland, you could consider taking Highway 5 or Highway 5A south. If you're not in a hurry, Highway 5A is your best choice for birdwatching and fine fishing lakes. Both routes are covered in *Coquihalla Trips & Trails*.

Kamloops Lake from the "Steamboat Saga" viewpoint.

An American Fur Trade Post

Kamloops has been an important Shuswap First Nations community and trade centre for thousands of years. Its European history goes back to late in 1812, when the Native peoples welcomed fur traders from John Jacob Astor's Pacific Fur Company. The Astorians spent the winter here and established the first and only American fur trading post on what is now British Columbia soil. The American presence was short-lived, however, and the post was soon sold to the Montreal-based Northwest Fur Company which, in 1821, merged with the Hudson's Bay Company.

The fur trade, gold rush, and railway construction, along with ranching, mining, and logging has kept Kamloops growing since then. Today, the city of 85,000 also serves as a distribution centre for much of the British Columbia Interior with all the amenities of a "big" little city.

Kamloops also serves as the east end of the "Thompson River Road." If you are still interested in following highways or waterways, you can follow the Yellowhead Highway and the North Thompson River more than halfway to Jasper or the

The Thompson River Road

Trans-Canada Highway and the South Thompson River into the heart of the Shuswap. Either way, there's a lot more to explore.

Note: See the *Information Sources* chapter at the end of the book for contact information on the services mentioned here.

CHAPTER 7

Whitewater Weekend: Rafting the Thompson and Fraser Rivers

The sun was high overhead when Bernie Fandrich cracked open the throttle on the 25-horsepower outboard, and the 6.7-metre-long whitewater raft slipped into the swift-flowing current. Beneath us churned British Columbia's Fraser River, throbbing with energy as it prepared to push through one of the most dangerous constrictions on its 1,370 kilometre run from the Rocky Mountains to the Pacific Ocean.

Bernie adjusted his stance, bracing his feet firmly on the plywood floorboards, and twisted the throttle a little more, his knuckles white with tension.

I glanced at my fellow passengers. Despite our varied ages and backgrounds, the dozen men and women aboard Bernie's raft were — for this moment — united. Clad in orange life jackets, we were going through the Fraser River rapid aptly named Hell's Gate.

Bernie studied the swirling waves beneath our feet. Here, through a channel a mere 35 metres wide, roars an untamed river five to ten times larger than the famed Colorado. Peak flows of 10,000 cubic metres per second have been recorded during the late-June runoff. During the safe rafting season, flows vary from 3,500 to 5,500 cubic metres per second. Even though the water is more than 30 metres deep, the awesome power of the river can create six-metre standing waves.

We were at the mercy of the Fraser River within seconds. This was the point of no return; all Bernie could do now was try to keep the waves from flipping our raft.

My heart stopped when we plunged deep into a wave and cascades of water tumbled over the bow, drenching everyone on board. A second later the raft bounced into the air, carried aloft by its buoyancy. As it slid back into the river, we were weightless for a moment; our hands tightly clenching the ropes were our only contact with the raft.

Screams of fear and delight echoed off the sheer canyon walls, threatening to drown out the roar of the rapid.

The river bounced us again and again before depositing us in the whirlpools and eddies at the foot of Hell's Gate. The rollercoaster ride through the most exciting rapid of the lower Fraser Canyon was over. What seemed like an eternity was only a matter of moments.

Releasing my grip from the gunwale ropes, I wiped the muddy water from my eyes and looked up at the whitewater behind me. The sun was still out, but now the sweltering canyon suddenly felt cool.

Thompson River Whitewater

Ever consider spending a three-day weekend drifting down British Columbia's Thompson and Fraser rivers on a seven-metre rubber raft? The idea sounds relaxing, doesn't it?

After making your reservations in advance, you park your vehicle at the Kumsheen Rafting Resort base just off the Trans-Canada Highway (Highway 1) six kilometres northeast of Lytton. Then, at the appointed hour, the outfitter's bus whisks you and your new-found friends 75 kilometres up the highway to the village of Ashcroft. Here, on the sun-drenched banks of the Thompson River, your guide for the weekend explains the intricacies of whitewater rafting, the features of your craft, and the hydraulics of the river. Then, after one last check of your over sized life jacket and your waterproof camera bag, you say goodbye to the shore crew and push off into the clear green water.

Eagles, osprey, hawks, and the occasional turkey vulture can be seen soaring above the river or resting on the riverbank stumps and trees.

Semi-Desert Canyon

Close your eyes and visualize the colourful rock formations that cling to the dry canyon wall. Smell the sage brush and the wildflowers as you drift through one of the hottest and driest valleys in British Columbia. Let your mind paint pictures of the hardships faced by the travellers who passed this way on their way to the Cariboo goldfields more than a century ago.

It all sounds serene — almost boring — until you drive along the Trans-Canada Highway and take a closer look at some of the 50 large rapids on the Thompson River. Names such as Jaws of Death, Washing Machine, and Cauldron are among the more exciting and — to the weak-hearted — frightening.

Don't be frightened! Aside from the occasional dousing with cold spray, an expertly guided raft trip down the Thompson River is probably less dangerous than rush hour traffic in Vancouver, Seattle, or Los Angeles. Experienced white-water guides, multi-compartment rubber rafts, and special whitewater life jackets reduce the risk without reducing the thrill.

"It's like riding a roller coaster in a washing machine!" says Bernie Fandrich, one of British Columbia's most experienced rafting outfitters. Bernie's Lytton-based Kumsheen Rafting Resort has operated on the Thompson and Fraser rivers since 1973 and is one of several outfitters offering one, two, and three day trips that encompass either or both rivers.

The rough-and-tumble Thompson, a major tributary of the Fraser River, is one of the most-travelled and largest whitewater rivers in the Pacific Northwest. Peak flows of over 3,000 cubic metres per second have been recorded during the June runoff — many times more than the famed Colorado.

Itineraries vary, depending on demand and the outfitter, but Kumsheen's three-day trip takes in the Thompson River from Ashcroft to the junction at Lytton and the Fraser River from Boston Bar to Yale. After the initiating run through the rapids of the Black Canyon, the first day's journey is one of relaxation, broken by relatively easy rapids. Remnants of the original 1860s Cariboo Waggon Road and 1930s placer mining activity are visible along the river. Tall, multi-coloured clay spires, typical of the region's dry climate, guard the waterway. With an average annual precipitation of 15 to 25 centimetres, the odds of good sunbathing weather are excellent.

The first night may be spent in a white canvas tent cabin or your own camping facilities at Kumsheen's private riverside campground six kilometres northeast of the historic village of Lytton. You will have time to set up your camp and meet your new neighbours before you settle down to dinner. Food on the river and at Kumsheen's restaurant is first class.

Pulpit Rock on the Fraser River near the mouth of the Chilcotin River. Kumsheen Rafting Resort occasionally runs week-long rafting trips through the Fraser Canyon. Check their brochures or website for details.

If you have any energy left, you can check out the swimming pool, hot tub, volleyball courts, or self-guided walking trails.

After a shuttle back to the rafts, day two takes in the section between Spences Bridge and Lytton, the climax of the Thompson River whitewater and the choice of those who prefer to spend only one day of whitewater rafting. The rafting begins with an easy ride for the first hour or two, and then the river begins to twist and tumble more violently. Life jackets are snugged up and double-checked, hats tied down, rain suits buttoned up, and then you are off to ride the whitewater roller coaster.

The infamous Frog Rapids near Nicoamen mark the start of "serious" whitewater. Named after a huge frog-shaped boulder that splits the river, the choice of best channel depends on the current and can vary from day to day. The guide uses the motor to hold the raft for a moment, then the choice is made and the big rig slips into the current.

The laughter and screams echo off the canyon walls as the big waves cascade over the bow of the craft. It rides through the water like a giant porpoise, leaping skyward then diving into the waves. Then there is a moment of quiet when you can wipe your eyes before nosing into the next rapids, your white knuckles firmly gripping the safety ropes.

There are approximately 30 major rapids in the 35 kilometres between Spences Bridge and Lytton. And just to keep their customers happy, the expert guides seldom avoid the biggest thrills of all of them. Though more hectic than day one, there is time for conversation and bird watching between rapids.

Silt-Laden Fraser River

After a stop for lunch at Nicoamen and a pullout at Lytton, you are again shuttled the few minutes back to your waiting accommodation at Kumsheen's resort.

The scenery is different on your third day on the river. Where the Thompson had carved a path through clay and gravel left behind by the glaciers that once covered the northern half of the continent, the Fraser's path is through solid rock — a narrow canyon carved through a mountain barrier. Though never far from the two railways and the highway that share the Fraser canyon route, the sheer cliffs that rise straight up from the water bring even the strongest people back to the reality of the strength of Nature.

In this area, the Fraser Canyon was an almost insurmountable barrier to human travel before the introduction of blasting powder. When fur trader Simon Fraser explored the canyon in 1808, he scrambled along the cliff face on a narrow Native footpath and over pole ladders held together with sage or cedar roots. The river itself was even less hospitable, overpowering all manner of craft before the introduction of the multi-compartmented, multi-pontooned rubber raft.

Compared to the Thompson River, the whitewater of the Fraser seems almost tame — that is until the concrete fishways come into view and the roar of Hell's Gate blocks out any hope of conversation. Man may have tamed the canyon walls, but the river remains untamed.

Hell's Gate

Rafting outfitters only run Hell's Gate in the late summer, generally avoiding the high-water months of June and July when whirlpools can swallow even the largest rafts. These restrictions were self-imposed in 1979 and later followed by government regulations after rafting accidents near Hell's Gate.

The drenching, exhilarating slide through the Hell's Gate rapid is over in a moment, but before your hearing has completely recovered from the noise, more standing waves and whirlpools toss and twist the whitewater raft. The Fraser's Black Canyon is suitably ominous, and then after a lunch break near the foot of the Alexandra Bridge, the last leg of the whitewater weekend is underway.

With names that reflect the 1860s gold rush period, the Sailor Bar rapid forms a narrow chute followed by a hydraulic jump. Saddle Rock Island and Steamboat Island, named thusly because of their shape, create twin channels with no easy way around. Then, just before four p.m., the raft bounces down the channel around Lady Franklin Rock and the village of Yale comes into view.

The shore crew waits with their giant trailers, ready to haul the whitewater rafts back to Kumsheen's headquarters six kilometres north of Lytton. But before they can go anywhere, they will need your help to load the cumbersome craft. And before you leave town, there is a short break at the parking lot to get your "River Rat" certificates and exchange addresses with all your new-found friends.

You are now a river rat. It has taken you three days to travel less than 180 kilometres, and it has cost you a little less than $200 per day to do it. You've been wet and cold, slept in a tent, and had the s... scared out of you — but you will be back.

"Most of our guests are in the 30- to 45-year-old range," says Bernie Fandrich.

Whitewater Weekend

"But we also have tour groups, for example, where the age range is 65 to 70. These people stop by and do our three-hour 'quickie' on the Thompson River.

"The trip that I think would appeal to most people trying whitewater rafting for the first time would be the one-day trip," suggests Fandrich. "Because we use motorized rafts primarily, all our passengers have to do is sit there, enjoy themselves, and hang on. Our clients are not required to row or take part in the actual operation of the raft. The choice is theirs."

For *detailed information* on whitewater rafting trips on British Columbia's Thompson and Fraser rivers, contact:

Kumsheen Rafting Resort
Trans-Canada Highway
(5 km east of Lytton)
PO Box 30
Lytton, BC V0K 1Z0
Tel: (250) 455-2296
Fax: (250) 455-2297
Reservations: 1(800) 663-6667
E-mail: rafting@kumsheen.com
Website: http://www.kumsheen.com

CHAPTER 8

Hat Creek Loop: A Scarce Natural Treasure

STATISTICS

	Map see page 102.
Distance:	62 km, Hwy 1 south of Ashcroft to Hwy 97 north of Cache Creek.
Travel Time:	Minimum two to three hours.
Elevation Gain:	850 metres plus another 736 metres to the top of the Cornwall Hills.
Condition:	Two-thirds gravel, one-third pavement (Hwy 99).
Season:	Best in dry weather. Some sections may be closed in winter.
Topo Maps:	Ashcroft, BC 92 I/11 (1:50,000).
	Lillooet, BC 92 I/12 (1:50,000).
	Pavilion, BC 92 I/13 (1:50,000).
	Cache Creek, BC 92 I/14 (1:50,000).
Communities:	Spences Bridge, Ashcroft, Lillooet, and Cache Creek.

If you are looking for a dry-weather backroad that will take you away from most of the trappings of civilization, consider a loop through the Upper Hat Creek Valley, west of Ashcroft. In addition to visiting a couple of BC's newest parks, you'll have the opportunity to explore one of the oldest ranching areas of the Interior.

For the most part, the road is narrow and gravel, with some steep sections on the Oregon Jack Creek route between Upper Hat Creek and Highway 1. On a dry summer day, the family sedan should have no problems navigating Hat Creek Road. However, it can be pure hell when wet or icy. In this case, a four-wheel-drive — with a set of chains tucked away for insurance — might be the vehicle of choice.

With the warnings out of the way, the route does have many redeeming features — if bird-watching, wildlife, wildflowers, grassland vistas, and the occasional glimpse of history past, present, and future interests you.

South to North

We have travelled the route numerous times, going either direction, depending on which terminus we were closest to when we started. For the sake of this

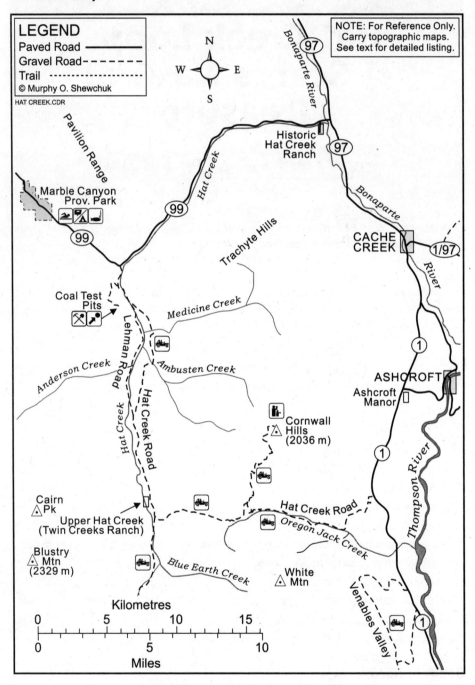

Cattle range on the slopes overlooking the south end of the Upper Hat Creek Valley.

discussion, we will start off on Hat Creek Road at its junction with Highway 1, 28 kilometres north of Spences Bridge or 20 kilometres south of Cache Creek. Reset your odometer here in order to follow my narrative.

If you travelled Highway 1 a couple of decades ago, you may remember a busy fruit and vegetable stand across from the junction, backed by a waving sea of corn. In later years, the sheltered field next to the beginning of the road became a feed lot. As time progressed, the fruit stand disappeared, the feed lot now shows little sign of use, and the cornfields have been seeded to grain and alfalfa.

Hat Creek Road winds through the old feedlot and soon begins the steady climb away from the grasslands and cultivated fields. Bunchgrass, prickly pear cactus, and the occasional struggling pine dominate the view in these first few kilometres. Then, near km 5.5 the gravel road leaves the open hillside and begins to follow Oregon Jack Creek upstream.

"Oregon Jack" Dowling

Jack Dowling came to British Columbia along with the major wave of gold seekers in 1858. Mining didn't hold his interest long, and he soon turned to the more reliable business of packing supplies to the miners. Branwen C. Patenaude in *Trails to Gold* writes, "By 1862 he and a partner, Dominic Gavin, had pre-empted land about 16 miles [25 kilometres] northwest of Cook's Ferry [Spences Bridge] where they opened a wayside house beside the trail, at the top of a long hill." I suspect it was located just south of the present rest area alongside Highway 1.

It seems that Oregon Jack's Hotel did not have a particularly splendid reputation, in character with Jack himself. "A reference made to Oregon Jack by a passerby in the 1880s described him as a vile-looking man with a red face, bald head and bowed legs. His chief claim to fame was the fact that he had not drawn a sober breath since arriving in B.C."

Oregon Jack Provincial Park

The valley varies in width as you continue climbing westward. Here and there hayfields and homes stand tucked up against the marble cliffs that dominate the valley wall. Park boundary signs at km 11.6 warn of something ahead, but that "something" had yet to be developed at the time of writing. Instead, watch for a short side road on your left on a corner at km 12.1. If you don't miss it, you can park in a small clearing just off the road and explore the rough trails to the base of a huge perpendicular boulder as well as the base of a magnificent cliff.

According to BC Parks, the primary role of 233-hectare Oregon Jack Provincial Park is to protect the geological features, wetlands, upland forest habitats, and cultural features associated with the setting and environs of Oregon Jack Creek. The park is one of a number of small parks in the BC Parks Thompson River District (Cornwall Hills, Blue Earth Lake, Bedard Aspen, and Harry Lake Aspen) and larger parks in Cariboo District (Marble Range and Edge Hills) that together represent the diverse ecosystems of the Pavilion Ranges Ecosection. A secondary role is to continue providing traditional low profile recreation opportunities for viewing the geological and waterfall features, hiking, hunting, and nature appreciation.

The rock and ice climbing and bouldering opportunities in the eastern section of the park appeal to the more agile (or foolhardy) recreationists, while those of us not quite up to climbing a perpendicular cliff can enjoy the birdwatching in the meadows near km 16.

Cornwall Hills Provincial Park

A junction at a switchback turn near km 13.5 marks an opportunity for a detour and some serious wildflower viewing — if your timing is right. Cornwall Hills Forest Service Road leads to the right (north) at the junction. Reset your odometer here again if you decide to explore the route to the subalpine grasslands.

The first kilometre of this road was particularly rutted and muddy when we made one mid-June drive to the top. Good clearance and four-wheel-drive were more a requisite than merely an asset on this section. However, the road improves once beyond the tiny Three Sisters Recreation Site and the creek by the same name.

A sign near km 5 marks the boundary of the new 1,188-hectare Cornwall Hills Provincial Park. The province created it on April 30, 1996, to protect a rich diversity of habitats, including rare Engelmann spruce/subalpine fir parklands and grasslands with patches of old-growth forest. The road ends at the Forest Service fire lookout on top of the mountain ("hills" seems somewhat inadequate) at an elevation of 2,036 metres. From the parapet of the lookout, you can look east over the vast grasslands that were once the domain of the brothers Cornwall. You may be able to pick out Ashcroft Manor, their headquarters and a family operation for more than a century. Farther below, the Thompson River winds through the bottom of the canyon. Tucked out of sight is the village of Ashcroft.

Cornwall Brothers

Clement Francis Cornwall and his brother, Henry Pennant Cornwall, of British aristocratic stock, first pre-empted two adjoining 160-acre (65-hectare) parcels on July 1, 1862. Hearing word of the gold discoveries in the Cariboo, they had left England several months earlier and travelled westward, reaching Lillooet via Port Douglas. There they were dissuaded from pursuing gold and decided to take up farming and ranching. Leaving Lillooet, they travelled to what is now the Ashcroft area via Hat Creek and the Bonaparte River.

According to Branwen Patenaude, within a decade they had built up a thriving farm "extending over 6,000 acres [2,428 hectares], on which were kept over 1,500 head of cattle, an operating sawmill, grist mill, a market garden, and a popular roadhouse."

While digging through the old *Journals of the Colonial Legislatures*, I discovered a reference to an 1870 Crown lease application for land in the Hat Creek Valley by the "Messrs. Cornwall." It was approved "at 3 1/3 cents per acre . . ." There was also another reference to the Cornwall brothers a few months earlier. This application was for 6,000 acres (2,428 hectares) and was granted at a yearly rental of

The south end of the Upper Hat Creek Valley as the first snow of the fall dusts the grasslands.

$200, although it isn't clear where the land was situated.

Canyons and Marshes

Beyond the Cornwall Hills Forest Service Road junction, Hat Creek Road continues to climb, steeper and narrower than before. After a kilometre or two it levels off, having cleared the marble cliffs. It then begins the descent to the marshes that straddle the divide between Oregon Jack Creek and Upper Hat Creek. A marker a few minutes farther along indicates the west boundary of 233-hectare Oregon Jack Provincial Park.

Hat Creek

Approximately 22 kilometres from Highway 1, the road comes out of the pass and into the main Hat Creek Valley.

According to the Akriggs in *1001 British Columbia Place Names*, Hudson's Bay Company trader and explorer A.C. Anderson wrote that: ". . . the Rivière aux Chapeaux, a feeder of the Bonaparte — now called Hat Creek . . . derives its name from an Indian habitation connected with a large granitic stone on its left bank, indented with several hat like cavities . . ."

The stone outcropping referred to is probably the one that hems in Highway 99 just before it reaches Highway 97, some 11 kilometres north of Cache Creek.

Meanwhile, back at Upper Hat Creek and heading north, on the topographical map the black dot marked "Upper Hat Creek" is now one of the recently refurbished buildings of the Twin Creeks Ranch. Peter and Bernadette McAllister have turned the old post office into an excellent bed and breakfast accommodation. A former tool shed has become Bernadette's art studio.

The McAllisters have taken a keen interest in the wildlife of the valley, particularly the birds that are attracted to the upland marshes and the predators they attract in return.

"The small wetland restoration project we did a stone's throw from our ranch house has given us a wonderful close-up window on the bountiful waterfowl and wildlife that Hat Creek attracts to its myriad ponds and wetlands," says Peter McAllister. "Cavity-nesting species that rely on old growth and snags get a boost from the dozens of duck boxes placed in trees around the ranch. Wood duck, barrows goldeneye, and the mergansers take advantage of them as well as flickers and kestrels. We put up owl boxes to attract saw-whet and flammulated owls.

"From our window, we can see an active golden eagle nest in a cliff. Bald eagles often roost in our big cottonwood near the house or sit on the gate posts in the barnyard. They appear to be dreaming about our yellow-bellied marmots and the native rainbow trout and muskrats in the creeks and ponds. An osprey will plunge for a trout in the creek and almost immediately will be dive-bombed by the eagles who generally grab the prize."

The Gordon Parke Ranch

In the 1860s, while the Cornwall brothers were building their ranch near Ashcroft, a young man from County Sligo in Ireland was doing the same thing in the Bonaparte Valley, a mile north of Cache Creek. Philip Parke was in his early 20s, but apparently wise enough to realize that the lasting gold was in the grass, not in the gravel of the creeks. However, the creeks are also essential to ranching.

In 1900, Philip Parke traded water rights on a creek crucial to the Cornwall operation for land the Cornwalls owned in the Upper Hat Creek valley. The descendants of Philip Parke have ranched in Upper Hat Creek ever since.

Duck Ranch

Although the Duck Ranch, near the centre of the Upper Hat Creek valley, has ideal habitat for these feathered creatures, it was not named after them. Pat Foster, in *Historic Ashcroft: For the Strong Eye Only*, explains the name. She writes that Ashcroft had a large, successful Chinese community. "Ah Duck, also known as Tong Sing, Joe Duck or Old Duck, opened a general store called Tong Sing in Cache Creek in the 1880s. He was sufficiently successful that in the early 1900s he was able to buy hundreds of acres of land in the Upper Hat Creek Valley. He brought a number of men from China to help in the venture, and soon had one of the largest cattle herds in the area — over 2,000 head — as well as fields of timothy and clover . . . and a huge potato garden." In that same period, Kwan Yee, a Chinese widow in her 40s, also homesteaded a quarter section of land (65 hectares) in the Upper Hat Creek area.

Hat Creek Coal

The road splits about 7.5 kilometres from where it first enters the valley from Oregon Jack Creek. Lehman Road rejoins Hat Creek Road near the 3K marker (km 40 from the Trans-Canada Highway). Whichever route you take, you should see the telltale signs of Hat Creek's foundation.

The giant 35-million-year-old coal deposit that lies beneath the Upper Hat Creek valley was first discovered in the 1870s. BC Electric recognized it as a possible power source in the 1950s. In 1974, BC Hydro began serious environmental and engineering studies for a 2,000-megawatt power plant — at that time large enough to supply the BC Lower Mainland. BC Hydro's reports indicated that there were two deposits in the area totalling approximately two billion tons of high-ash, low-sulphur, sub-bituminous B coal. The deposits are unique in physical terms, with the north deposit "approximately two square miles [5.2 square kilometers] and more than 1,000 feet [305 metres] thick in places." As work progressed the numbers changed, suggesting as much as 15 billion tons of low-grade coal in deposits up to 2,000 feet [610 metres] thick.

In addition to the electricity produced by the coal, there was mention of a $200 million aluminum smelter to process the alumina in the three million tons of fly ash that would be produced each year. While the electricity and aluminum were on the plus side of the equation, some details on the minus side bothered a lot of

BC Hydro made several excavations to obtain large test samples of the Hat Creek coal.

people. In addition to the disruption of a ranching community that supplied enough beef to keep 10,000 people in burgers and steaks, there was the concern of fallout that could affect a quarter of the province. Sulphur dioxide and nitrogen oxide emissions were major concerns as well mercury, which one report suggests could exceed 20 tons over the 35-year life of the operation.

By April 1977, a design contract had been granted for a $1.2 billion generating plant. Work progressed with exploratory trenching and test burns of the coal. In the meantime, the project approval date kept getting pushed back until, a decade and $70 million after the initial drilling work, BC Hydro shelved the project indefinitely.

The "shelving" hasn't spared the valley inhabitants from continuing concern. Peter McAllister says, "Hat Creek may be one of the least known jewels of the southern interior but it is hardly a secret to the timber industry, the coal industry, and now the gas drilling companies. The remaining old growth forests nurturing the water and wildlife of Hat Creek are on the chopping block. BC Hydro still owns the rights to vast undeveloped coal beds under the valley floor, and a Calgary

Historic Hat Creek Ranch contains several pioneer log buildings.

outfit wants to drill for methane gas all over the rich grasslands where unique acquifers abound."

"Scenic" View

Finney Creek Forest Service Road, to the left about a kilometre north of the Lehman Road junction, offers access to a couple of the test pits. Follow the road as it climbs southwest, turning left at a cattleguard at about 1.8 kilometres. Follow the track through the sagebrush for another kilometre and you should find your-self on the rim of a large trench. Use extreme caution because of the unstable banks.

Highway 99

At one time designated Highway 12, Highway 99 is a continuation of the road that winds north from the Canada-US border through Squamish and Whistler, ending at Highway 97 near Hat Creek House. If you are looking for a spot to camp or try some fishing, you could head west about seven kilometres to Marble Canyon Provincial Park. For the sake of this discussion, we will follow Hat Creek east another 21 kilometres to the Bonaparte River and Highway 97.

Hat Creek House

A junction to the south about a half a kilometre before Highway 97 marks the entrance to the Historic Hat Creek Ranch, a restored ranch museum and tourist attraction. The property began attracting "tourists" of another sort as early as July 16, 1861, when British Columbia Governor James Douglas reported that "Mr. McLean, a native of Scotland, and lately of the Hudson's Bay Company, has recently settled on a beautiful spot, near the debouch of the Hat River, and is rapidly bringing his land into cultivation."

"McLean's Restaurant" became a regular stopping place on the road to the goldfields. Unfortunately, Donald McLean was killed in the "Chilcotin War" in 1864. The property went through a succession of owners and managers until 1990, when it was acquired by the British Columbia Heritage Trust.

The ranch grounds are open from May 1 to mid-October. The attractions include the historic buildings, First Nations displays, a free stagecoach ride, a restaurant, and an RV park.

A Scarce Natural Treasure

While you can make the trip through the Hat Creek Valley in a few hours, it can take much longer to gain an understanding of what this 25-kilometre-long oasis has to offer. Peter McAllister sums it up best. "Few places in the southern interior have managed to preserve as much historic ranching charm and natural beauty as the Upper Hat Creek. What's more, the diversity of habitat, including just about everything from bunch grass and ponderosa pine ecosystems all the way up to alpine meadows, makes this watershed a scarce natural treasure."

Note: See the *Information Sources* chapter at the end of the book for contact information on the services mentioned here.

GPS References for major points of interest
Ref: WGS 84 - Lat/Lon hddd.ddddd
Allow +/-100 metres due to data conversions

Wpt	Km	Description	Latitude	Longitude	Elev.
001	0	Jct Hat Creek Rd and Hwy 1	N50.65354	W121.35656	471 m
002	8.0	Wun Day Ranch	N50.64288	W121.44429	878 m
003	10.0	10K marker	N50.64542	W121.46725	1,011 m
004	11.2	Three Sisters Ranch	N50.64412	W121.47291	1,043 m
005	11.6	Oregon Jack Park boundary	N50.64430	W121.47672	1,077 m
006	12.1	Parking area for cliffs	N50.64249	W121.48180	1,116 m
007	13.3	Cornwall Hills FS Rd	N50.65071	W121.48184	1,187 m
008	14.3	Oregon Jack Park boundary	N50.64398	W121.48579	1,267 m
009	16.4	Marshes	N50.63738	W121.49995	1,185 m
010	17.6	Oregon Jack Park boundary	N50.63963	W121.51586	1,180 m
011	21.4	Lake and marsh	N50.63926	W121.56502	1,159 m
012	22.2	Brand 88, Hat Creek Ranch	N50.63919	W121.57421	1,131 m
013	23.6	Twin Lakes Ranch	N50.65038	W121.58101	1,133 m
014	38.8	View of coal pit	N50.77174	W121.59637	911 m
015	39.3	Lehman Rd	N50.77487	W121.60206	869 m
016	40.4	Hat Creek Bridge	N50.78263	W121.60887	859 m
017	40.8	Jct to coal trench	N50.78412	W121.61298	846 m
018	42.0	Jct Hat Creek Rd and Hwy 99	N50.79611	W121.61087	823 m
019	61.5	Historic Hat Creek Ranch	N50.88616	W121.40974	512 m
020	62.0	Jct Hwy 99 and Hwy 97	N50.88778	W121.40066	516 m

CHAPTER 9

Deadman-Vidette Road: Red Cliffs and Blue Lakes

STATISTICS

	Map see page 114.
Distance:	65 km, Trans-Canada Highway to end of road.
Travel time:	Two to three hours.
Elevation gain:	700 metres.
Condition:	Mostly gravel road; rough in places.
Season:	Best in dry weather.
Topo maps:	Tranquille River, BC 92 I/15.
(1:50,000)	Criss Creek, BC 92 P/2
	Cache Creek, BC 92 I/14.
Communities:	Savona, Cache Creek, and Kamloops.

Deadman Valley is one of the least commercialized of BC's many beauty spots. The Deadman-Vidette Road sign and the fishing camp billboards only hint of attractions that include desert plants, waterfalls, and a string of fine fishing lakes, historic relics, hoodoos, and giant sand castles.

According to sketchy records of the North West Fur Company, the valley acquired the basis for its name about 1815 when Monsieur Charette, a clerk or senior labourer temporarily in charge of the post at Kamloops, met an untimely death near here. As the story goes, Charette was travelling through the area with a Native companion when an argument developed over where they should camp. A knife in the hands of Charette's companion ended the discussion.

Older names for the river reflect this episode, most notably Riviere des Defunts (River of Death) and Knife River. The present, rather gloomy name of Deadman River was adopted during the gold rush of the 1860s.

The start of this interesting backroad (km 0) is marked by the Deadman-Vidette Road sign at its junction with the Trans-Canada Highway, 5 kilometres west of Kamloops Lake. Look carefully at the sagebrush-covered western slopes for the weathered wooden flumes that once carried water to the Walhachin orchards high

Deadman-Vidette Road

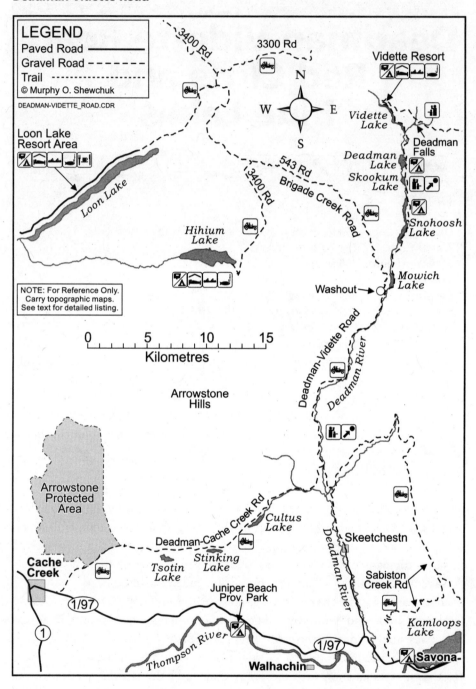

LEGEND
Paved Road
Gravel Road
Trail
© Murphy O. Shewchuk

DEADMAN-VIDETTE_ROAD.CDR

3400 Rd

3300 Rd

N
W   E
S

Vidette Resort

Vidette
Lake

Deadman
Falls

Loon Lake
Resort Area

Loon Lake

543 Rd

Brigade Creek Road

Deadman
Lake

Skookum
Lake

Snohoosh
Lake

NOTE: For Reference Only.
Carry topographic maps.
See text for detailed listing.

Hihium
Lake

3400 Rd

Mowich
Lake

Washout

0   5   10   15
Kilometres

Deadman-Vidette Road

Deadman River

Arrowstone
Hills

Arrowstone
Protected
Area

Deadman-Cache Creek Rd

Cultus
Lake

Skeetchestn

Cache
Creek

Tsotin
Lake

Stinking
Lake

Deadman River

Sabiston
Creek Rd

Kamloops
Lake

1/97

Juniper Beach
Prov. Park

1/97

Savona

1

Thompson River

Walhachin

Remnants of the flumes that once carried Deadman River water to the orchards of Walhachin.

above the Thompson River. Watch for logging trucks on weekdays and keep headlights on for safety.

Skeetchestn First Nation Village

The Skeetchestn village, at km 7.5, marks the last opportunity for fuel or supplies before you continue north on your Deadman Valley backroad adventure. The valley gradually narrows beyond the village. Modern flumes and pipes carry water to the fields at the base of the blood-red rock bluffs and deeply eroded clay banks. Lush, green hayfields grow on the bottomland, while only a few metres outside the reach of the sprinklers, scrub pine and sagebrush survive in summer temperatures that reach 40°C.

On the west side of the valley, a short distance up the eroded hillside near the junction of the Criss Creek Road (km 12.6), sun-bleached and decaying flumes serve as a reminder of irrigation methods of the past. A dam on Deadman Creek was the source and the long-abandoned orchards of Walhachin were the destination of these wooden flumes and the water that they once carried. To distribute the much-needed water, the promoters of Walhachin hired Chinese and Native labourers, supervised by a few young Englishmen, to build a network of flumes and ditches that stretched for more than 190 kilometres.

Red Lava Cliffs

The rock formations of the lower Deadman Valley, red and stark at km 14, are part of what geologists call the Nicola Group. They are approximately 180 million years old and are principally of volcanic origin, containing green, red, and grey lavas plus bands of argillite and limestone.

The Deadman-Vidette Road crosses the Deadman River at km 14.8, and just upstream from the bridge is a small dam that was part of the valley irrigation system. Deadman – Cache Creek Road, at the crest of the hill just beyond the bridge, winds westward through Pass Valley to Cache Creek.

While the colourful eroded cliffs are a stark reminder of the distant past, more recent geological disturbances have also left their mark. Watch the roadside cuts near km 16 for a thin layer of creamy white volcanic ash about a metre below the surface. Similar ash layers elsewhere have been associated with the 7,000-year-old eruption of Oregon's Mount Mazama, which formed what is now Crater Lake.

Hoodoos of Deadman Valley

Local volcanic activity once blanketed the area with lava. Slow erosion in the dry climate has worn away the lava beds, leaving the cliffs to the west and a Deadman Valley landmark. Corrals near a bend in the road at km 18.1 mark the Hoodoos of Deadman Valley, a rock formation that is easily missed. However, with the aid of binoculars, they are visible about halfway up the eastern side of the valley. The five majestic clay and gravel columns stand like guards under stone hats. Each narrow sentinel is 10 to 12 metres high and about three metres in diameter at the base. Joined together at the bottom, somewhat like the fingers on a hand, this close-knit group of royal guards can lead one's imagination on a merry chase.

Old Hihium Lake Road

A rough four-wheel-drive road at km 19.9 follows the natural gas pipeline route

Deadman Valley has a wide variety of intriguing and colourful rock formations.

northwest to Hihium Lake. Hihium-Scottie Creek Road was once the main road to the lake, but there is now easier access via Loon Lake, north of Cache Creek. However, this area is also of interest to rockhounds, because the cliffs along the west side of the valley contain petrified wood, agate, and multi-coloured jasper. The prime rock-hunting area is about 1 kilometre up the old road.

The valley narrows more near the Circle W Ranch/Hihium Fishing Camp headquarters (km 22.4), and the forest begins to squeeze out the hayfields. In spring and early summer, the river splashes between the rock bluffs on either side of the valley. By October, the water barely gurgles as it flows beneath the boulders of the river bed.

Brigade Creek Road

The Brigade Creek Road (551 Road), at km 33.5, once provided access to Hihium Lake, Loon Lake, and Cariboo Highway 97 at Chasm. However, a land slump a few years ago blocked the road a hundred metres off of Deadman-Vidette Road. We discovered this blockage recently when making a fall trip from the Cariboo south to Savona. While it may have been possible to take a Hummer or Jeep through the convoluted section of road, I wasn't prepared to risk my truck and camper. After considerable jockeying, we were able to turn around and head back up the narrow road and return to Highway 97 via Loon Lake.

A few hundred metres beyond the junction, the canyon opens into Mowich Lake, the first of half a dozen lakes that grace the valley floor. The road follows along the east side of the lake for a short distance and then passes around a small lakeshore community.

Polar Springs

A clearing on the left side of the road at the crest of a short hill (km 38.3) marks Polar Springs, aptly named because of the cold, clear water flowing out of the mountain. A short side road leads west, down the hill to the dam at the outlet of Snohoosh Lake.

A dam had originally been built at Snohoosh Lake in 1910 to store water for Walhachin, but when Walhachin failed, it lay idle for over 30 years before being breached to prevent an accidental collapse and flooding of the valley. In the 1970s, a new dam was built to control the water flow for the ranches in Deadman Valley.

There is a small forest recreation site at the head of Snohoosh Lake (km 43.1). Shore fishing is particularly easy in late summer when the drop in water level leaves plenty of room to cast.

The sand castles of Castle Rock Hoodoos Provincial Park are a fragile reminder of the dry climate of Deadman Valley.

Sand Castles of Skookum Lake

On the east side of the road, at km 44.7 near Skookum Lake, is another unusual feature of Deadman Valley. An outcropping on the west slope has been eroded into a giant sand castle. Standing over 60 metres tall, this creamy-white structure has been sculpted by wind and rain in a manner that rivals the best medieval craftsmen. With imagination, trees become fair maidens and shadows become lurking crossbowmen.

Thirty-four hectare Castle Rock Hoodoos Provincial Park was established in 1997 to protect this yellow to white hoodoo formation comprised of eroded fluvial deposits of volcanic ash. Although a short trail leads around to the right of the castle and climbs among the turrets, BC Parks recommends viewing the sand castles from the safety of the road. A slip and the pain of scraping across rock-hard volcanic ash will quickly bring you back to reality. It could also damage the fragile castle.

After a slow, distracting drive up Deadman-Vidette Road, the user-maintained recreation site on Deadman Lake (km 46.4) will be a pleasant destination. This site is largely undeveloped, but it has a number of tables and ample space to camp among the timber. A boat is useful when fishing Deadman Lake, but launching facilities preclude anything larger than a car-topper.

Vidette Lake

Vidette Lake, at km 49.5, is the last and prettiest of the lakes on the valley floor. It is an excellent food source for fish and has been known to provide some lively kokanee and rainbow trout to the diligent angler. The lake was rehabilitated in 1973, to remove the coarse fish that had endangered the trout. A small recreation site has been carved out of the timber partway up the lake.

In addition to its reputation as an excellent fishing lake, Vidette was in the news as a promising gold-producing area in the early 1930s. A report in the *Kamloops Sentinel* of December 4, 1934, stated that mining "reached considerable development during the summer. It is estimated that during the past season a payroll of between $70,000 and $75,000 has been maintained in the Vidette Lake area." One mining company engineer "expected it to become one of the major gold producing areas in the province." These vast expectations did not materialize, and a lonely group of buildings at the north end of the lake appear to be all that remains of the mining operation.

Deadman Falls

The gravel road leaves the floor of Deadman Valley at Vidette Lake and climbs up to the aspen-dotted grasslands of the Kukwaus Plateau. Deadman Falls Recreation Site (km 57.3) marks the head of a short trail that leads to the lip of Deadman Falls. For a better view, continue up the road for half a kilometre to Joe Rich Creek.

Just beyond the creek crossing, a little-used road swings off to the right toward a gate a few hundred metres along. On a warm spring morning, visitors can park at the gate and follow the far side of Deadman Creek a short distance downstream. The thunder and spray of a wall of water hurtling 45 metres to the rocks heralds Deadman Falls. Game trails follow the edge of the volcanic escarpment to an excellent view of the magnificent canyon and falls.

As hot, dry summer turns into autumn, the torrent diminishes and the water splits into long silvery strands that justify its unofficial name of "Three Witches Falls." An exceptionally dry season can reduce the water flow to a trickle — barely enough to keep the hanging moss alive.

Deadman Falls is the end of the road for most casual travellers. Beyond this

In spring, Deadman Falls resembles the famous Helmcken Falls in Wells Gray Park.

point, the road leads to several active and inactive ranches. At one time there was four-wheel-drive access to some of the fly-in fishing lakes on the Bonaparte Plateau, but because of vandalism, efforts have been made to block these roads.

Deadman – Cache Creek Road

If you aren't in a hurry to get back to the blacktop of the Trans-Canada Highway, you could take Deadman – Cache Creek Road west from km 15.1 on Deadman-

Deadman-Vidette Road

GPS References for major points of interest
Ref: WGS 84 - Lat/Lon hddd.ddddd
Allow +/-100 metres due to data conversions

Wpt	Km	Description	Latitude	Longitude	Elev.
		Deadman–Vidette Road			
W01	0	Jct Hwy 1 and Deadman-Vidette Rd	N50.77625	W120.92393	471 m
W02	5.2	Deadman River Bridge	N50.82111	W120.94078	480 m
W03	7.5	Skeetchestn Indian Reserve	N50.84141	W120.94871	505 m
W04	10.2	Colourful rock formations	N50.86155	W120.96004	511 m
W05	12.6	Jct Criss Creek Rd	N50.88265	W120.96423	528 m
W06	14.8	Deadman Creek bridge and dam	N50.90004	W120.97506	545 m
W07	15.1	Jct Deadman – Cache Creek Rd	N50.90255	W120.97458	563 m
W08	18.1	Hoodoos across valley	N50.92594	W120.98100	611 m
W09	19.1	Cross Deadman Creek	N50.93528	W120.98673	601 m
W10	19.8	Jct Hihium – Scottie Creek Rd	N50.93899	W120.98954	625 m
W11	22.4	Circle W and Hihium fish camp	N50.95941	W120.97959	625 m
W12	30.1	Enter canyon	N51.00302	W120.92230	683 m
W13	33.5	Jct 551 Rd – washout	N51.02782	W120.90272	788 m
W14	38.4	Snohoosh Dam Rd	N51.06228	W120.88309	861 m
W15	43.2	Snohoosh rec site	N51.09771	W120.87577	836 m
W16	44.5	Skookum Lake and Castle Rock Hoodoos Park	N51.10928	W120.87533	875 m
W17	44.7	Clay castles	N51.11126	W120.87563	877 m
W18	46.1	Deadman Lake	N51.12220	W120.87663	884 m
W19	46.4	Deadman Lake rec site	N51.12515	W120.87708	879 m
W20	49.1	Cross Joe Ross Creek	N51.14465	W120.87816	880 m
W21	49.6	Vidette Lake	N51.14913	W120.87929	884 m
W22	52.1	Vidette Lake rec site	N51.16462	W120.89906	887 m
W23	52.6	Vidette Lake Resort	N51.16651	W120.90505	900 m
W24	57.5	Joe Ross Creek	N51.15302	W120.86176	1,053 m
W25	58.0	Deadman Falls	N51.15158	W120.86386	1,040 m

Vidette Road to Cache Creek. The road climbs approximately 285 metres in elevation as it winds west up Charette Creek to Cultus Lake before beginning the descent via Back Valley to Cache Creek.

This scenic route offers a different ecological perspective than slightly wetter

GPS References for major points of interest
Ref: WGS 84 - Lat/Lon hddd.ddddd
Allow +/-100 metres due to data conversions

Wpt	Km	Description	Latitude	Longitude	Elev.
		Deadman – Cache Creek Road			
W07	0	Jct Deadman – Cache Creek Rd	N50.90255	W120.97458	563 m
W26	4.0	Charette Creek	N50.88388	W121.00300	688 m
W27	5.7	Jct Silver Springs meadows	N50.87960	W121.02528	759 m
W28	8.6	Cultus Lake	N50.86354	W121.05058	834 m
W29	11.0	Height of land	N50.84474	W121.08322	848 m
W30	12.9	Stinking Lake	N50.84007	W121.09544	829 m
W31	15.9	Battle Creek FS Rd	N50.84014	W121.13382	832 m
W32	21.9	Cache Creek crossing	N50.84216	W121.21381	827 m
W33	25.0	Arrowstone Protected Area boundary	N50.82838	W121.25007	682 m
W34	27.0	Pavement and houses	N50.82215	W121.27459	617 m
W35	29.4	Jct Hwy 1 and Back Valley Rd	N50.80718	W121.29379	546 m

Deadman Valley, with scattered Interior Douglas fir and ponderosa pine as well as frequent clumps of juniper. Arrowleaf balsamroot blossom in the spring while rabbitbrush blossom in September.

Arrowstone Protected Area

The west end of the road skirts Arrowstone Protected Area, a 6,203-hectare wilderness area in one of the largest undisturbed valleys in the dry southern Interior. Vehicles aren't allowed in the park, but backcountry camping, nature appreciation, wildlife viewing, photography, and hunting are permitted in the park. Additional information is available on the BC Parks website at http://www.env.gov.bc.ca/bcparks/.

Note: See the *Information Sources* chapter at the end of the book for contact information on the services mentioned here.

CHAPTER 10

Red Lake Road: (Tranquille — Criss Creek Road) Kamloops — Red Lake — Savona

STATISTICS

	Map see page 125.
Distance:	86 km, North Kamloops to Trans-Canada Highway near Savona.
Travel time:	Three to four hours.
Elevation gain:	660 metres.
Conditions:	Gravel road; some steep hills.
Season:	May be impassable in winter and slippery in wet weather.
Topo maps:	Kamloops 92 I/9.
(1:50,000)	Cherry Creek 92 I/10.
	Tranquille River 92 I/15.
Communities:	Kamloops and Savona.

G old panning, hiking, fishing, rockhounding, and backroads exploring are all part of the "Red Lake Road" north of Kamloops Lake. The shortest route from Kamloops to Savona via Red Lake is about 65 kilometres and could take you three or four hours, depending on how easily you are distracted.

Although we have done it as a day trip on several occasions — including one where I had an opportunity to photograph a beautiful rattlesnake — allow a weekend or more to really explore the high country. On one weekend trip through the area, we racked up over 120 kilometres and found more than half a dozen interesting upland lakes.

Most of the road is maintained throughout the year, but despite the intermittent application of gravel, the steep hills between Red Lake and Savona will probably be slippery during spring thaw and after a heavy rain.

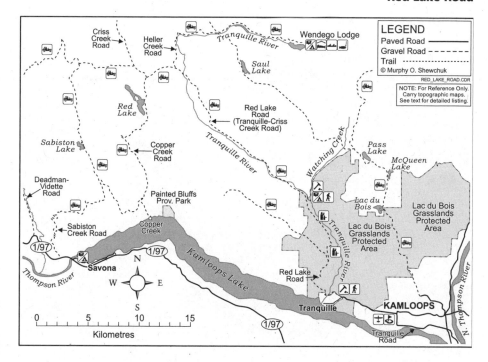

North Kamloops Starting Point

The intersection of Tranquille Road, 8th Street and Fortune Drive, amid the shopping centres in North Kamloops, serves as the km 0 reference point for the start of this trip. Follow Tranquille Road west, bearing in mind that this is your last chance for supplies or fuel. Once you leave Kamloops, there are no stores or gasoline stations along this backroad route.

Kamloops Airport (Fulton Field), at km 5.7, is named after F.J. Fulton, the patriarch of a long, political family line, who came to Kamloops as a lawyer in 1889. He served as City Solicitor before serving in the BC Provincial Parliament from 1900 to 1909. He was a member of the federal Unionist Government in 1917 and died in 1936.

Tranquille School

Keep right at the intersection (km 11.5) just before the grounds of the former Tranquille institution for the mentally handicapped. The buildings also were once home to a sanatorium and are now being seriously considered as a base for a new resort. This intersection also marks the start of the Tranquille – Criss Creek Forest Service Road. Kilometre markers along the route are based on this point.

The pavement ends a kilometre west of the junction, and the gravel road loops

Efforts are underway to turn the old Tranquille School into a resort community.

to the north of the Tranquille establishment. The long row of buildings to the right near km 13 was once part of the Tranquille pig farm, providing employment and food for the patients. A short side road near here leads north to a parking area for a trail up Tranquille River. Recreational gold panning is permitted in Tranquille River below the canyon — no sluicing or power equipment.

The lower portion of Tranquille River is part of 15,000-hectare Lac du Bois Grasslands Protected Area, established in 1996 to protect the delicate rangeland north of Kamloops Lake.

Hill Climb

This backroad soon crosses Tranquille River and the CNR tracks and begins a northerly climb away from Kamloops Lake. There is a viewpoint near km 14.5, and your first opportunity for a detour is into the Dewdrop Range at km 15.7. This area is a protected home for deer and California bighorn sheep as well as a favourite haunt for mountain bicyclists and orienteering enthusiasts.

Viewpoints and Trails

A short side road leads to the right (east) near the crest of the hill at km 18.6. There is space to park and hike south to the top of a knoll that provides an excellent view of Kamloops and the surrounding area. The good gravel road then swings northwest, following the benches high above Tranquille River.

The viewpoints mentioned on this backroad trip are not formal fenced-off enclosures; they are more often merely wide spots in the road to pull over safely and photograph the magnificent scenery. There are several locations near km 20 to take in the badlands scenery of the Tranquille Canyon.

Although there are few landmarks left to tell the story, Tranquille River played an important part in the development of British Columbia. Gold was discovered in the river gravel as early as 1852. Despite the Hudson's Bay Company's efforts to keep the discovery quiet, the news leaked out, helping to spark the gold rush of 1858. The miners found richer lodes in the gravel bars of the Fraser and the creeks of the Cariboo, but small companies and individual miners continued to work Tranquille River until 1948.

Watching Creek Recreation Site and Trails

The main road dips down into a hollow near km 25 where an easily missed side road cuts off to the right (north). It is only a short drive down to a parking and camping area and then a short walk down to Tranquille River and the site of an

Gold panning in Tranquille River near the Tranquille School.

old footbridge. This is the eastern approach to a series of hiking trails known collectively as the Watching Creek Trail. The trails have been developed over the past few years to allow ready access for hikers, fishing enthusiasts, goldpanners, and rockhounds. Watching Creek has some nodules of apple-green common opal in the rock bluffs a short distance upstream. Some prospectors also suggest that the gold in the lower Tranquille River may have been carried down Watching Creek.

Tranquille River Recreation Sites

The Lac du Bois Park boundary is near the roadside 15K marker. Red Lake Road again crosses Tranquille River at the top end of the Tranquille Canyon (km 28.3). The bridge also marks the head of the northwest end of a very rough road down to Watching Creek. There is also a small Forest Service recreation site upstream of the bridge. While space is severely limited at the Tranquille Creek crossing recreation site, the Tranquille Meadow site, near km 30, has considerably more room.

Tranquille Falls

Although it is not marked on present topographical maps, there is a waterfall a short distance up Tranquille River from the bridge at km 43.5. Drive or hike up

Wendego Lodge, near the east end of Tranquille Lake.

the old logging road to the north, about half a kilometre before the bridge, keeping west at all the junctions, to find a most interesting canyon and waterfalls. Logging roads and cattle trails make the hike an enjoyable way to spend a morning or afternoon. A map and GPS, as well as a good ear for the sound of the falls, will be helpful.

Truda and Tranquille Lakes Side Trip

The Heller Creek Forest Service Road junction, near the 33K marker and 44.5 kilometres from North Kamloops, marks a side road that swings to the north and then east as it follows Tranquille River up past Truda Lake to

Tranquille River canyon near Tranquille School.

Tranquille Lake. Truda Lake, 10.5 kilometres from Red Lake Road, is a dammed lake that doesn't show up on most of the maps. There are places to park a camper near the west end of the lake. Wendego Lodge, at the east end of Tranquille Lake, is 17.7 kilometres from the junction. At last check, the last few kilometres of the road were narrow and rough, but for the avid fishing enthusiast, the Kamloops trout and Kokanee may be worth the bouncing.

Criss Creek – Red Lake Junction

Meanwhile, back on the Red Lake Road (a.k.a. Tranquille – Criss Creek Forest Service Road) at the 33K marker, continue west another three kilometres to the junctions of Criss Creek and Copper Creek roads (47.5 kilometres from North Kamloops). The first settlers in this area established a small community at Criss Creek, little over five kilometres to the north, in the early 1900s. They carved their

Pacific rattlesnakes live in the Thompson and South Cariboo region.

farms out of the pine forest and raised cattle and grain, alternately fighting early frost and drought. The final blow came in the late 1960s when their post office closed, forcing them to travel to Savona or Kamloops for their mail. While the schoolhouse no longer has regular classes, a large arena is a strong sign that the community was not wiped out.

If you are interested in serious backcountry exploring, you can head north about 1.7 kilometres from the Criss Creek – Red Lake junction to the Seven Lakes Road junction near Cayuse Lake. If you keep right at a junction north of Sparks Lake, you should reach Sabiston Creek Forest Service Road, about six kilometres west of the Cayuse Lake junction. If you head south on Sabiston Creek Forest Service Road, you should join up with the more direct route from Red Lake to Savona, 3.5 kilometres south of Sabiston Lake.

"Should" is a key word in backroads exploring. Locked gates, washouts, and de-activated roads can block your way. A wrong turn can also add to the "interest." A full tank of fuel and lots of time makes these unexpected detours interesting rather than a disaster.

Head South to Red Lake

The Criss Creek – Red Lake junction (47.5 kilometres from North Kamloops) is also the high point in this backroad jaunt, with an elevation of about 1,000 metres. The south fork (Copper Creek Road) continues to Red Lake and Savona over a sometimes narrow and twisting road. Watch for cattle and oncoming vehicles. Red Lake (km 50) has Kamloops (rainbow) trout and brook trout that often respond to the patient fish enthusiast. Camping is limited and boat launching is restricted to those carrying car-toppers or canoes. South of Red Lake, the road now begins a steady, sometimes steep, descent to the Carabine Creek valley. Crushed rock and gravel has been spread over the clay surface, but the road is still narrow and must be driven with caution.

Pine and aspen give way to grassland and sagebrush on the approach to the dry Thompson Valley. Deer and brown bear frequent the area as do the occasional Pacific rattlesnake. The normally shy rattlesnakes can occasionally be seen sunning themselves on the warm, dusty road. They eat mice and generally do no harm to man. Wear good boots and jeans while scrambling around the grasslands. Give the snakes an opportunity to get out of the way and they will quickly do so.

A relic of past transportation sits in a meadow near Criss Creek Road.

Copper Creek Junction

There are photogenic old log buildings near km 61 that are worth exploring, but remember to respect private property and leave fences and gates the way you find them. A junction near km 62.5 marks an option for another detour. Copper Creek, once an important Hudson's Bay Brigade stopping point and later a settlement on the CNR, is now virtually a ghost town. It is located two kilometres south of the junction, on the shores of Kamloops Lake. Copper Creek was named after native copper was found near here. The First Nations peoples used the copper for tools and ornaments. The colourful rocky hillsides, now part of Painted Bluffs Provincial Park, also show traces of cinnabar, a wine-red mercury ore. A mine waste dump is visible west of the road near the bottom of the hill.

From the Copper Creek junction, the road to Savona continues west and then loops north to the previously mentioned Sabiston Creek Road. A knoll near a cattleguard at km 66 provides an excellent view of Savona and Kamloops Lake to the east and south. Watch for a herd of California bighorn

The Copper Creek area as viewed from the south side of Kamloops Lake.

GPS References for major points of interest
Ref: WGS 84 - Lat/Lon hddd.ddddd
Allow +/-100 metres due to data conversions

Wpt	Km	Description	Latitude	Longitude
		Kamloops to Savona via Red Lake		
W01	0	Fortune Dr and Tranquille Rd	N50.69945	W120.36290
W02	5.7	Airport Rd and Tranquille Rd	N50.70853	W120.43064
W03	11.0	Tranquille Slough	N50.72430	W120.49980
W04	11.5	Red Lake Rd 0K	N50.72536	W120.50528
W05	12.9	Jct to Tranquille River Trail	N50.72762	W120.52052
W06	13.2	Tranquille River Bridge	N50.72680	W120.52543
W07	15.7	Jct to Dewdrop Range	N50.74031	W120.54810
W08	18.6	Parking for knoll hike	N50.75520	W120.52409
W09	24.9	Jct to Watching Creek rec site	N50.79946	W120.55276
W10	28.3	Tranquille River Bridge	N50.82057	W120.58069
W11	32.3	Tranquille River Guest Ranch	N50.84133	W120.62357
W12	35.8	Tranquille Valley School	N50.85887	W120.66093
W13	43.5	Tranquille River Bridge 32K	N50.91032	W120.72230
W14	44.5	Jct Heller Creek Rd	N50.91570	W120.73379
W15	46.5	Red Lake Rd 35K	N50.91397	W120.75781
W16	47.5	Jct Criss Creek and Copper Creek Rds	N50.90752	W120.77250
		Copper Creek Road		
W17	50.0	Red Lake	N50.88618	W120.77452
W18	55.5	Carabine Creek	N50.85828	W120.80683
W19	62.5	Jct Copper Creek and Kamloops Lake	N50.80621	W120.77603
W20	66.0	Viewpoint knoll	N50.79307	W120.80326
W21	70.0	Jct to Sabiston Lake	N50.82292	W120.83688
W22	74.5	Jct Steam Shovel Forest Service Rd	N50.79429	W120.87084
W23	75.0	Corrals and start of descent	N50.79434	W120.87649
W24	86.0	Jct Hwy 1 and Sabiston Creek Rd	N50.75723	W120.88858
		Side trip to Tranquille Lake		
W14	0	Jct Heller Creek Rd and Red Lake Rd	N50.91570	W120.73379
W25	4.1	Jct Wendego Lodge to right	N50.94401	W120.72719
W26	8.1	Jct Sawmill Lake Forest Service Rd	N50.94584	W120.67751
W27	10.3	Truda Lake and dam	N50.95250	W120.65442
W28	16.2	West end of Tranquille Lake	N50.93925	W120.58018
W29	17.7	Wendego Lodge	N50.93661	W120.56038

sheep. Cattle-loading chutes mark the junction of a rough gravel road that winds north a few kilometres to Sabiston Lake. The fishing is worth a try, but drifting along in a canoe and listening to the song of the loon is also an enjoyable way to spend an evening.

Long Descent Begins

After passing the Copper Creek junction (km 62.5), the road maintains a relatively level course. Here, however, the long descent to the Thompson River and the Trans-Canada Highway begins near km 75. The road soon resembles a combination roller coaster track and slalom course with eight switchback turns in a few kilometres. The Thompson River is visible far below, and to the west lays Deadman Valley.

Trans-Canada Highway and Sabiston Creek Road

Sabiston Creek Road, 86 kilometres from North Kamloops and one kilometre west of the Thompson River Bridge at Savona, forms the west end of the "Red Lake Road" route. The creek, lake, and road were named after James Sabiston, an Orkney Islander who was in charge of the Hudson's Bay Company warehouse at Savona's Ferry in the 1870s. Sabiston took up ranching in the area after leaving the Hudson's Bay Company.

Note: See the *Information Sources* chapter at the end of the book for contact information on the services mentioned here.

Cariboo Roadhouses: The "Waggon" Road to Barkerville

B ritish Columbia's colourful history manifests itself in many ways, but few are more intriguing than the roadhouses that dot the highways and backroads of the Cariboo from Yale to Barkerville.

Freight wagons carried thousands of tons of equipment and supplies along the Cariboo Waggon Road.

Cariboo Roadhouses

Names such as Hat Creek House, 100 Mile House, and Cottonwood House attract the curious visitor.

Why were these settlements named this way? Where or what is the starting point that lies 100 miles (160 kilometres) from 100 Mile House?

The answers lie in a very short span of British Columbia's history; a decade in the middle of the nineteenth century that abruptly changed this mountainous land from the domain of the Native peoples and the fur trader to a rich gold-mining province.

Starting in March 1858, tens of thousands of miners began tramping northward in search of a golden mother lode. The quiet Cariboo became gold rush country, establishing the names of many of its villages and physical features during the late 1850s and early 1860s.

Governor James Douglas

British Columbia Governor James Douglas quickly recognized the need for better roads through the mountainous terrain. He assigned the task of creating these roads to the Royal Engineers. Their first obstacle was the treacherous Fraser Canyon. A Lake Trail route was chosen that started on the lower Fraser River near present day Chilliwack and linked Harrison, Lillooet, Anderson, and Seton lakes by a series of trails and portages, bypassing the Fraser Canyon completely. The Lake Trail ended at Cayoosh Flats (now Lillooet), an arid bench lying between Seton Lake and the Fraser River. A community quickly developed, and in 1858 it became the supply centre for the upper Fraser River.

Lillooet was Mile 0

As Mile 0 of the Cariboo Trail, Lillooet grew into a boom town boasting a population of four to five thousand and all the amenities of civilization, including a brewery.

The River Trail, as it was also known, crossed the Fraser River and then climbed northeastward over Pavilion Mountain. From Kelly Lake, west of Clinton, it paralleled the Fraser northward through Jesmond, Big Bar, Dog Creek, and Alkali Lake, joining the old fur brigade trail at Williams Lake. See *Exploring the Fraser River Trail: Lillooet to Williams Lake* for details.

Cariboo Waggon Road

The Lake Trail from Port Douglas to Lillooet, with its many portages, proved to be a tough and expensive route, prompting the Royal Engineers to begin work on a wagon road from Yale to the Cariboo, through the Fraser Canyon. The Royal

St. John the Divine Church at Yale, built in 1863, is considered to be the oldest church on the British Columbia mainland still standing on its original foundation.

Cariboo Roadhouses

Engineers surveyed the first section of the road from Yale to Lytton in 1861. Construction of the Cariboo Waggon Road began in the lower Fraser Canyon in 1862.

This road followed much the same route presently used by the Trans-Canada Highway from Yale to Cache Creek. North of Cache Creek, the wagon road followed much of the route traversed by present-day Cariboo Highway 97. The first connection was made from Cache Creek to 47 Mile House (Clinton), where it linked up with the earlier trail from Lillooet.

In 1863, the Cariboo road was surveyed between Clinton and Soda Creek, north of present-day Williams Lake, and construction contracts were let. Clinton also had the dubious honour of being the toll office for the portion of the wagon road north to Soda Creek. The government under James Douglas was unable to finance the road construction and the contractors collected tolls to recover their costs.

By September of 1863, the wagon road was completed from Yale northward 480 kilometres (300 miles) to Soda Creek. The project was an instant success and soon

Roger Porter drives the BX stage coach at Hat Creek House.

Isabel holds up a wagon wheel at Barkerville.

freight wagons and mule trains were transporting supplies to the goldfields.

Barnard Express Stage Coach

In May 1864, the first stage coach was driven up the new road. A ride on Frank Barnard's stage, from Yale to Soda Creek, originally cost $65 and took 52 hours to travel the 480 kilometres (300 miles).

During the height of the gold rush, 150 Mile House became famous as the departure point for the instant towns on the banks of the Horsefly, Keithley, and Antler creeks. From 150 Mile House, the Cariboo Road swung north, deviating from the present route of Highway 97.

Cariboo Roadhouses

Sternwheel Steamboats Carried Freight
The River Trail and the Cariboo Waggon Road both ended at Soda Creek, the foot of the upper Fraser navigation, approximately 32 kilometres north of William's Lake. The first steamer to slip into the muddy Fraser was the stern-wheeler *Enterprise*. The *Enterprise* made her maiden voyage between Soda Creek and Quesnel on May 9, 1863, and continued running three trips per week from May to October.

In 1863, a 100-kilometre trail was cut from Quesnel to Barkerville, tying the rich mining district to the head of the sternwheeler travel on the upper Fraser River. Cottonwood House, located on the road to Barkerville, was constructed in 1864 and 1865.

Largest Town West of Chicago
Barkerville became the destination of the gold rush: "the largest town west of Chicago and north of San Francisco." In 1865, the wagon road was completed from Yale to Barkerville, closing the gap between Soda Creek and Quesnel and reducing the freight load on the paddlewheel steamers. Huge freight wagons, each carrying several tons, brought in the supplies. Passengers rode the stagecoaches, covering the distance from Yale in six and one-half days.

Ashcroft New Gateway
In 1885, the Canadian Pacific Railway was completed through the Fraser and Thompson canyons, destroying much of the original wagon road and establishing Ashcroft as the new gateway to the Cariboo. In 1899, the British Columbia government attempted to change the names of the mileposts by measuring from Ashcroft. The local people refused to change, as they undoubtedly would today, should a modern-day government attempt to introduce metrification into the Cariboo roadhouse system and, for instance, change 70 Mile House to 112.6 Kilometre House.

CHAPTER 11

Highway 97:
The Cariboo Road
Cache Creek to Quesnel

STATISTICS

	Map see page 142.
Distance:	112 km, Cache Creek to 100 Mile House.
	90 km, 100 Mile House to Williams Lake.
	120 km, Williams Lake to Quesnel.
Travel time:	Four to five hours.
Conditions:	Paved throughout.
Season:	Maintained all year, could be slippery in winter.
Topo maps:	Clinton 92 P/SW (1:100,000).
	Churn Creek 92 O/SE (1:100,000).
Communities:	Cache Creek, Clinton, 100 Mile House, Williams Lake, and Quesnel.

Lillooet Was Original Mile 0

When the Royal Engineers completed the Lake Trail from Port Douglas (Harrison) to Cayoosh Flats (Lillooet) this bustling community on the banks of the Fraser River became Mile 0 of the original trail to the goldfields of the Cariboo. See *Exploring the Fraser River Trail* for details.

Cariboo Waggon Road

The Lake Trail from Port Douglas to Lillooet was soon abandoned in favour of the wagon road being built up the Fraser Canyon. The River Trail came closest to the new wagon road at Kelly Lake, 16 kilometres southwest of Clinton. It didn't take much to build a wagon road through Cutoff Valley, and the upper Fraser Canyon traffic soon diverted to the new wagon road.

Cache Creek Junction Start

It would take a book or two to do more than touch on the history of the wagon road north to Barkerville — and Branwen C. Patenaude has done just that in her

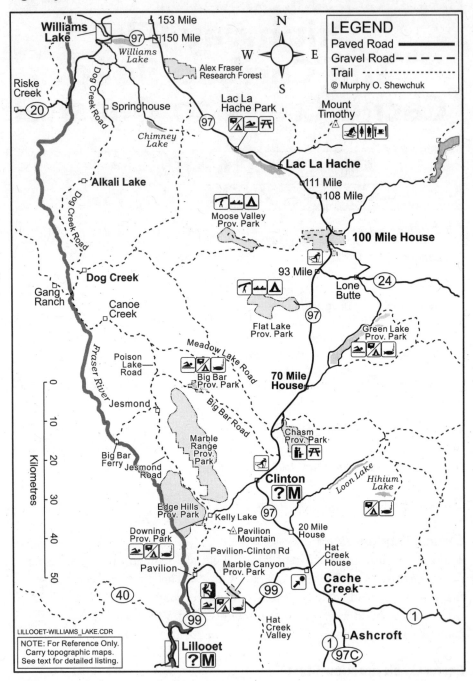

LEGEND
Paved Road
Gravel Road
Trail
© Murphy O. Shewchuk

Williams Lake
153 Mile
150 Mile
Williams Lake
Alex Fraser Research Forest
Riske Creek
Springhouse
Chimney Lake
Lac La Hache Park
Mount Timothy
Lac La Hache
Alkali Lake
111 Mile
108 Mile
Moose Valley Prov. Park
100 Mile House
93 Mile
Lone Butte
Dog Creek
Gang Ranch
Canoe Creek
Flat Lake Prov. Park
Green Lake Prov. Park
Meadow Lake Road
Big Bar Prov. Park
70 Mile House
Poison Lake Road
Jesmond
Big Bar Road
Marble Range Prov. Park
Chasm Prov. Park
Hihium Lake
Loon Lake
Big Bar Ferry
Jesmond Road
Clinton
Edge Hills Prov. Park
Kelly Lake
20 Mile House
Downing Prov. Park
Pavilion Mountain
Pavilion-Clinton Rd
Marble Canyon Prov. Park
Hat Creek House
Cache Creek
Pavilion
Hat Creek Valley
Ashcroft
Lilloooet

Kilometres
0
10
20
30
40
50

LILLOOET-WILLIAMS_LAKE.CDR
NOTE: For Reference Only. Carry topographic maps. See text for detailed listing.

Trails to Gold series. As my objective here is to turn this chapter into a backbone for a series of chapters on the backroad diversions off Highway 97, I won't attempt to provide the detail that long-time resident Branwen Patenaude has done in her books.

Cache Creek is a good place to double-check your supplies and get that last ice cream or burger fix before heading for the hills. If ice cream and burgers aren't on your preferred menu, the Bonaparte Bend Winery, on the north outskirts of town, can add a touch of class with fine fruit wines. Horsting's Farm Market, a few minutes farther north, has fresh homemade soup and sandwiches and fresh vegetables that attract a steady clientele. If you arrive in mid-June, you may catch a glimpse of prickly pear cactus in full bloom on the hillsides to the east of the Horsting orchards.

Hat Creek Ranch

The next major junction is Highway 99, 11 kilometres north of Cache Creek. Highway 99 to Lillooet and Pemberton is covered elsewhere in this book, but Historic Hat Creek House is well worth a visit. Hat Creek House, 11 kilometres north of Cache Creek, was among the first roadhouses established on the new wagon road. Donald McLean, previously chief trader at the Hudson's Bay Company post at Kamloops, established McLean's Farm and Restaurant near the confluence of Hat Creek and the Bonaparte River in 1860. Unfortunately Donald McLean became involved in one of the few battles with the Native peoples and died near Anahim Lake in 1864 in what has become known as the Chilcotin War. McLean's wife Sophia and her family remained at Hat Creek for several years before new owners took over. As road traffic increased, so did the size of the operation, with the present Hat Creek House roadhouse and ranch buildings dating back to the 1880s.

The property served a variety of landowners until it was purchased by BC Hydro in the 1970s when interest peaked in turning the massive Hat Creek coal deposit into a supply base for a thermal electric plant. Interest in the historical aspect of the property also began to grow and the heritage site opened to the public in 1987.

The B.X. stop-of-interest sign near km 15.5 pays tribute to the Barnard's Express stage coaches that served the Cariboo for over 50 years. It is also a landmark for a colourful rock and clay formation on the west side of the Bonaparte River.

20 Mile House, at the junction of Loon Lake Road and the foot of the long climb to Clinton, was one of the few roadhouses that took its reference from the CPR station in Ashcroft. Loon Lake Road also serves as access to a resort area on

The museum attendant plays the pump organ at the Clinton Museum.

Loon Lake, some 20 kilometres to the northeast. The pavement runs out on Loon Lake Road 30 kilometres from Highway 97, and there is another eight kilometres of rough road before you can join the smoother logging roads that serve to haul timber north to Chasm. With a little bit of exploring, you can access Hihium Lake and the west end of Bonaparte Lake. See the *West Bonaparte Loop* chapter for details.

Lord Henry Pelham Clinton

The next major "house" is located 40 kilometres north of Cache Creek, at the junction of the old River Trail and the new wagon road. The first 47 Mile House opened on New Year's Day, 1861. It was reported as "A fine two-story hewn-log building of seven rooms (and not a nail in it) . . . with a well stocked bar, good food and kindly generous hosts." Originally known as "47 Mile" because of its distance from Mile 0 at Lillooet, the name was changed to "Clinton" in honour of Colonial Secretary, Lord Henry Pelham Clinton.

Clinton Museum is well worth a stop for a glimpse of local history. Across the street, the Cariboo Lodge sits near the site of the original 47 Mile House.

Clinton also serves as a base for a network of backroads that can take you west to the Fraser River in several locations. To the southwest is Lillooet with Pavilion

Mountain limiting access to the dry summer months. To the northwest is the old River Trail and access to the canyon at the Big Bar Ferry. See the *Fraser River Trail* and *Southwest Cariboo Loop* chapters for details. While Edge Hills Provincial Park is a wilderness area with no services, there is a campground at Downing Provincial Park on Kelly Lake, 16 kilometres southwest of Clinton.

Big Bar Road, near km 50, also provides access to a provincial park campground on Big Bar Lake, 31 kilometres northwest of Highway 97. If you are interested in cross-country skiing (or mountain cycling), the home base of the Clinton Cross Country Ski Trails is only six kilometres to the northwest.

The Chasm

Chasm Road, to the east at km 55.5, provides another opportunity for a diversion into the back country as well as a view of a major remnant of the last ice age. The "Chasm" is about 4.5 kilometres off Highway 97. The eight-kilometre-long chasm is protected by a 3,067-hectare provincial park. The main feature is the 600-metre-wide by 300-metre-deep canyon carved through numerous layers of red, brown, yellow, and purple lava. Although camping isn't permitted, there are picnic tables,

The Clinton Museum is an excellent place to stop for local information and history.

a pit toilet, and undeveloped trails along the southern edge of the chasm. After taking your photos, you can return to Highway 97 near km 62.2, adding less than a kilometre to your northward trip.

Chasm Road is also the departure point for a backroad that once headed across the Bonaparte plateau to Deadman Valley, north of Savona. "Once" is the key word. The Chasm–Loon Lake Road (3400 Road) was one of our favourite backroads until a land slump a few hundred metres from Deadman-Vidette Road blocked the way to all but 4x4 Jeeps or Hummers. Although the last leg down to Deadman Valley is or was blocked by a washout, there is still an opportunity to explore the plateau and return to Highway 97 via Loon Lake.

Meadow Lake Road

There is another opportunity to get sidetracked little more than a kilometre north of the south entrance to Chasm Road. Meadow Lake Road heads northwest across the Cariboo Plateau to join up with Poison Lake Road, part of the previously mentioned Fraser River Trail. If you aren't in a hurry, you can take a break at the Beaver Dam Lake Forest Service recreation site or try fishing at several lakes along the way to the Fraser River at the Gang Ranch.

There is also a network of backroads that will take you northwest past Meadow Lake and White Lake, then circle north of Gustafson Lake to Holden Lake and the Moose Valley area. You can then return to Highway 97 at 100 Mile House. With all the logging taking place on the plateau, the old topographic maps won't be a lot of help; however a good GPS and compass will help you find your way through the maze. I suggest you be sure to fill your larder and fuel tank before leaving Clinton. When we last "did" the route, it totaled 114 kilometres, doubling the distance to 100 Mile House and much more than doubling the time. My wife muttered loudly about the dust, but I enjoyed exploring the parkland and grasslands.

70 Mile House

The North Bonaparte Road junction at 70 Mile House (km 72) is an opportunity for more diversions into the Cariboo Plateau. If you are underwhelmed by dusty roads, you will appreciate the *Green Lake Loop* route that can take you northeast to Green Lake, then north along Green Lake and Watch Lake to Highway 24 near Lone Butte. After a short drive along Highway 24, you can continue your backroads exploring via Horse Lake into the heart of 100 Mile House.

Although dustier, 70 Mile House is also the departure point for a series of backroads that loop north and east to Bonaparte Lake and then south and west to

Chasm Provincial Park protects the eight-kilometre-long, 600-metre-wide, and 300-metre-deep Painted Chasm. The chasm is believed to have been carved through the layers of lava by the meltwaters of the retreating glaciers some 10,000 years ago

The Forest Fire Lookout on the summit of Mount Begbie provides a view of most of the Cariboo plateau.

Loon Lake and Highway 97. See the *Green Lake Loop* and *West Bonaparte Loop* chapters for more information.

Begbie Summit Trail

Sir Matthew Baillie Begbie was one of a handful of officials sent out from Great Britain in 1858 to administer the new Colony of British Columbia. Begbie travelled constantly, mainly on horseback, serving as a judge in the makeshift courtrooms of the gold rush towns, drafting legislation and advising Governor James Douglas on policy that was successful in maintaining law and order in this wild land. After the gold rush waned, he went on to become the Chief Justice of British Columbia, a post he held until his death in 1894.

It is only fitting that the highest point along Highway 97 was named after this hard-working pioneer judge. There is a fire lookout building on the top of the 1,276-metre peak that, according to the Forest Service, on a clear day provides a view of almost all of the Cariboo — a range of just under nine million hectares.

There is a trail to the summit around the south face of the mountain. After a view of the countryside and a chat with the lookout personnel, you can hike back down to your vehicle via an old road around the north side of the mountain. The circle tour is under a kilometre in length with a 50-metre difference in elevation.

Highway 24: The Bridge Lake Road

Highway 24, 104 kilometres north of Cache Creek, is an important link across the plateau to Yellowhead Highway 5 at Little Fort. It is also the starting point for backroads to dozens of Cariboo fishing lakes, many with fishing resorts or campgrounds. In addition to Bridge Lake Provincial Park, there is access to the west end of Mahood Lake, part of much larger Wells Gray Provincial Park. See the *Bridge Lake Road* and *Wells Gray Park West* chapters for details.

99 Mile Ski Trails

As you descend to 100 Mile House and the Bridge Creek Valley, a side road leads west to the 99 Mile Cross-Country Ski Trails. Volunteers from the 100 Mile Nordic Ski Society maintain a day lodge and a network of Nordic trails including 3.5 kilometres of trails that are lit for night skiing. For up-to-date information on the Cariboo Marathon, Gold Rush Trail Loppets, and ski conditions, visit their website at http://www.100milenordics.com.

100 Mile House and the Barnard Express Stage Coach

Nestled at the foot of 99 Mile Hill is the roadhouse stop of 100 Mile House, one of the Cariboo's largest communities to spring from roadhouse beginnings. The original Barnard Express (BX) stage coach, refurbished and painted red, is on display in front of the Red Coach Inn at 100 Mile House. A ride on the Barnard Express stage, from Yale to Soda Creek, originally cost $65 and took 52 hours to travel the 480 kilometres (300 miles). Frank Barnard was purser on the sternwheeler Fort Yale when its boiler exploded at Union Bar, near Hope. The incident must have frightened Barnard. He quit the steamers and began packing letters the

240 kilometres from Yale to Barkerville on foot before forming the famous Barnard Express and Stage Line.

Picnic Tables and Waterfalls

If you are looking for a break from driving, Centennial Park and the Bridge Creek Waterfall Trail are only a few steps from downtown 100 Mile House. To find the park, take 4th Street or 5th Street east of Highway 97 (across from the Information Centre) east to Cedar Avenue South. Look for the Centennial Park

Bridge Creek Falls at 100 Mile House in September.

entrance road next to the daycare centre less than one hundred metres south of 4th Street. The parking lot is two hundred metres east of Cedar Avenue.

The Bridge Creek Waterfall Trail starts at the south end of the lot and follows the creek upstream about 350 metres to the falls. The trail climbs up to the bench above the canyon before winding northward and back to the parking lot. Allow half an hour to meander along the 1.2-kilometre loop trail.

If you brought your lunch, there are picnic tables in the meadow northeast of the parking area.

Stock up Before Exploring the Backroads

100 Mile House continues to serve Cariboo travellers with most of the services they are likely to need. And as previously stated, it is wise to take advantage of the opportunity before heading out to explore the backroads. One such road leads west some 30 kilometres to Moose Valley Provincial Park, famous for the Moose Valley Canoe Route, described in the *Moose Valley Canoe Route* chapter. If you are equipped with topographic maps, a GPS, and a good sense of direction and adventure, you can continue west to Dog Creek and the Fraser River.

Canim Lake Road, a couple of kilometres north of downtown 100 Mile House, leads northeast to another network of lakes and backroads. Again, with a stock of maps, fuel, grub, and adventure, you could work your way east and north to Horsefly, Likely, and Barkerville.

The fine old log buildings of the original 108 Mile Roadhouse still stand overlooking 108 Lake. Now a resort community, the 108 Ranch offers modern recreation in a historic setting.

Lac La Hache

In 1863, Judge Matthew Baillie Begbie put his official signature to the deed of the McKinley family holdings in Lac La Hache. Archibald McKinley was not a newcomer to the district. He had travelled the brigade trails with the fur traders more than a decade before the gold rush. He and his brothers established 115 Mile House on the shores of Lac La Hache and built it up to a successful roadhouse and cattle ranch. The roadhouse stayed in the family for almost 80 years before they sold it.

Mount Timothy Ski Hill

Today, Lac La Hache is one of the busiest resort areas along Highway 97. Timothy Lake Road, near the south end of the lake, leads east to a series of fishing lakes and the Mount Timothy Ski Hill. "Mt Timothy offers a variety of terrain for every

Saddle Bronc Riding is one of the more than a dozen events at the Williams Lake Stampede.

age and level of ability. Take an easy glide down a long rolling cruiser, or head off to challenge the Diamondback trails. The popular terrain park on Morningside offers boxes, rails and jumps in a progressive design allowing park users to learn at their own pace — no matter what your style, Mount Timothy has it." For up-to-date information on the Mount Timothy ski conditions, visit their website at http://skitimothy.com.

Lac La Hache Park

Lac La Hache Provincial Park, near the north end of the lake, has an 83-unit campground north of Highway 97 and a picnic ground with beach access south of the highway. Cariboo Nature Provincial Park, an undeveloped area set aside to protect Woodfrog Lake, is located about 3.5 kilometres northwest of Lac La Hache Park. There are no services, but it could be a good location for some quiet birdwatching.

150 Mile House

During the height of the gold rush, 150 Mile House became famous as the departure point for the instant towns that had grown overnight on the banks of the Horsefly, Keithley, and Antler creeks. From 150 Mile House, the Cariboo Road swung north, deviating from the present route of Highway 97. You too can deviate from Highway 97 and head northeast to Barkerville via Horsefly or Likely. Don't forget to take in the ghost town of Quesnel Forks, a decaying mining community that predates Barkerville. See the *Backroad to Barkerville* chapter for details.

Williams Lake

Williams Lake, situated on the old fur brigade trails, was a major supply centre for the miners using the Fraser River Trail to the Cariboo in the late 1850s and early 1860s. When the Cariboo Waggon Road was being constructed, one story is that a quarrel between a contractor and a local settler resulted in William's Lake being bypassed.

However, as neither the railway nor Highway 97 bypass Williams Lake, it has

The Scout Island Nature Centre is operated by the Williams Lake Field Naturalists in cooperation with the Nature Trust of BC and the City of Williams Lake. The boardwalk and trails provide an opportunity to view a wide variety of wetland wildlife.

The Williams Lake River Valley Trail winds through ancient glacial silt deposits and crosses the river more than two dozen times on the way from Williams Lake to the Fraser River.

become the central supply community for much of the Cariboo and the Chilcotin. It can also become the central point for a wide variety of backroads trips and hiking trails.

Scout Island Nature Centre Trails

The closest to the highway is the Scout Island Nature Centre, a few minutes south of the junction of Highway 97 and Highway 20. Access is via Mackenzie Avenue and Borland Road from either Highway 97 or 20. The centre is open year-round from 8:00 a.m. to dusk and the Nature House is open daily from May to August. Operated by the Williams Lake Field Naturalists, Scout Island has a selection of trails with wildlife-viewing opportunities plus indoor displays and a summer interpretive program.

Williams Lake River Valley Trail

The Williams Lake River Valley Trail is a little farther from the highway, but is still part of the community. The 12-kilometre-long trail follows the river from just north of the outlet of Williams Lake to the Fraser River. It initially passes through an industrial area and then winds through a broad valley beneath the clay cliffs.

The upper (south) section of the trail is accessible from a parking area on the west side of Mackenzie Avenue, across from the community cemetery. The lower (northwest) section of the trail is accessible via a gravel road that switchbacks across the cliffs and winds down to the valley floor.

I wouldn't recommend this route to anything larger than a pickup truck. However, if the weather is dry, there isn't any sign of rain or snow, *and* your heart pills are handy, give it a try. With the junction of MacKenzie Avenue and Highway 20 as your 0 km reference, head north on Mackenzie Avenue and Soda Creek Road for 5.6 kilometres to Frizzi Road and cross the railway tracks. Turn right and follow Frizzi Road past the landfill and through the industrial area. The pavement ends and the gravel road switchbacks down to the valley bottom, crossing a one-lane bridge. Continue west along the south side of Williams Lake River for one kilometre to a parking area, keeping right at a fork in the road.

The parking lot is at km 7 of the 12-kilometre trail system. The trail initially passes a couple of ponds before winding west along the river to the Fraser. In addition to birdwatching opportunities (hundreds of species have been reported), the meandering river supports a healthy wildlife population including deer, beaver, and the occasional bear.

The Fraser Canyon near the Rudy Johnson Bridge.

The Road to Bella Coola

Highway 20 starts (or ends) at Williams Lake and winds 456 kilometres westward across the Chilcotin Plateau to Bella Coola. At least a dozen books have been written about the area. They range from serious non-fiction histories to personal autobiographies to colourful fiction. A quick look through my library reveals authors such as Cliff Kopas, Ralph Edwards, Paul St. Pierre, Irene Stangoe, Trudy Turner and Ruth McVeigh, Mel Rothenburger, and many others. See the *Highway 20: Williams Lake to Bella Coola* chapter for a brief overview of the route to the Pacific.

Highway 97 shifts away from the Fraser as it continues north of Williams Lake. If you are interested in a closer look at the magnificent canyons, you could follow Mackenzie Avenue North, the Soda Creek Road, and Williams Lake Cutoff Road along the canyon benches to Soda Creek. Prior to the early 1990s, you could follow the gravel road along the river benches all the way to Macalister. However, a bridge was taken out just south of the old Soda Creek townsite for safety reasons, and you will now have to detour east to Highway 97 for a few kilometres before returning to the river road via Soda Creek Townsite Road.

If you follow this route, you can also cross the Rudy Johnson Bridge

Soda Creek, approximately 32 kilometres north of Williams Lake, was the departure point for northbound sternwheel steamers in the early years of the Cariboo gold rush.

approximately 24 kilometres north of Williams Lake and work your way back down the west side of the Fraser River to Highway 20 via Meldrum Creek Road.

Bull Mountain Ski Area

Watch for the Bull Mountain X-C Ski Trails signs and Bull Mountain Road approximately 18 kilometres north of the junction of Cariboo Highway 97 and Highway 20. The Williams Lake Cross Country Ski Club maintains a total of 28 kilometres of cross-country ski trails including 3.5 kilometres of lighted trails. A warming hut, complete with wood stove, plus large trail maps and a stadium are part of the facilities. For up-to-date information, a printable map, and ski conditions, visit their website at http://www.bullmountain.ca.

A cairn marks the head of navigation of the Fraser Canyon as well as the vicinity of a North West Company fur trade fort erected in 1821.

Soda Creek

The River Trail and the Cariboo Waggon Road both ended at Soda Creek, the foot of the upper Fraser navigation, approximately 26 kilometres (16 miles) north of Williams Lake. The first steamer to slip into the muddy Fraser was the sternwheeler *Enterprise*. Built at a cost of $75,000 from local hand-hewn lumber, the boiler, engines, and hardware were packed by mules from Port Douglas. The *Enterprise* made her maiden voyage between Soda Creek and Quesnel on May 9, 1863, and continued running three trips per week from May to October.

Highway 97 dips down toward the Fraser near Soda Creek before climbing north again as it skirts the east side of McLeese Lake. On the way north, you have the opportunity to explore the Bull Mountain X-C Trails or visit the Xats'ull Heritage Village on the banks of the Fraser.

One of the many displays in the Quesnel Museum.

Basalt Cliffs

Richard Wright, in his book *Cariboo Mileposts*, suggests that the basalt columns east of the highway, 65 kilometres north of Williams Lake, are known as the Devil's Palisades. With a little care, you can pull off the road and get a closer look at these volcanic remnants. Other fine examples in the BC Interior include the Keremeos Columns and the Devil's Woodpile in Cathedral Provincial Park.

Fort Alexandria

Although there is some debate regarding the exactness of the location, a stone cairn a kilometre north of the basalt cliffs commemorates the site of a fur trade fort built in 1821. It is also believed to be the farthest south point that Alexander Mackenzie travelled on his 1793 journey to the Pacific at what is now Bella Coola.

Quesnel

On his return journey from the mouth of the Fraser River, Simon Fraser noted in his journal for August 1, 1808, "Debarked at Quesnel's River." Jules Maurice Quesnel was one of two clerks of the North West Company who accompanied Fraser on his historic journey.

The City of Quesnel, with a population of 11,000, has changed significantly since Simon Fraser "debarked" here. It has grown from a fur trade stop to a sternwheeler stop on the gold trails to a major forest resource and area supply centre. The Quesnel Museum and Information Centre is a good base to begin any exploration of Quesnel and the surrounding area. While the downtown has retained much of the character of the 1980s, the southern approach to the city is lined with shopping centres and "big box" stores.

The Moffat Bridge across the Fraser River near the city centre provides access to West Quesnel and a variety of backroads to explore. West Fraser Road can take you south approximately 90 kilometres to the Rudy Johnson (Buckskin) Bridge and your next opportunity to cross the Fraser. To the west, my maps suggest that the Nazko Road and its various logging road tributaries can take you two hundred kilometres west to the north boundary of Itcha Ilgachuz Provincial Park. Although we have made a couple of forays into the Itcha and Ilgachuz mountains from Anahim Lake, we have yet to explore this route so you are on your own.

If you are interested in 12-million-year-old "hoodoo" rock formations, Pinnacles Provincial Park, on the west side of the Fraser River six kilometres from downtown Quesnel, is well worth a visit. Camping isn't allowed, but it's a pleasant hike along a well-maintained trail to a scenic viewpoint.

To the north, Highway 97 continues to Prince George and beyond, providing

Cross the Fraser River on the Moffatt Bridge at Quesnel and take Baker Driver north, 0.5 kilometres west of the bridge. Follow Baker Drive, which soon becomes Pinnacles Road, for 5.8 kilometres to the Pinnacles Park parking area. The 2.4-kilometre round trip trail to the Pinnacles viewpoints could take an hour, particularly if you have a camera and kids.

**GPS References for major points of interest
Ref: WGS 84 - Lat/Lon hddd.ddddd
Allow +/-100 metres due to data conversions**

Wpt	Km	Description	Latitude	Longitude	Elev.
C01	0	Cache Creek – Highway 1 and 97	N50.80866	W121.32532	460 m
C02	3.0	Horstings Farm Market	N50.82650	W121.35322	469 m
C03	4.8	Bonaparte church	N50.83568	W121.37400	471 m
C04	11.0	Jct Hwy 99 – Hat Creek Ranch	N50.88754	W121.39993	495 m
C05	15.5	BX stop-of-interest	N50.91746	W121.40964	508 m
C06	21.5	Jct Loon Lake Rd	N50.96751	W121.45817	532 m
C07	40.0	Clinton	N51.09134	W121.58789	878 m
C08	49.5	Jct Big Bar Rd	N51.14680	W121.50197	1,047 m
C09	55.4	Jct Chasm Rd S	N51.19302	W121.52932	1,083 m
C10	56.7	Jct Meadow Lake Rd	N51.20517	W121.53598	1,091 m
C11	62.2	Jct Chasm Road N	N51.24356	W121.48712	1,090 m
C12	71.7	70 Mile House	N51.30266	W121.39719	1,086 m
C13	89.6	83 Mile House	N51.45778	W121.37005	1,111 m
C14	91.7	Begbie Summit	N51.47769	W121.37038	1,205 m
C15	104	93 Mile House – Hwy 24	N51.57670	W121.33386	1,180 m
C16	112.4	100 Mile House	N51.64188	W121.29748	925 m
C17	113.5	Jct Exeter Stn Rd	N51.65009	W121.29635	919 m
C18	115.3	Jct Canim Lake Rd	N51.66408	W121.28928	966 m
C19	120.7	Jct Back Valley Rd	N51.70577	W121.31823	895 m
C20	123.4	Jct 108 Mile Resort	N51.72764	W121.32703	938 m
C21	127	108 Mile Historic Ranch	N51.75134	W121.34580	892 m

access to northern British Columbia and the Yukon.

To the east, backroads follow the Quesnel River upstream toward Likely and Horsefly. However, one of the Cariboo's richest roads — one that might well be paved with gold — is Highway 26, the Barkerville Road, which we will cover in the next chapter.

Note: See the *Information Sources* chapter at the end of the book for contact information on the services mentioned here.

GPS References for major points of interest
Ref: WGS 84 - Lat/Lon hddd.ddddd
Allow +/-100 metres due to data conversions

Wpt	Km	Description	Latitude	Longitude	Elev.
C22	133	Big Country RV Campground	N51.79003	W121.40685	853 m
C23	151	Lac La Hache Prov Park	N51.85938	W121.64072	832 m
C24	161	130 Mile Wetlands	N51.90883	W121.73798	800 m
C25	165	To the goldfields stop-of-interest	N51.93933	W121.77117	787 m
C26	188	150 Mile House	N52.11431	W121.93510	747 m
C27	194	Chief Will Yum Campground	N52.11750	W122.00577	621 m
C28	202	Williams Lake	N52.12730	W122.12689	614 m
C29	220	Bull Mountain X-C Trails	N52.24661	W122.11847	804 m
C30	235	Jct Xats'ull Heritage Village	N52.33213	W122.26095	655 m
C31	245	McLeese Lake Store	N52.41990	W122.29574	689 m
C32	246	McLeese Lake Resort	N52.42580	W122.29842	677 m
C33	254	Paddle Wheels North stop-of-interest	N52.44411	W122.39817	520 m
C34	256	Jct Soda Creek – Macalister Rd	N52.45301	W122.40463	481 m
C35	267	Basalt columns	N52.55120	W122.46055	461 m
C36	268	Fort Alexandria Historic Site	N52.56211	W122.46279	490 m
C37	285	Highway Rest Area	N52.70966	W122.45641	521 m
C38	319	Quesnel River bridge	N52.98363	W122.48159	486 m
C39	326	Jct Highway 26 to Barkerville	N53.01475	W122.49533	547 m

CHAPTER 12

Highway 26: The Barkerville Road Quesnel to Barkerville

STATISTICS

	Map see page 166.
Distance:	81 km, Highway 97 at Quesnel to Barkerville.
Travel time:	One hour.
Elevation gain:	710 metres.
Conditions:	Paved throughout.
Season:	Maintained year-round; could be slippery in winter.
Topo maps:	Cottonwood, BC 93 G/1.
(1:50,000)	Wells, BC 93 H/4.
Communities:	Quesnel, Wells, and Barkerville.

The Road to Barkerville

Gold was discovered in the tributaries of the Quesnel River as early as 1859. In the summer of 1861, Williams Creek, east of Quesnel, became an important prospect. By the summer of 1862, about 2,000 men were working the gravel of Williams Creek at Richfield, recovering more than $2 million in gold. In mid-August, William "Billy" Barker, a stubborn Cornishman, struck a hoard of gold nuggets 12 metres below the creek bed, a short distance downstream from Richfield. Barker recovered an amazing $1,000 worth of gold in 48 hours, and the Barker Company claim rapidly became the centre of a new gold rush town.

Cottonwood House

In 1863, a one-hundred-kilometre trail was cut from Quesnel to Barkerville. While the reference points may be a little different than in 1863, it is little more than 80 kilometres from Highway 97 to Barkerville via Highway 26. Straightening numerous twists and turns and filling in dozens of swamps has turned the route into a pleasant hour-long drive.

The first major landmark, Cottonwood House, is located 26 kilometres east of

The historic Cottonwood House, built in 1864, stood as an oasis of civilization on the frontier of a rich new land.

Highway 97. It was constructed in 1864 and 1865. From the beginning, it established a reputation among travellers as a stopping place of the highest quality. Clean rooms and good food met the needs of two-legged travellers while the four-legged beasts of burden were housed in large barns and fed locally grown oats and hay. As well as the "hotel," a store and post office were established at Cottonwood House.

In 1963, the BC government created Cottonwood House Provincial Historic Park, includ-

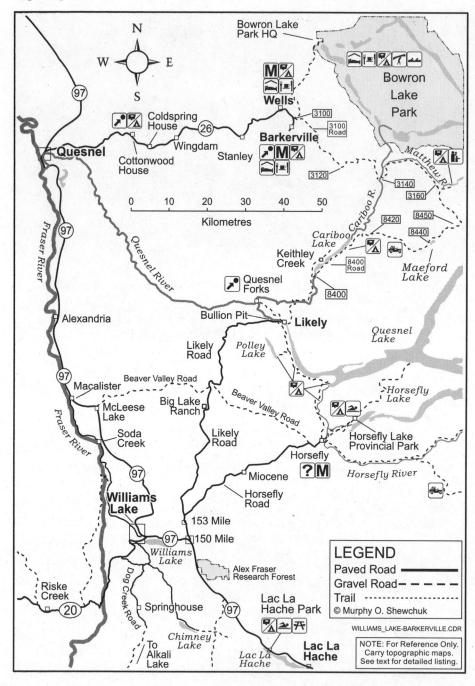

Bowron Lake
Park HQ

Bowron
Lake
Park

Wells

Coldspring
House

Quesnel

Cottonwood
House

Wingdam

Stanley

26

3100

3100
Road

Barkerville

3120

Matthew R.

3140

3160

8450

8420

8440

Cariboo R.

Cariboo
Lake

Keithley
Creek

8400
Road

Maeford
Lake

8400

Quesnel River

Fraser River

Quesnel
Forks

0   10   20   30   40   50
Kilometres

Alexandria

Bullion Pit

Likely

Quesnel
Lake

Likely
Road

Polley
Lake

Macalister

Beaver Valley Road

Horsefly
Lake

McLeese
Lake

Big Lake
Ranch

Beaver Valley Road

Soda
Creek

Fraser River

Likely
Road

Horsefly Lake
Provincial Park

97

Williams
Lake

Miocene

Horsefly

Horsefly River

?M

Horsefly
Road

153 Mile

97

150 Mile

Williams
Lake

Alex Fraser
Research Forest

Riske
Creek

20

Dog Creek Road

Springhouse

97

Lac La
Hache Park

Chimney
Lake

To
Alkali
Lake

Lac La
Hache

Lac La
Hache

ing Cottonwood House and most of the major buildings. Restoration work continues, but while the "hotel" no longer caters to travellers, the park and campground opens its gates to thousands of visitors each summer.

Lightning Creek and Wingdam

From just east of Cottonwood House (km 32) to the east end of Stanley Road, the Barkerville Road follows Lightning Creek, considered by many to be the second richest gold creek in the Cariboo.

A plaque in the Quesnel Museum, probably salvaged from the Wingdam area (km 40),

Charles Morgan Blessing's grave marker sits in the trees near the Barkerville Highway.

presents some examples of Lightning Creek gold production:

1861 – 1700 ounces of gold were produced by three men in three days.

1875 – 13 claims produced $2,179,000.

1934 – 1937 – Mines at Wingdam produced 11,139 ounces of gold.

The same plaque indicates that to the end of 1945, the Cariboo yielded 538,070 ounces of gold and 59,149 ounces of silver. (It is worth noting that gold was worth about $16 per ounce in the 1800s and about $30 per ounce in the 1930s.)

Blessing's Grave

According to Harbour Publishing's *Encyclopedia of British Columbia*, Blessing's Grave (km 43) is BC's smallest provincial historic site. Charles Morgan Blessing was an Ohioan who came to the Cariboo in the 1860s. On May 31, 1866, while on the way to Barkerville, he was murdered by another prospector, James Barry, who stole his gold tie pin and a large amount of cash. Thanks to the efforts of Blessing's friend, Wellington Moses, a barber in Barkerville, Barry was arrested while fleeing south by stagecoach. He was tried by Judge Matthew Begbie, convicted by a jury, and hanged. Moses erected the headstone and fence that now surround the grave.

Troll Mountain Ski Resort

While Blessing's Grave may be one of BC's smallest historic sites, Troll Mountain Ski Resort, less than a kilometre east, may also qualify as one of BC's smallest ski resorts. The base is next to the highway and the T-bar tows take you up to the

1524-metre elevation. The resort offers cross-country trails, snowboarding, and night skiing from early December to mid-April.

Stanley Road

A road to the right (south) at km 59.3 leads down to Lightning Creek and the former mining community of Stanley. Post offices were established in Stanley and nearby Van Winkle in 1874 and 1875, respectively. There were a large number of workings near Stanley along Lightning Creek, and the area threatened to eclipse Barkerville in the early 1900s.

A fine example of axe work is visible in the corner of this cabin at Stanley.

In this vicinity, gold-bearing gravels lay mainly on bedrock, in some cases, at a considerable depth below the present creek level. In other cases, the gold gravels occur on bedrock benches along the sides of and above the present creek level. In either case, pick and shovel manpower was replaced by dredges and giant "monitors" that washed the gravel into sluices where the heavier gold was captured by the riffles.

A graveyard atop a hill overlooking Lightning Creek and a few cabins (or remnants) are all that is left of Stanley.

Wells

Named after Fred Wells, the prospector who discovered the Cariboo Gold Quartz Mine, Wells began life in the 1930s as a company town. Unlike the

The Wells Hotel.

Amy Lee Newman, musical director of Barkerville's Theatre Royal.

placer gold mining that took place in the creek beds and glacial gravel, this was "hard rock" mining that lasted until 1967 and at its peak, supported a town of 4,500. One source suggests that the Cariboo gold fields produced over 3.3 million ounces of gold, including more than 1.2 million ounces of "lode" gold produced from the Cariboo Gold Quartz, Island Mountain, and Mosquito Creek mines. While prospecting continues for new placer and lode gold deposits, the town of Wells (population 250) serves as a home base for nearby Barkerville and a base for local artistic enterprises such as Island Mountain Arts.

Largest Town West of Chicago

With continuing success, Barkerville became the destination of the Cariboo gold rush. The town that sprang up on the banks of Williams Creek was full of contradictions. German hurdy-gurdy dancing girls sold their favours in the bars while travelling actors played Shakespeare in the Theatre Royal. It was a hodge-podge of humanity, many from the wild American west, kept under control by British justice, personified in the stern but fair Judge Matthew Baillie Begbie.

A fire destroyed Barkerville on September 16, 1868, but rebuilding started immediately. Within six weeks, over 90 buildings were rebuilt. Although the gold rush soon waned, Barkerville lived on, experiencing a revival during the depression of the 1930s.

According to N.L. "Bill" Barlee, a noted gold rush historian and raconteur, Williams Creek "produced somewhere in the neighborhood of $25 million in gold." Unofficial estimates were as high as $40 million — and this was at a time when gold was roughly $16 per troy ounce.

In 1958, Barkerville was designated a Historic Park, and restoration and reconstruction of the town as it existed in 1870 began. Only 15 of some 120 original buildings still stood, the others having been modified or torn down. However, photographs and other information have allowed the restoration to continue, turning the town into a live museum.

Today, the historic town is open from 8:00 a.m. to 8:00 p.m. from mid-May to the end of September. A variety of services are open to the public in the heritage buildings, including restaurants, a bakery, and various shops. While the hurdy-gurdy girls have retired, the Theatre Royal, operated by the Newman & Wright Theatre Company, puts on as many as three shows a day.

Judge Begbie last held court here nearly a century and a half ago. However, the walls of the Richfield Court House, a half-hour walk beyond the Barkerville gates, still echoes the voices of stern judges and infamous criminals.

GPS References for major points of interest
Ref: WGS 84 - Lat/Lon hddd.ddddd
Allow +/-100 metres due to data conversions

Wpt	Km	Description	Latitude	Longitude	Elev.
QB01	0	Jct Hwy 97 and Hwy 26	N53.01545	W122.49394	557 m
QB02	20.0	20K marker	N53.05147	W122.22967	894 m
QB03	24.5	Cottonwood River bridge	N53.05393	W122.17730	788 m
QB04	25.6	Cottonwood House	N53.05122	W122.15384	780 m
QB05	27.2	Cottonwood General Store	N53.04164	W122.13928	787 m
QB06	34.0	Viewpoint	N53.02443	W122.05605	966 m
QB07	40.5	Wingdam and Lightning Creek	N53.04374	W121.96999	942 m
QB08	42.0	Robber's Roost	N53.05421	W121.95555	968 m
QB09	43.0	Blessing's Grave	N53.06192	W121.94873	992 m
QB10	43.7	Troll Mountain Ski Resort	N53.06570	W121.94190	1,008 m
QB11	59.3	Stanley Rd W	N53.04655	W121.73157	1,171 m
QB12	61.3	Stanley Rd E	N53.04953	W121.70606	1,245 m
QB13	64.0	Devil's Canyon	N53.06923	W121.69039	1,287 m
QB14	72.0	Jack of Clubs Lake Boat Launch	N53.09031	W121.59925	1,206 m
QB15	73.3	Wells Info Centre	N53.09790	W121.58069	1,200 m
QB16	77.3	The Meadows	N53.09709	W121.53333	1,206 m
QB17	78.1	Reduction Rd to R	N53.09222	W121.52580	1,215 m
QB18	78.8	Lowhee Campground	N53.08851	W121.51743	1,222 m
QB19	79.5	Bowron Lake Park Rd	N53.08405	W121.51117	1,232 m
QB20	80.7	Government Hill Campground	N53.07246	W121.51220	1,272 m
QB21	81.0	Barkerville entrance parking	N53.07099	W121.51416	1,269 m

More to Explore

A junction a few hundred metres before the Barkerville gates provides a couple more options for the intrepid backroads explorer or canoeist. Bowron Lake Park Road winds 27 kilometres north to Bowron Lake Park and the departure point for the world-famous canoeing circuit. The 116-kilometres Bowron Lake circuit is a chain of lakes, waterways, and connecting portages that takes from six to ten days to complete, depending on your time frame and skill level. For those looking for a shorter trip, the west side of the circuit can be paddled in two to four days. BC Parks recommends that those who attempt the circuit have some wilderness canoeing experience. The number of daily departures is limited and advance reservations are highly recommended. Visit the BC Parks

Bowron Lake Park website for detailed information including maps.

Backroad to Likely

If you are looking for an alternate route back to "civilization," Bowron Lake Park Road is also the point that you would leave Highway 26. Look for Cunningham Pass Forest Service Road (3100 Road) a few hundred metres east of Highway 26. This is the beginning of a circuitous route that will take you southeast before swinging southwest to Likely. It's 147 kilometres to Likely — most of it gravel — and another 82 kilometres of pavement to Highway 97 at 150 Mile House. Check out the *Backroad to Barkerville* chapter for more details.

Note: See the *Information Sources* chapter at the end of the book for contact information on the services mentioned here.

Southwest Cariboo Loop

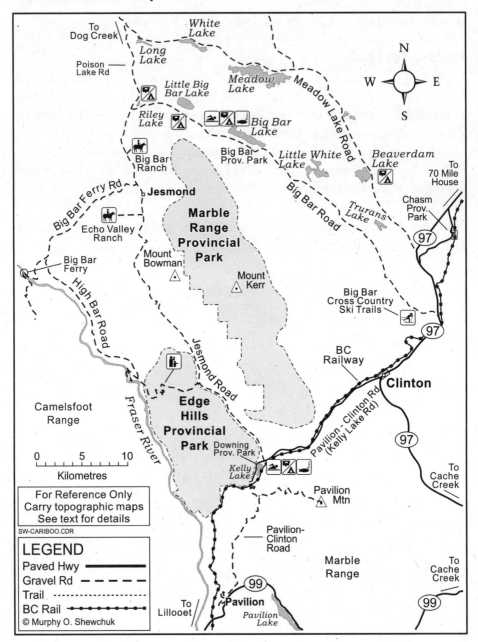

CHAPTER 13

Southwest Cariboo Loop: Clinton — Kelly Lake — Big Bar — Clinton

STATISTICS

	Map see page 174.
Distance:	120 km, Clinton – Kelly Lake – Big Bar – Clinton.
Travel time:	Three to four hours.
Elevation gain:	600 metres.
Conditions:	Variable gravel road with some paved sections.
Season:	Maintained year-round, could be slippery in spring.
Topo maps:	Clinton, BC 92 P/4.
(1:50,000)	Big Bar Creek, BC 92 O/1.
	Jesmond, BC 92 P/5.
	Empire Valley, BC 92 O/8.
Communities:	Clinton and 100 Mile House.

If you are looking for an all-season backroad getaway that includes fishing, camping, and horseback riding in summer (and winter) and snowmobiling, cross-country skiing, and snowshoeing in winter, consider a back-country scenic loop west of Clinton. The 120-kilometre trip around the Marble Range will take at least three hours. You could easily stretch it into a long weekend or a week, if you take advantage of some of the many attractions and distractions along the way, including spectacular Fraser Canyon scenery, high-country grasslands, and well-established guest ranches.

Top-Up Before You Leave Clinton

With the junction of Highway 97 and the Pavilion-Clinton Road as your km 0 reference, prepare to head southwest toward Kelly Lake. *Prepare* is the key word here. Clinton is the best place for a final replenishment of all your supplies because there are no services along the way.

As the Pavilion-Clinton Road winds southwest through the base of Cutoff

The Cariboo ponds and lakes are rich with waterfowl such as this bufflehead pair.

Valley, the elevation here is about 1,000 metres and the valley floor is a mix of hay-fields, aspen groves, ponderosa pine, and the occasional small lake. BC Hydro's Kelly Lake Substation (km 14.5) is the first major landmark along the way. Kelly Lake Sub is an important power distribution point on the high voltage lines that link the Peace River generating stations to the BC lower mainland.

Take a Break at Downing Provincial Park

A few minutes beyond the substation, this circle tour leaves the Pavilion-Clinton Road (km 17) and heads north up Jesmond Road. If you are looking for a place to camp, swim, or fish, delay your northward trip and continue southwest for less than a kilometre to Kelly Lake and Downing Provincial Park. With its cool, clear water, Kelly Lake provides a welcome respite at the end of a hot, dusty day and is the favourite haunt of local fishing enthusiasts. Downing Park is equipped with picnic tables (set in the meadow among the willows) and plenty of room to park an RV or pitch a tent. A land donation by C.S. Downing forms the basis for the developed portion of the park that was established in 1970.

Westward to Lillooet

If you're curious — and the weather is agreeable — you can follow Pavilion-Clinton Road over Pavilion Mountain and westward to Lillooet, a distance of about 56 kilometres. The Kelly Lake – Pavilion section of this road is steep and narrow and not usually maintained in the winter. Parts of it can be particularly slippery and muddy in wet weather. The gravel road across the plateau benchland played a major part in the early years of the Cariboo Gold Rush. In 1859, it was the main route to the gravel bars of the upper Fraser Canyon and the gold creeks of the south Cariboo. The Fraser Canyon north of Lillooet was, and for the most part still is, impassable as a road of commerce. The Fraser River Trail, with Lillooet as Mile 0, followed what is now Highway 99 to Pavilion and then climbed up through the Carson Ranch to Kelly Lake before continuing north to Big Bar and Dog Creek.

Kelly Lake Ranch

Meanwhile, back at the Jesmond Road junction, the weather-beaten buildings of the Kelly Lake Ranch, originally established by Edward Kelly in 1866, serve as a landmark for the junction of the road north. Part of the original Fraser River Trail, the Jesmond Road lost its place in inland commerce when the Cariboo Waggon Road opened to traffic in 1864. In the past couple of decades it has undergone several name changes. Known earlier as the Dog Creek Road, it became the Kelly Lake – Canoe Creek Road and, as of the fall of 2007, it is the Jesmond Road.

Edge Hills Provincial Park

With Clinton still as your km 0 reference, continue north up Porcupine Creek. A low, wooded mountain range known as the Edge Hills separates this valley from the steep-walled Fraser Canyon. This spectacular wilderness, including panoramic canyon vistas, gentle forested slopes, and rolling grasslands, was given park status in 1995. Of special note is that 11,882-hectare Edge Hills Provincial Park is an undeveloped wilderness with no facilities.

In addition to the placer mining that took place on the Fraser River bars, there was some hard-rock mining in the area. The Grange Mine, a gold mine located just outside Edge Hills Provincial Park at the mouth of Kelly Creek, was in operation until the late 1940s. While it is not easily accessible, whitewater rafts or jet-boats on the Fraser River can reach it.

Cougar Point

For a graphic illustration of just how steep and deep the canyon is, take a short detour west on High Bar Road (km 28). With an elevation at the junction of about 1,450 metres, you'll climb about 100 metres to a barely discernible pass before starting a steep winding descent along the edge of Barney Creek canyon. The road is narrow and can be slippery when wet. From what is locally known as Cougar Point, 5.5 kilometres from Jesmond Road, the view of the canyon is absolutely spectacular. There is just enough room to turn a small vehicle around at the viewpoint. Use caution, as it is over 1,000 metres to the river — with damn few bounces along the way.

Circle H Mountain Lodge
Twenty-four kilometres north of Kelly Lake (km 40) is the Circle H Mountain Lodge. The ranch was first surveyed and registered to the Hallers of Big Bar Creek in the 1890s. The Circle H was once a year-round guest ranch operation with over 90 kilometres of horse and cross-country ski trails. Now their operation is primarily available as a group accommodation.

The Circle C Ranch (Mt. Bowman), at km 48, marks another local landmark. Mount Bowman, at 2,243 metres, is an impressive sight and is one of the highest mountains in the region.

Marble Range Provincial Park
Mount Kerr, about seven kilometres to the southeast is, at 2,270 metres, less than 30 metres higher. Mount Kerr is near the geographical centre of 17,920-hectare Marble Range Provincial Park. The Marble Range gets its name from its unusual karst (limestone) ridges. The park protects populations of California bighorn sheep and mule deer. Like Edge Hills Park, it was established in 1995. There are some rough trails, popular with local hikers, hunters, and horseback riders. Otherwise, it has no organized facilities.

Horseback Spa
The Echo Valley Ranch, accessible from a junction at km 52.5, is far from your average rustic wilderness retreat. With its own private, paved airstrip and regularly scheduled flights to Vancouver, dusty Jesmond Road isn't the only way to get here. However, if you are following this backroad adventure, the main lodge lies in a secluded vale 3.5 kilometres west of the road. With guest facilities that can handle up to 26 people, Norm Dove and his staff offer a variety of "soft adventures," from guided whitewater rafting on the Fraser and Chilcotin Rivers to exploring the nearby mountains on horseback. Echo Valley's season is from the end of March to the end of October, except for a

The slowly decaying Grange Mine buildings cling to the Fraser Canyon walls west of Kelly Lake.

Riders at the Echo Valley Ranch.

couple of weeks at Christmas. Reservations are required with a minimum stay of three nights.

Jesmond

The former Jesmond Store and Post Office (km 53) is now just a private residence. I stopped here once, a few decades ago, after an exciting drive from the Bridge River, up the Yalakom River, around Poison Mountain, over China Head Mountain, and down to the Fraser River at Big Bar Ferry. (Note that the Poison Mountain – China Head Mountain route is now closed to vehicular traffic.) Metal rural-route boxes sit alongside the road where I hand-pumped the tall glass measure on the Jesmond gasoline pump.

Big Bar Ferry

Little more than a kilometre beyond the former Jesmond Post Office is the junction of the road to the Big Bar ferry. The Big Bar reaction ferry has been in operation since 1894 and serves several ranches and homesteads on the west side of the Fraser. It is a steady descent of about 800 metres in the 19 kilometres to the Fraser

Loading horses on the Big Bar Ferry.

River at the ferry crossing. The first 14 kilometres follows Big Bar Creek down through a beautiful, sheltered valley. Then the vistas change to the multi-coloured clay and rock formations of the Fraser Canyon benches, and the switchback descent gets serious. Be prepared to use your lowest gear on the way down — and on the way back up.

Big Bar Guest Ranch

Across the valley to the east, about five kilometres north of the Big Bar Ferry junction, the Big Bar Guest Ranch offers family ranch vacations, supervised trail rides, and everything from hiking to gold panning in a Cariboo ranch atmosphere. With the Limestone Mountains at their back door and the Fraser River far below, the ranch has the terrain that has made the Cariboo famous. The experienced crew offers horseback riding 365 days a year with no lower age limit for young riders. When the horses have on their winter shoes, you can strap on a pair of cross-country skis or snowshoes and check out the trails with them.

Greg "Junior" Loring checks a cinch at the Big Bar Guest Ranch.

The Red Dog Saloon

North of the junction to the Big Bar Guest Ranch, the old River Trail dips into a hollow that shelters the green buildings of the former OK Ranch.

Joseph Haller, the first settler at this location, was born in Pittsburgh, Pennsylvania, in 1825 and came to British Columbia via Sacramento, California, in July of 1858. He worked in the mines of the Fraser and Cariboo for two years before buying a dozen donkeys and going into the packing business. In 1862, Haller established "a house for travelers and a store with grub" on Big Bar Creek. His winter supplies included 8,000 pounds (3,600 kilograms) of flour and "90 gallons [340 liters] schnapps of different kinds." Known locally as the Red Dog Saloon, Haller's roadhouse was a popular stopping place for miners and packers.

Pioneer ranchers Harry Marriott, author of *Cariboo Cowboy*, and George Harrison consolidated several smaller ranches to form the well-known OK Ranch.

Go East

A junction at km 64 marks the beginning of the swing around the north end of the Marble Range and the southeastward drive to Clinton on Big Bar Road. If you

A log barn near Big Bar Road.

aren't in a hurry, you can continue north on what seems to be a little used road (Poison Lake Road joins Meadow Lake Road in 10 kilometres) and explore the Fraser Canyon benchlands all the way to Williams Lake.

Riley Lake, at km 65, has an inviting, semi-open Forest Service recreation site. The Little Big Bar Lake junction near km 68 marks the access to another Forest Service recreation site with rainbow trout fishing potential.

Big Bar Lake Park

Big Bar Lake Provincial Park, near km 76, is probably one of the most attractive, yet under-utilized lakeside campgrounds in the south Cariboo. The 332-hectare park was originally set up as a recreation reserve in 1944 and enlarged in 1958. But it was not officially established as a park until 1969. Now equipped with a 46-unit campground, picnic area, and boat launch, the 4.5-kilometre-long lake has become a popular swimming and fishing hole.

Cross-Country Skiing

While Jesmond Road winds north through a valley, Big Bar Road crosses the Green Timber Plateau, part of the much larger Fraser Plateau. The elevation here is about 1130 metres, contributing to colder winters and moderate snowfalls.

Cariboosters don't hide when the snow comes out. They bundle up, strap on the planks, and head out on the ski trails. The Clinton Snow Jockey Club has 15 kilometres of groomed trails, part of a 50-kilometre trail system suitable for beginners to advanced recreational skiers. If it does get a little chilly, there are several shelters on the trail system. Trail maintenance is done by volunteers funded by a donation box at the trailhead. Your $5 per person per day contribution will help buy fuel for the club's twin-track snowmobile.

After passing the access to the Big Bar cross-country ski trails, Big Bar Road begins the descent to the junction with Highway 97 (km 110), 10 kilometres north of Clinton.

For most backroad explorers, the Southwest Cariboo Loop is an ideal three-season getaway. Summer, fall, and winter all have their attractions; however, spring breakup can be a challenge on the clay and gravel sections of Jesmond Road and Big Bar Road.

Note: See the *Information Sources* chapter at the end of the book for contact information on the services mentioned here.

GPS References for major points of interest
Ref: WGS 84 - Lat/Lon hddd.ddddd
Allow +/-100 metres due to data conversions

Wpt	Km	Description	Latitude	Longitude	Elev.
SW01	0	Downtown Clinton	N51.09134	W121.58789	878 m
SW02	14.5	Kelly Lake Sub	N51.02409	W121.74029	1,076 m
SW03	17.0	Jct Jesmond Rd	N51.01286	W121.76974	1,102 m
SW04		Downing Prov Park	N51.01058	W121.77904	1,089 m
SW05	27.5	Jct High Bar Rd	N51.07952	W121.85873	1,432 m
SW06	39.5	Circle H Ranch	N51.16010	W121.93595	1,357 m
SW07	52.9	Jesmond Post Office	N51.25679	W121.95374	1,168 m
SW08	54.2	Jct Big Bar Ferry	N51.26667	W121.96271	1,148 m
SW09	59.0	Big Bar Guest Ranch	N51.30225	W121.98338	1,036 m
SW10	64.0	Jct Poison Lake Rd and Big Bar Lake Rd	N51.33588	W121.97127	1,048 m
SW11	65.0	Riley Lake	N51.33715	W121.96038	1,022 m
SW12	76.0	Jct to Big Bar Lake Park	N51.30938	W121.82353	1,122 m
SW13		Big Bar Lake Park	N51.31276	W121.82005	1,082 m
SW14	93.5	Isadore Rd	N51.22665	W121.62896	1,126 m
SW15	101.0	Big Bar X-C Trails	N51.17157	W121.56851	1,146 m
SW16	107.5	Jct Hwy 97 and Big Bar Rd	N51.14566	W121.50247	1,055 m
SW17	117.0	Downtown Clinton	N51.09134	W121.58789	878 m

Green Lake Loop

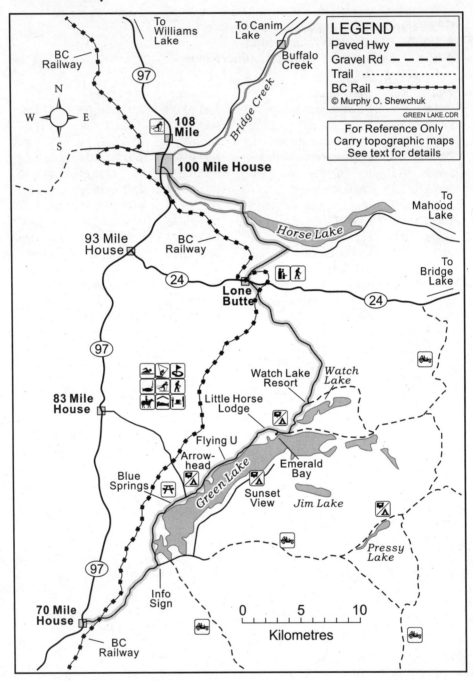

LEGEND
Paved Hwy
Gravel Rd
Trail
BC Rail
© Murphy O. Shewchuk

GREEN LAKE.CDR

For Reference Only
Carry topographic maps
See text for details

Green Lake Loop: 70 Mile House to 100 Mile House via Green Lake, Lone Butte, and Horse Lake

STATISTICS

	Map see page 186.
Distance:	62 km.
Travel Time:	One to two hours.
Conditions:	Paved throughout.
Season:	Open year-round.
Topo Maps:	Green Lake, BC 92 P/6.
(1:50,000)	100 Mile House, BC 92 P/11.
Communities:	70 Mile House, Lone Butte, and 100 Mile House.

Historic Route

The backroad from 70 Mile House to 100 Mile House via Green Lake has much to offer today's traveller — without the hardship faced by the Native peoples, fur traders, and gold seekers who passed this way in centuries past. It is now a two-lane paved secondary highway, with ample opportunity to enjoy the outdoors by day and the amenities of indoor living by night.

The Fur Brigades

While details are understandably sketchy, there is strong evidence that this area may have been part of the North West Company's supply route as early as October 1814, when supplies from England were delivered to Fort St. James via Astoria, on the Columbia River. By 1821, when the Hudson's Bay Company absorbed the North West Company, this had become an important fur trade route. Prior to the gold rush of the 1860s, the Brigade Trail passed through the Okanagan Valley to Monte Creek and then west to Fort Kamloops and on to the foot of Kamloops

Green Lake Loop

The Cariboo ponds add a picturesque touch to the landscape.

Lake. Then it continued north to the Bonaparte River and travelled along it, Green Lake, and Horse Lake to Lac La Hache.

Trails to Gold

While botanist David Douglas had found traces of gold in the soil of some of the plants he had collected in 1833, it was a quarter of a century before the hordes of gold seekers began their relentless migration to the Cariboo. The rush to the gravel bars of the Thompson and Fraser rivers began in 1858. Lieutenant H.S. Palmer of the Royal Engineers summed up the trail conditions faced by the gold seekers of the early 1860s: "It is difficult to find language to express in adequate terms the utter vileness of the trails of Cariboo, dreaded alike by all classes of travellers; slippery, precipitous ascents and descents, fallen logs, overhanging branches, roots, rocks, swamps, turbid pools and miles of deep mud."

By the mid-1860s, the Cariboo Waggon Road had changed all that — and had bypassed — Green Lake with a route straight through the timber. At about six metres wide, the new wagon road could have been compared to today's freeways. Although, as one writer put it, it was still "stony, dusty, muddy, pitted with holes, and constantly subject to slides, washouts and other hazards."

70 Mile House Starting Point

Cariboo Highway 97 follows much the same route as the Cariboo Waggon Road of the mid-1860s. According to Branwen Patenaude, in *Trails to Gold — Volume Two*, 70 Mile House was built in September 1862. It served the miners heading to the gold fields as well as G.B. Wright's road crews. The roadhouse saw a variety of owners and some good times as well as bad.

In the late 1910s and early 1920s, it became the service centre for the railway crews and settlers of the North Bonaparte region. In the 1940s, owner "Ma" Porter cooked for the construction crews on the "new" Cariboo Highway. The original 70 Mile House lasted nearly a century before disappearing in a fiery blaze in May 1956.

Today, 70 Mile General Store serves travellers on Highway 97, visitors to the parks and resorts of the region, and local residents. It is, good location to stock up on groceries, fuel, and refreshments. While you are there, you can renew your fishing licence and restock your tackle box and camping kit.

With the junction of Green Lake Road and Highway 97 as km 0, head east and then northeast across the plateau. The elevation here is over 1,080 metres above sea level so be prepared for cool evenings, even after the warmest summer days.

Your first point of interest will be the BC Rail crossing near km 1.5. The Pacific Great Eastern Railway (PGE) — Pigs Go East on the Please Go Easy — was constructed through the Cariboo after World War I, reaching Lone Butte in 1919 and Williams Lake in 1920. It has since undergone a name change or two, but the route has changed little.

Green Lake Provincial Park Junction

A junction with an information sign and a sani-dump near km 8.5 marks the first of many choices. The road to the east continues across the south end of Green Lake with options to explore the Hutchison Lake area to the south or the east shore of Green Lake, including the BC Parks Sunset View campground (with 54 campsites) to the north. If you like, you can also continue east to Pressy Lake and the Bonaparte Lake area.

For the sake of this discussion, we will take North Green Lake Road along the west side of Green Lake.

West Shore Facilities

The Blue Springs picnic site, near km 14.5, is the first developed part of Green Lake Park that we pass. According to BC Parks, Green Lake Provincial Park is made up of 13 parcels of land, five of which have developed facilities.

Guest ranches offer a taste of the old west in more ways than one.

A crossroads near km 16 presents more options. The road to the northwest leads to Highway 97 at 83 Mile House. About one kilometre straight ahead is the Arrowhead campground, the smallest of the park camping facilities. A short drive (or walk) farther along is the Little Arrowhead picnic site. Both are located between the road and the lake and have boat launches.

Flying U Guest Ranch

While one of the oldest and largest of the Cariboo guest ranches, the Flying U Ranch (at km 21) is a working cattle ranch that combines the old with the new. A museum, 1890s saloon, log cabins, and 16,000 hectares of rangeland are part of the operation as well as a float plane dock and private airstrip, should you decide that driving in by car is too much like work.

Little Horse Lodge

Little Horse Lodge, four kilometres farther up the road, is virtually a community unto itself. It offers cabins, a fine restaurant, a store, public showers, a laundromat, gasoline and propane, a campsite, a sani-dump, plus boats, motors, and canoe rentals.

Emerald Bay Campground

With 51 campsites, Emerald Bay campground (near km 26) is the second largest of the BC Parks facilities on Green Lake. It is also ranks as one of our favourite campgrounds in all of the BC Parks system. The design of the park offers a fair degree of privacy for each camper and an excellent children's playground. The shelter at the beach picnic area can serve as a retreat from the hot summer sun or a sudden Cariboo shower.

While Emerald Bay may be aptly named, the whole of Green Lake takes its name from the emerald colour created by the way that the chemical composition of the water refracts and reflects the sunlight.

Watch Lake Road

A junction about a kilometre past Emerald Bay campsite offers another alternative. To the right lie Green Lake Lodge and the northeast end of Green Lake. A

Boats in the morning mist at Watch Lake.

Green Lake Loop

short side road will also take you to Ace High Resort on the south shore of Watch Lake. If you are in no rush to continue north, you can explore the backroads leading to Sheridan Lake, the Bonaparte Plateau, and Highway 24. To the right is Watch Lake Road and the continuing route to Lone Butte and 100 Mile House.

Watch Lake is reported to be a better fishing lake than Green Lake. And Tall Timbers Resort, at the southwest end, is your first chance to prove or refute the theory.

Less than two kilometres farther up the road is Watch Lake Lodge. Here the specialty is a charming log lodge that was built in the late 1930s, rustic cabins, and supervised horseback trail rides.

Beyond Watch Lake Lodge, the road gradually changes to a northwest direction, again crossing the BC Rail tracks near km 42.3. When we recently drove this route, a beautiful log building was under construction in the Pacific Log Homes Ltd. yard. It was a Sunday, so we didn't have the opportunity to ask, but the struc-

Geese are frequent visitors to Horse Lake.

ture looked to be far more than a home. It reminded me of the beautiful log buildings at the Echo Valley Ranch Resort near Jesmond.

Lone Butte

Watch Lake Road ends at Highway 24 (Bridge Lake Road), less than a kilometre to the north of the railway crossing. If you are the least bit observant, you should have seen the lone butte that rises nearly 80 metres above the surrounding plateau. If you have time for some exploring and a bit of scrambling, take Highway 24 northwest for about half a kilometre and then take the first road to the right. Backtrack along the service road about two hundred metres to where it ends near a communications building. If my directions are correct and you followed them properly, you should be at the base of the butte. A trail winds around the south foot of the old volcanic core, gradually gaining altitude as you continue to the east face. A short scramble up the rocks should take you to the top. Use caution because there are no safety fences or guard rails on the trail or on top of the rock. The 360-degree view from the top presents a better feeling for the overall flatness of the Cariboo plateau than almost anywhere else on the ground.

On the way from Highway 24 to the communications building, you should have passed a pioneer cemetery. A stroll through a cemetery can reveal much about the past, particularly when you pay attention to the ages of those who are buried there.

The community of Lone Butte has served as a supply centre to the local ranches and resorts since the arrival of the PGE Railway (BC Rail) in 1919.

Horse Lake Road

From Lone Butte, take Horse Lake Road 4.4 kilometres northeast to Horse Lake and then another nine kilometres northwest to 100 Mile House. Horse Lake is also a popular resort area, as is the network of lakes to the east, stretching all the way to Mahood Lake and Wells Gray Provincial Park.

The route through the Bridge Creek valley was used by the Hudson's Bay Company fur brigades for more than 40 years. It was also one of the routes used by the early gold seekers. Hay and water was an essential ingredient for transportation then, but are no less important to agriculture in the region today.

100 Mile House

According Branwen Patenaude, Bridge Creek House was built in the summer of 1861. The name was changed when the Cariboo Waggon Road descended 99 Mile Hill and into the Bridge Creek valley. Since then, the community has grown to become the largest centre in the region.

GPS References for major points of interest
Ref: WGS 84 - Lat/Lon hddd.ddddd
Allow +/-100 metres due to data conversions

Wpt	Km	Description	Latitude	Longitude
W01	0	Jct Hwy 97 and Green Lake Rd	N51.30353	W121.39655
W02	8.5	Jct and Park info signs	N51.34512	W121.30648
W03	14.5	Blue Springs picnic site	N51.39071	W121.28515
W04	15.8	Jct to 83 Mile House	N51.39531	W121.27026
W05	16.6	Arrowhead campground	N51.39888	W121.25826
W06	25.1	Little Horse Lodge	N51.44463	W121.17044
W07	25.8	Jct to Emerald Bay campsite	N51.44325	W121.15949
W08		Emerald Bay campsite	N51.44078	W121.15935
W09	26.8	Jct Watch Lake Rd	N51.44135	W121.14704
W10	28.4	Jct Tall Timbers Resort	N51.45352	W121.13757
W11	30.0	Jct Watch Lake Resort	N51.46307	W121.12126
W12	42.3	BC Rail crossing	N51.54622	W121.18071
W13	43.2	Jct Hwy 24 and Watch Lake Rd	N51.55181	W121.18824
W14		Foot of Lone Butte	N51.55329	W121.19071
W15	43.6	Jct Lone Butte – Horse Lake Rd	N51.55454	W121.19460
W16	48.0	Jct Horse Lake Rd	N51.57669	W121.14379
W17	53.4	Bridge Creek Bridge	N51.60459	W121.19785
W18	62.3	Jct Hwy 97 – Horse Lake Rd	N51.63840	W121.29845

If you've had enough back-country exploring, Highway 97 will take you north or south. If you still want more adventure, you can head northeast to Canim Lake or west to Dog Creek and the Fraser River — or you can hole up in 100 Mile House for a while. The decision is yours.

Note: See the *Information Sources* chapter at the end of the book for contact information on the services mentioned here.

CHAPTER 15

West Bonaparte Loop: 70 Mile House – Bonaparte Lake – Loon Lake – 20 Mile House

STATISTICS

	Map see page 196.
Distance:	67 km, Highway 97 at 70 Mile House to Bonaparte Lake.
	81 km, Bonaparte Lake to Highway 97, south of Clinton.
Elevation Gain:	Approximately 600 metres.
Travel Time:	Four to five hours.
Condition:	Some pavement, mostly gravel industrial road, rough in spots.
Season:	May be closed in winter.
Topo Maps:	Green Lake, BC 92 P/6.
(1:50,000)	Bridge Lake, BC 92 P/7.
	Criss Creek, BC 92 P/2.
	Loon Lake, BC 92 P/3.
	Cache Creek, BC 92 I/14.
Communities:	100 Mile House, 70 Mile House, Clinton, and Cache Creek.

70 Mile House Starting Point

There are thousands of backroads and lakes in British Columbia's Cariboo region. Checking out all of them would take a lifetime of hard "work" with little time for the pleasures of life, such as punching the clock at the local factory. If, however, you are up to such an assignment, here is a backroad loop that will give you the opportunity to get acquainted with some of the finer large and small lakes of the south Cariboo. If you really can't leave "life in the fast lane," you can do it in a day. Should you find it not too difficult to adjust to a slower pace, leave the cellphone at home and take a long weekend or a week — just don't forget your grub and refreshments.

If you are wondering where the heck 70 Mile House is, the mileage back in the 1860s Cariboo gold rush was measured from Lillooet. Today the kilometrage (my

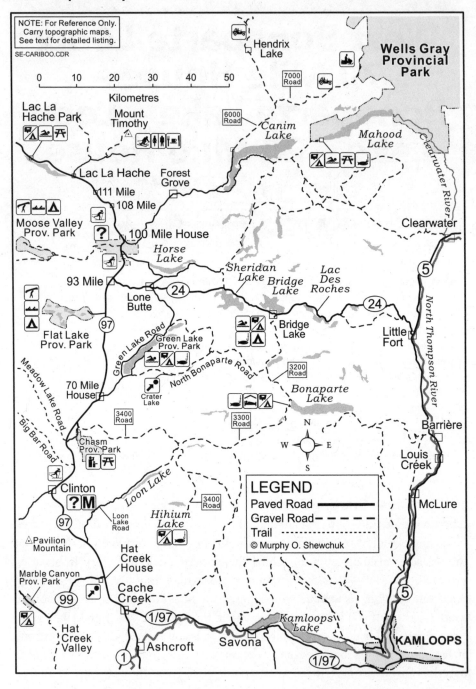

NOTE: For Reference Only. Carry topographic maps. See text for detailed listing.

SE-CARIBOO.CDR

Kilometres

0 10 20 30 40 50

Hendrix Lake

Wells Gray Provincial Park

7000 Road

6000 Road

Lac La Hache Park

Mount Timothy

Canim Lake

Mahood Lake

Clearwater River

Lac La Hache

Forest Grove

111 Mile

108 Mile

Moose Valley Prov. Park

100 Mile House

Horse Lake

Sheridan Lake

Bridge Lake

Lac Des Roches

Clearwater

93 Mile

Lone Butte

24

Bridge Lake

24

Little Fort

Flat Lake Prov. Park

97

Green Lake Road

Green Lake Prov. Park

North Bonaparte Road

3200 Road

Bonaparte Lake

Barrière

North Thompson River

70 Mile House

Crater Lake

3400 Road

3300 Road

N
W   E
S

Louis Creek

McLure

Meadow Lake Road

Big Bar Road

Chasm Prov. Park

Loon Lake

3400 Road

Clinton

? M

Loon Lake Road

Hihium Lake

LEGEND
Paved Road
Gravel Road - - -
Trail ·······
© Murphy O. Shewchuk

97

Pavilion Mountain

Marble Canyon Prov. Park

99

Hat Creek House

Cache Creek

Kamloops Lake

KAMLOOPS

Hat Creek Valley

1

Ashcroft

1/97

Savona

5

1/97

spell-checker doesn't like that word) places it about 410 kilometres northeast of Vancouver.

70 Mile General Store serves travellers on Highway 97, visitors to the parks and resorts of the region, and local residents. It is a good location to stock up on groceries, fuel, and refreshments. While you are here, you can renew your fishing licence and restock your tackle box and camping kit.

With the junction of Green Lake Road and Highway 97 as km 0, head east and then northeast, across the plateau. The elevation here is over 1,080 metres above sea level so be prepared for cool evenings, even after the warmest summer days.

Green Lake Park Junction

A junction with an information sign and a sani-dump near km 8.5 marks the first of many choices. The road to the north follows the west shore of Green Lake past Watch Lake to Highway 24, a few minutes east of Lone Butte. See the *Green Lake Loop* chapter for details.

The lava layers create steep cliffs around Crater Lake.

West Bonaparte Loop

Green Lake is one of the larger water bodies in the southern Cariboo. The lake is about 19 kilometres long with an average width of 1.5 kilometres and an irregular shoreline of approximately 57 kilometres. The greenish hue (and its name) is due to the chemical composition of the warm, shallow waters. There are two BC Parks campgrounds and two picnic sites on the northwest side of the lake, along with a variety of guest ranches, lodges, and other services.

The road to the east continues across the south end of Green Lake with options to explore the Hutchison Lake area to the south or the east shore of Green Lake, including the BC Parks Sunset View campground (with 54 campsites) to the north. Sunset View campground and the campgrounds on the northwest side of the lake have a total of 121 sites. Be warned — they could be busy in the summer months.

Crater Lake

For the sake of this discussion, we will take North Bonaparte Road (3200 Road) east to the Bonaparte Lake area, sneaking off for a few detours along the way.

Crater Lake is the first of these detours — and one that could easily turn into a two-hour ramble. Watch for a side road to the right (south) marked with a snowmobile sign near km 24.3 (32–39 on the roadside markers).

It had rained the day before we first explored Crater Lake, so we chose to park at a wide spot on the main road and walk the short distance down the steep, rutted, muddy road to the lake. It turned out to be a wise decision because we were able to enjoy exploring the trails and the many waterfalls without worrying about how we would get back out of there.

Crater Lake is not named on any of the many maps we have on hand. It is not even shown on most of the larger-scale maps. However, this hole in the plateau bears a strong resemblance to a volcanic crater. Although I suspect it was created by the massive runoff as the glaciers melted in the waning years of the last ice age, it is still an intriguing landform. Equally as intriguing is the series of waterfalls on Rayfield River where it flows into the lake. It will take a bit of exploring and scrambling to find the trails to them, but they will be well worth the adventure. (Hint: Look for a narrow path down the hill and through the trees to the left (east) when you first arrive at the edge of the crater.)

Pressy Lake

If you have reached the junction (km 25 or 32–40 on the roadside markers) with the Eagan-Bonaparte Forest Service Road (3700 Road) without finding the trail to Crater Lake, you'll have to backtrack. Otherwise, continue east on the North

There are a series of waterfalls on the Rayfield River upstream from Crater Lake.

Bonaparte Road (3200 Road). 3700 Road should also take you to Bonaparte Lake. However you'll bypass Pressy Lake and the opportunity to take a break at the fine little Forest Service recreation site on the east end of the lake.

If you are looking for another detour, Green Lake – Pressy Forest Service Road (321 Road) heads north near the midpoint of Pressy Lake. With a little exploring, it will take you to Watch Lake and more fishing opportunities. Beyond Pressy Lake, follow North Bonaparte Road eastward to km 41.3 (32–57) and the junction with Eagan Lake Road. Then swing south through the tall timber and past the hayfields on the plateau. You'll begin to descend at marker 32–65 and you'll have another opportunity for a detour at the Sharpe Lake Road junction at marker 32–69 (km 52). Go left here, following the Bonaparte River (and 3200 Road) upstream for about 3.3 kilometres before swinging south and crossing the river near the west end of Eagan Lake.

Bonaparte Lake

If I haven't managed to get you totally confused, you should still be on 3200 Road and heading south and then southeast to Bonaparte Lake. A marker at 32–80 (62 kilometres from 70 Mile House, by my calculations) signals the end of 3200 Road. Fortunately you can continue south on 3300 Road and begin a countdown to Bonaparte Lake and, if you are truly optimistic, Loon Lake.

A junction at km 66.3 (between 33–78 and 33–77) marks the main access road to the west end of Bonaparte Lake. It is about 0.4 kilometres to Reeder Road and the three-kilometre access road to Thunderbird Resort. If tenting isn't your strong suit, you can rent a cabin and a boat and enjoy your break while the kids check out the beach. (Bug repellent might be a good investment.)

A couple hundred metres past the Reeder Road junction is the Bonaparte Lake Forest Service recreation site. This relatively small site is sheltered in the trees with a gravel boat launch and several trails down to the lake. It could serve as a base for exploring Bonaparte Lake and several nearby lakes.

Eighteen-kilometre-long Bonaparte Lake is a little shorter than Green Lake, but the east-west lie of the lake and the lack of significant bays can make it hazardous for small boats. It is also about one hundred metres higher in elevation and significantly deeper, reaching a maximum depth of 98 metres. If fishing is your reason for fighting the dusty backroads, reports suggest this lake can produce rainbow trout to 5.5 kilograms with 1.6 kilograms being the norm.

Meanwhile, back on 3300 Road, if you continue south of the junction, you'll soon cross the Bonaparte River (you can check out the new dam) and the junction to Bonaparte Lake Fishing and Hunting Resort. Again, cabins, boats, and a small beach offer a respite to fast-paced city life.

Hammer Lake

Continue the countdown on 3300 Road for another 3.2 kilometres south of Bonaparte Resort and you'll have another opportunity for a detour. Hammer Lake hosts a well-treed Forest Service recreation site. This is the last one on this loop as you swing south of the lake and start the journey west to Loon Lake and Highway 97. However, if you are really serious about detours, you can explore 3700 Road

The numerous small lakes attract trout fishing enthusiasts.

northwest to Scot Lake, Moose Lake and Pressy Lake.

The trek westward begins in earnest south of Hammer Lake. Watch for the Clinton-Upper Loon Forest Service Road sign and continue the 3300 Road countdown. Although the Cariboo Region Forest Service recreation site map doesn't show them, there are more roads to get lost on before you make the switchback descent into the Coal Creek canyon.

Loon Lake

The climb west out of the canyon is a little less steep, and around km 106 (33–37) you should come to a junction. Again it is decision-making time. To the northwest lies Chasm and 70 Mile House, completing the loop. To the southwest, the descent continues to Loon Lake and Highway 97, at the foot of the long hill up to Clinton. If you are going to follow this description, go left at this junction and right at the next junction two kilometres down the road, following the Loon Lake signs. The well-maintained industrial road gives way to a rough country road for about six kilometres before emerging on pavement at the east end of the Loon Lake resort area. It is a little more than five kilometres to Loon Lake Provincial Park, a small campground nestled between the road and the lake.

Bonaparte River

Ten minutes drive farther along and you'll begin the winding descent through the spectacular Loon Creek canyon. After leaving Bonaparte River back at the outlet of Bonaparte Lake, you'll have an opportunity to renew acquaintances at km 141 when you emerge from the canyon. By now you should have noticed that the vast sea of lodgepole pine has turned into clumps of sagebrush and the occasional hardy juniper. If your timing is right (mid-June to mid-July), you may even see an elusive prickly-pear cactus blossom (the blossoms are elusive — the cacti are plentiful).

Continue southwest on the paved road to Highway 97 (km 147), emerging 21 kilometres north of Cache Creek and 18.5 kilometres south of Clinton.

This time I'll leave the choice to you. You'll also have other choices to make even before you set out, such as "Will I take a day, a weekend, or a week to make this loop?" Whatever your decision, go well prepared.

Note: See the *Information Sources* chapter at the end of the book for contact information on the services mentioned here.

GPS References for major points of interest
Ref: WGS 84 - Lat/Lon hddd.ddddd
Allow +/-100 metres due to data conversions

Wpt	Km	Description	Latitude	Longitude
WB01	0	70 Mile House	N51.30266	W121.39719
WB02	8.5	Jct and Park info signs	N51.34527	W121.30635
WB03	9.6	Hutchinson Lake Rd	N51.34996	W121.29184
WB04	11.0	South Green Lake Rd	N51.35202	W121.27244
WB05	19.7	Komori Lake	N51.35728	W121.15655
WB06	24.3	Crater Lake Trail	N51.35299	W121.09590
WB07	25.0	Egan-Bonaparte Forest Service Rd	N51.35372	W121.08682
WB08	28.0	Green Lake Forest Service Rd to north	N51.36599	W121.05278
WB09	30.0	Pressy Lake rec site	N51.37819	W121.03098
WB10	32.0	Boule – Young Lake Forest Service Rd	N51.38460	W121.00591
WB11	34.7	Little Green Lake (Bonaparte) Rd	N51.39868	W120.97559
WB12	39.6	32-55	N51.39994	W120.91507
WB13	41.3	32-57 Jct Eagan Lake Rd	N51.40523	W120.89544
WB14	48.0	32-65	N51.36590	W120.83365
WB15	52.0	32-69 Sharpe Lake Rd	N51.34267	W120.79977
WB16	55.0	Jct to Bonaparte Resort	N51.35763	W120.76294
WB17	62.3	32-80 end of 3200 Rd	N51.31412	W120.70971
WB18	62.7	Start 3300 Rd	N51.30740	W120.70412
WB19	63.3	33-80	N51.30399	W120.69907
WB20	66.0	Jct to Bonaparte Lake rec site	N51.28537	W120.67889
WB21		Bonaparte Lake rec site	N51.28243	W120.67163
WB22	66.3	Bonaparte River Bridge	N51.28187	W120.67959
WB23	67.8	Jct to Bonaparte Resort	N51.26923	W120.68303
WB24		Bonaparte Resort	N51.26910	W120.67624
WB25	71.0	33-72 Jct to Hammer Lake	N51.24597	W120.69796
WB26	73.0	33-70	N51.23408	W120.70880
WB27	80.3	Jct Deadman River and 3800 Rd	N51.21131	W120.79720
WB28	82.7	33-60	N51.20268	W120.82631
WB29	90.6	Coal Creek valley	N51.18009	W120.92498
WB30	92.4	33-50	N51.17954	W120.94237
WB31	102	33-40	N51.19738	W121.06994
WB32	105	Jct 3400 Rd (34-37) Go left	N51.19236	W121.10788
WB33	107	Jct 3400 Rd to south	N51.17816	W121.11490
WB34	110	Private ranch – stay on road	N51.16017	W121.12946
WB35	116	Pavement starts	N51.13118	W121.19230
WB36	147	Jct Loon Lake Rd	N50.96751	W121.45817

CHAPTER 16

Bridge Lake Road (Highway 24): 93 Mile House – Bridge Lake – Little Fort

STATISTICS

Map see page 196.

Distance: 98 km, 93 Mile House to Little Fort.

Elev. Gain: Approximately 900 metres.

Travel Time: Two to three hours.

Condition: Paved throughout.
Long hill (8 percent) near Little Fort.

Season: Maintained all year; may be slippery in winter.

Topo Maps: 100 Mile House, BC 92 P/11.
(1:50,000) Deka Lake, BC 92 P/10.
Bridge Lake, BC 92 P/7.
Chu Chua Creek, BC 92 P/8.
Clearwater, BC 92 P/9.

Communities: 100 Mile House, Bridge Lake, and Little Fort.

One of my favourite Cariboo backroads is in the process of being changed from a backroad to a good secondary highway. I have enjoyed occasional trips along this route for more than three decades, exploring a different side road each time. The west end of Wells Gray Park (BC's waterfall wilderness park) lies to the northeast; the rolling timber lake country of the Bonaparte Plateau lies to the south; and Horse Lake (stocked with kokanee) lies to the north.

The Bridge Lake Road, the 100-kilometre-long route linking Cariboo Highway 97 with the North Thompson and Yellowhead Highway 5, has long had the Highway 24 designation. It is only in the past couple of decades that reconstruction of this road has changed it from a sometimes muddy wagon track to a highway that shouldn't frighten any traveller.

The reconstruction of the east end was completed in late 1980s, but straightening and paving of the remainder of the route has continued up to the time of writing.

The restored water tank at Lone Butte is a reminder of the Pacific Great Eastern Railway steam days.

Bridge Lake Road (Highway 24)

West-to-East Travel

In keeping with the apparent Ministry of Highways policy of placing kilometre posts at five-kilometre intervals along the major roads and highways in a south-to-north and west-to-east pattern, I have chosen to detail the Bridge Lake Road (Highway 24) on a west-to-east basis. This method makes it easier for you, the traveller, to check your references, particularly if you are travelling from British Columbia's Lower Mainland.

93 Mile House Starting Point

93 Mile House, like many of the communities in the Cariboo, got its name during the 1860s gold rush. Also like many of the roadhouse communities, 93 Mile House has seen its fortunes ebb and flow. The community seems to be currently in the growth phase with a major RV dealership across Highway 97 from the Highway 24 entrance.

Lone Butte

The first major stop is the community of Lone Butte at km 10.5. There are limited services and an information centre near the landmark railway water tank. The BC Railway line (now part of the CNR) winds through the Cariboo Plateau, reaching its highest point of 1,178 metres within sight of Lone Butte. Coincidentally, this is almost exactly halfway between North Vancouver and Prince George. Also near the water tank is a large map of the Interlakes Recreation Area. If you have a month to do some serious backroads exploring and lake fishing, this map will give you an overview of the lake-dotted plateau.

Lone Butte's landmark namesake is clearly visible as you approach from the west. Part of an ancient volcanic core, the lone butte is adorned (perhaps *desecrated* might be a better word) with radio towers. The butte is being promoted as a scenic point of interest and a hiking trail to the top is being marked.

Lone Butte – Horse Lake Road

The first of several side roads linking Highway 24 with 100 Mile House and Mahood Lake in Wells Gray Provincial Park winds its way north a few hundred metres east of the community. See the *Green Lake Loop* and *Wells Gray Park West* chapters for details.

Watch Lake Road, at km 11.5, winds south to Watch Lake and Green Lake providing access to a number of fishing resorts and guest ranches as well as Green Lake Provincial Park. If you are interested in exploring, fishing, lounging in the sun, or collecting a few blisters at a guest ranch, you can drive south to Green Lake

The Interlakes Recreation Area map at Lone Butte presents an overview of the wealth of fishing lakes in the area.

and then return to Highway 97 at 83 Mile House or 70 Mile House. See the *Green Lake Loop* chapter for details.

If you are continuing eastward on Highway 24, you'll soon have a few more distractions. Fawn Creek Road, near km 25, and Sheridan Lake West Road, near km 26, will take you into more fishing resorts. The latter also winds south to North Bonaparte Road and if you are persistent, Bonaparte Lake. See the *West Bonaparte Loop* chapter for more information.

Interlakes Corner Supply Stop

You can't spend your summer fishing the plateau lakes without restocking your larder. The services at Interlakes Corner (km 31) give you the opportunity to save a drive into 100 Mile House. This is an important junction with a well-maintained road leading 62 kilometres northeast to Mahood Lake in Wells Gray Park.

Bridge Lake Area

Bridge Lake North Road, at km 37.5, loops north around Bridge Lake, returning to Highway 24 at km 50, just east of Bridge Lake Provincial Park. The Bridge Lake community hall was once on the highway, but the highway was rerouted and it is now a short drive to the south near km 47. Also to the south are many more roads and fishing lakes to explore. To the east lies Montana Lake (14 km) and Machete Lake (21 km); to the south lies Eagan Lake (14 km), Sharpe Lake (24 km), and Bonaparte Lake (32 km).

Bridge Lake Provincial Park

This is a small park, 49.5 kilometres east of 93 Mile House. It has 13 vehicle campsites, picnic tables, a small beach, and a boat launching pad. Despite its small size, Bridge Lake Park does offer many attractions, particularly for the fishing enthusiasts with a young, curious family. There are several walk-in tenting sites near the lake shore and a trail that follows the lakeshore around and over the treed rocky point.

On one visit to the park we photographed ground dogwood (bunch berries), arnica, and roses in bright blossom, watched three young children playing a game of hide-and-seek among the trees and boulders, and photographed a young couple rowing an outrigger-equipped aluminum canoe on the glassy surface of the lake.

Lac Des Roches Rest Area

The first fur brigade trail from Fort Alexandria (on the Fraser River south of Quesnel) to Kamloops followed much the same route across the plateau as the Bridge Lake Road. It was in use during the 1820s and 1830s before the relocation of Fort Kamloops prompted the development of a new route via Green Lake, Loon Lake, and Criss Creek to Kamloops Lake.

Mary Balf, in *Kamloops: A History of the District up to 1914*, explains the role the fur trade played in opening travel routes in the Cariboo plateau country: "Furs were a very valuable and somewhat perishable cargo, and their transport was therefore a prime consideration with the traders."

The Hudson's Bay Company "used horse brigades. The furs were carefully counted, graded, and pressed into bales, usually of 80 pounds [36 kilograms]. Each horse carried two of these bales and there were sixteen horses in the care of each man. Up to 300 horses, or even more, formed the brigade, which travelled in slow stages, with regular camping grounds where there was good feed and water."

The open grassy slopes above Lac Des Roches may have made this a prime camping spot for the horse brigades. Today it is a highway rest area with an excellent view of the lake.

A Major Change

Phinetta Lake, near km 68, marks a major change in the Bridge Lake Road. To this point, the reconstructed highway follows much the same route as the pre-1980 gravel road. The original road follows closer to the lake shore, providing access to a pair of Forest Service recreation sites on Phinetta Lake. It also marks the west end of Eakin Creek Road, the original Highway 24. The old highway wound down through a narrow canyon, following Phinetta Creek and Eakin Creek down to Lemieux Creek.

The newer road (opened in 1983) now swings to the north up Eagle Creek. It passes north of Long Island (Janice) Lake, now part of the new 1,604-hectare

Lac Des Roches was part of the Hudson's Bay Company Brigade Trail route in the 1820s and 1830s.

Emar Lakes Park, before descending into the Nehalliston Creek valley. The park, established in 1996, takes in more than a dozen lakes with a variety of wilderness campsites and portages linking several of the lakes. There is parking and a boat launch site near km 75. There is also a detailed map on the BC Parks website. Search for Emar Lakes Park.

Check Your Brakes

The Bridge Lake Road crests at 1,310 metres, about one kilometre east of Long Island Lake, and then begins the long downhill run to Little Fort. Roadside signs note an eight percent grade for 10 kilometres. There are several runaway lanes on the steep grade; however, I wouldn't want to have to pilot a logging truck up any of them.

Thuya Lakes Lodge

The old road up Eakin Creek rejoins the new highway near km 90. A roadside sign advertises Thuya Lakes Lodge. What the sign doesn't say is that at the end of a 20-kilometre gravel road is a network of over 30 small mountain lakes. With an elevation of 1,200 to 1,600 metres, these aren't likely to be your first choice for a swimming hole except in the warmest summer days. However, if you are a fly fishing enthusiast, both you and the Kamloops trout will find the cool upland lakes to your liking.

If you aren't into roughing it, the lodge offers housekeeping cabins and full "American Plan" accommodations, which includes cabin, all meals, boat and motor or float tube equipment, and bedding.

Lemieux Creek Bridge

You can breathe easy when you reach the bridge at km 94. This is the bottom of the hill and it is easy travelling the next four kilometres through the farmland to Little Fort on Yellowhead Highway 5.

Little Fort

The Little Fort area first saw fur trade activity in the 1820s and 1830s with the brigades from the Prince George area, then known as New Caledonia. Paul Fraser, of the Hudson's Bay Company post at Kamloops, opened a winter post (the little fort) here in 1851 to facilitate trade with the Aboriginal peoples of the North Thompson valley. It was just a small cabin with Antoine Lamprant in charge, but it brought in a good yield of furs before being discontinued two years later.

When you reach Yellowhead Highway 5 at Little Fort, you have at least four options. If you prefer pavement to gravel roads, you can head north or south on the Yellowhead Highway. If a little dust doesn't bother you, you can cross the North Thompson on the Little Fort ferry and explore the backroads north to Clearwater or south to Barrière. The approaches to the two-vehicle ferry can be tricky so I would recommend double-checking before tackling it with a motorhome or a vehicle pulling a large RV trailer.

Note: See the *Information Sources* chapter at the end of the book for contact information on the services mentioned here.

GPS References for major points of interest
Ref: WGS 84 - Lat/Lon hddd.ddddd
Allow +/-100 metres due to data conversions

Wpt	Km	Description	Latitude	Longitude	Elev.
BL01	0	93 Mile House	N51.57673	W121.33315	1,195 m
BL02	10.5	Lone Butte – Horse Lake Rd	N51.55452	W121.19463	1,149 m
BL03	11.5	Watch Lake Rd	N51.55178	W121.18804	1,171 m
BL04	26.2	Sheridan Lake Rd W	N51.53811	W120.98536	1,139 m
BL05	31.0	Interlakes community	N51.54671	W120.91496	1,134 m
BL06	34.5	Sheridan Lake store	N51.53408	W120.87961	1,138 m
BL07	38.5	Sheridan Lake Rd E	N51.51381	W120.83566	1,134 m
BL08	46.8	Jct to Bridge Lake store	N51.48390	W120.73209	1,198 m
BL09	48.3	Jct to Bridge Lake store	N51.48168	W120.71147	1,146 m
BL10	49.0	Cottonwood Bay Rd	N51.48237	W120.70067	1,138 m
BL11		Bridge Lake Prov Park	N51.48507	W120.69959	1,141 m
BL12	58.0	Lac Des Roches rest area	N51.49874	W120.59446	1,182 m
BL13	60.0	Wavey Lake (2000) Rd	N51.49209	W120.56825	1,176 m
BL14	68.0	Phinetta Lake	N51.47497	W120.49637	1,141 m
BL15	75.7	MacDonald summit	N51.49619	W120.40200	1,300 m
BL16	81.0	Latremouille Lake	N51.49615	W120.33836	1,242 m
BL17	84.5	Roadside rest area	N51.49196	W120.29880	1,123 m
BL18	89.0	View of Dunn Peak and Monashees	N51.47174	W120.25592	736 m
BL19	90.5	Eakin Creek Rd	N51.46202	W120.24550	642 m
BL20	93.5	Lemieux Creek bridge	N51.45326	W120.21656	435 m
BL21	97.5	Little Fort	N51.42440	W120.20627	390 m

CHAPTER 17

Moose Valley Canoe Route: An Alternative to Bowron Lake Provincial Park

STATISTICS

	Map see page 124.
Distance:	30 km, Highway 97 at 100 Mile House to Marks Lake campsite.
	Canoe route approximately 10 km, Maitland Lake to Moose Lake.
Travel Time:	One to 1.5 hours, 100 Mile House to Marks Lake.
Conditions:	First part paved, then mostly gravel.
Season:	Best in dry weather, may be closed in winter.
Topo Maps:	100 Mile House, BC 92 P/11.
(1:50,000)	Gustafsen Lake, BC 92 P/12.
Communities:	100 Mile House.

Best Kept Secret

While I don't like to use the hackneyed phrase, "best kept secret," it certainly applies to the chain of lakes in the Moose Valley, some 30 kilometres west of 100 Mile House. It may be the size that counts. While 121,000-hectare Bowron Lake Provincial Park gets reams of press, 2,322-hectare Moose Valley Provincial Park seldom receives more than a paragraph or two.

Or it could be the age — Bowron Lake Park was established in 1961 and Moose Valley Park received its official sanction in 1995.

Maybe it is the challenge. The 116-kilometre-long Bowron Lake canoe circuit takes one to two weeks, depending on your level of fitness and weather conditions. The 10-kilometre-long Moose Valley circuit, on the other hand, takes one to three days, depending on how slothful you feel and how easily you are diverted by bird and wildlife watching.

It could also be the scenery. The Bowron Lake chain is surrounded by mountains reaching for the sky — Kaza Mountain, at 2,499 metres, does it quite successfully. On the other hand, Moose Valley is surrounded by forest-covered rocky outcrops that barely poke their spires above the 1,175-metre-high plateau.

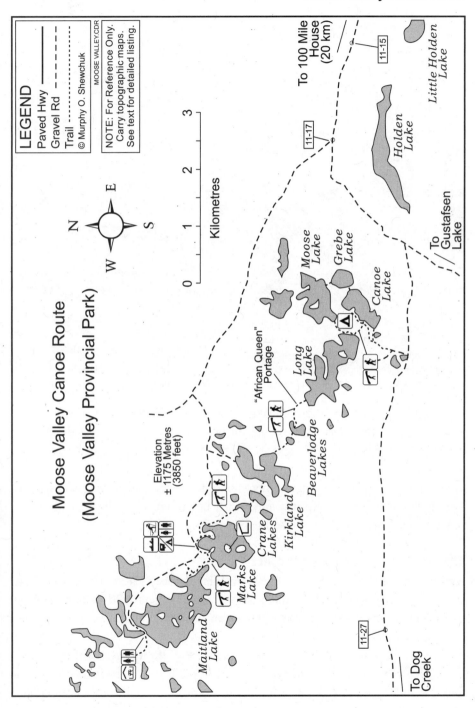

Moose Valley Canoe Route
(Moose Valley Provincial Park)

If you are fortunate, you might see a moose in Moose Valley.

It shouldn't be the number of lakes. The Moose Valley chain incorporates a dozen lakes, more or less, depending on water levels, with at least double that number within walking distance. You'll be stretching things to match that at Bowron.

I'm sure that there are a few other subtle differences, such as Bowron Lake's lengthy portages, busy campsites, and grizzly bears, but surely these shouldn't justify Moose Valley's banishment to the back pages.

Opportunities For Youth Project

While Bowron Lake takes its name from John Bowron (1837–1906), a member of the "Overlanders" of 1862, and, among other jobs, a gold commissioner at Barkerville in the 1880s, Moose Valley's name isn't nearly as auspicious — unless you are a moose.

The Moose Valley canoe route's beginnings rate right up there with the moose — wild and untamed. According to an article published in 100 Mile House on July 25, 1973, the route began as an Opportunities For Youth project undertaken that summer by three teenage boys. Eighteen-year-old project leader Stuart

Maitland was assisted by Hugh Kirkland, 17, and Kevin Marks, 15. The three lads' summer jobs cost the government $2,500, paying them each $80 per week. Included in the budget was another few hundred dollars for chainsaw rental, transportation, and supplies.

Unlike many of today's youth projects, the lads were on their own. They camped in a plastic-sheet tent during their work week and lived off the land as much as possible because the budget didn't include food. Roast beaver, spruce tip tea, and boiled lily pad roots supplemented their bacon and eggs, beans, chili, potatoes, and bread brought from home.

While the project may not have met today's stringent BC Parks standards, it certainly was a summer of growth for the three 100 Mile House lads. In a world far removed from city lights and noise, they coped with the black bear that literally fell through the wall of their tent, watched the wildlife that, in turn, watched them,

Morning reflections on Marks Lake.

and counted the loons lined up at their wharf.

While not "surviving," they blazed and cleared portage trails, dug miniature canals, and pulled vegetation to create a 10-kilometre-long canoe route through virgin Cariboo forest. Nature has reclaimed many of the wharves, shelters and canoe rests that they built nearly three decades ago. However, the lakes have changed little and the steady traffic and recent improvements have made the portages easier to find. The real lasting reminder of their summer's work is on paper — local maps, to be exact. The names of Maitland, Marks, and Kirkland lakes, plus most of the other lakes in the chain, bear witness to the Opportunities For Youth project.

Trapline and Canoe Outfitting

Stuart Maitland, now owner of Eureka Peak Lodge and Outfitters, didn't give up on the area after his summer of work and adventure. He purchased the local trapline and attempted to establish a canoe outfitting business. "We were ahead of our time," says his wife, Joyce, whom he enticed to join him in the wilderness.

Canoeists chat on the shores of Kirkland Lake.

There is a cabin at the west end of Maitland Lake. Unfortunately, the packrats have found a way to get into it. If nasty weather forces you to take cover in it, a broom or shovel would be a handy tool.

"There wasn't good fishing in the lakes and we couldn't make a successful business of guiding people just for the natural beauty of the place."

Stuart Maitland eventually gave up the trapline and moved to Forest Grove and built a base lodge for his Eureka Peak operation at Gotchen Lake, both northeast of 100 Mile House.

Job Trac Program

The Moose Valley again saw construction activity on the portages and wharves in 1987–88 under a provincial Job Trac program. If you are fortunate, you may still find a copy of the brochure and map that was also produced then. When we visited the area there was a signboard still standing with information and photos from that project.

Designated a Park

The efforts of Stuart Maitland, Hugh Kirkland, Kevin Marks, and countless others have been protected by park status since 1995. This is, however, a wilderness park with few facilities and no services. You won't find paved roads, fancy tables, neat camp sites, or an interpreter. You will have to bring in everything you need and pack out everything you brought in. You will have to look after yourself and your fellow campers as though your life depended on it — because it could.

With the proper attitude and suitable equipment, Moose Valley can be a wonderful place for a family to spend a leisurely weekend or more canoeing, bird watching and wildlife viewing. Suitable equipment means the usual life jackets (sometimes called "personal floatation devices"), camping gear, and water shoes appropriate for "wet-footing" it in the marshes and portages. Insect repellent is a must although one source suggests mosquitoes aren't as bad as elsewhere on the Cariboo Plateau.

Winter Wonderland

While the last stretch of road into Marks Lake isn't maintained in winter, the area is still a haven for cross-country skiing and snowshoeing.

Getting to Moose Valley

The 31-kilometre drive from 100 Mile House to Marks Lake, in the heart of Moose Valley Provincial Park, should take less than an hour. But don't bet money on it. Cariboo gumbo, high water, or dust can all make a difference. As previously mentioned, go prepared because there are no services once you leave town.

To get there, drive west on Exeter Station Road (it leaves Highway 97 just north of downtown 100 Mile House), past the BC Rail yard and the OSB mill to the junction with 1100 Road. Continue west on 1100 Road up the Little Bridge Creek valley. The occasional "Educo" and "Moose Valley Canoe Route" signs will be assurance that you are on the right route.

Continue past the Valentine Lake and Educo Adventure School junctions until you reach a junction to the right at the "11-17" marker, approximately 22 kilometres from 100 Mile House. Take the one-lane road to the right and follow it generally northwestward. You'll pass an access road to Kirkland Lake to the left (south) about 6.5 kilometres from 1100 Road. You should reach the Marks Lake campground and put-in about two kilometres farther along.

For most vehicles, the Marks Lake base is a good place to park. The road gets rougher and narrower, but it does continue toward the west end of Maitland Lake. After sorting out your gear, you can paddle south along the west shore of Marks

Lake to the portage to Maitland Lake. After a short portage and leisurely paddle northwest to the cabin at the end of Maitland Lake, you can take a break before retracing your strokes to Marks Lake and starting the route southeast. Depending on seasonal water levels, the portages may be wet enough to paddle or just muddy enough make you glad you wore an old pair of runners.

Rustic campsites at Long Lake or Canoe Lake can be a good base for your first night out. Then, after looping through Grebe and Moose lakes, you can retrace your route to Marks Lake and back to your vehicle.

Check out the Moose Valley Canoe Route. While it isn't Bowron Lake Park, it doesn't have a quota system either.

Note: See the *Information Sources* chapter at the end of the book for contact information on the services mentioned here.

GPS References for major points of interest
Ref: WGS 84 - Lat/Lon hddd.ddddd
Allow +/-100 metres due to data conversions

Wpt	Km	Description	Latitude	Longitude
W01	0	100 Mile House Info Centre	N51.64155	W121.29801
W02	1.0	Jct Hwy 97 and Exeter Rd	N51.64947	W121.29647
W03	4.0	Railway crossing	N51.65242	W121.33864
W04	5.0	OSB Mill	N51.65572	W121.35321
W05	6.9	Jct stay on 1100 Rd	N51.65322	W121.37863
W06	13.5	Jct to Valentine Lake	N51.62095	W121.43144
W07	15.7	Jct stay on 1100 Rd	N51.62059	W121.46063
W08	20.0	Educo Adventure School	N51.62895	W121.51846
W09	22.5	11 – 17 marker - go right	N51.63328	W121.55207
W10	24.5	Park Boundary	N51.64461	W121.57328
W11	27.8	Jct keep left	N51.65586	W121.61667
W12	29.0	Jct to Kirkland Lake	N51.65347	W121.63039
W13	31.0	Parking – Marks Lake	N51.65514	W121.65577

East Cariboo Loop

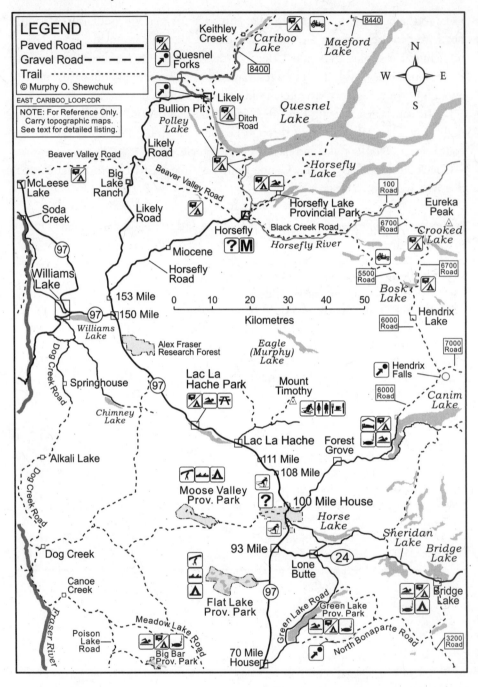

LEGEND
Paved Road ——————
Gravel Road — — — —
Trail - - - - - - - - -
© Murphy O. Shewchuk

EAST_CARIBOO_LOOP.CDR

NOTE: For Reference Only.
Carry topographic maps.
See text for detailed listing.

Keithley Creek
Cariboo Lake
Maeford Lake
8440
Quesnel Forks
8400
Likely
Bullion Pit
Polley Lake
Ditch Road
Quesnel Lake
Likely Road
Beaver Valley Road
Beaver Valley Road
Horsefly Lake
Big Lake Ranch
McLeese Lake
Soda Creek
Likely Road
Horsefly Lake Provincial Park
100 Road
Eureka Peak
6700 Road
Crooked Lake
Horsefly
Black Creek Road
Miocene
Horsefly River
6700 Road
Williams Lake
97
Horsefly Road
5500 Road
Bosk Lake
153 Mile
150 Mile
6000 Road
Hendrix Lake
Williams Lake
Alex Fraser Research Forest
Eagle (Murphy) Lake
7000 Road
Hendrix Falls
Canim Lake
Dog Creek Road
Springhouse
97
Lac La Hache Park
Mount Timothy
6000 Road
Chimney Lake
Lac La Hache
Forest Grove
Alkali Lake
111 Mile
108 Mile
Moose Valley Prov. Park
100 Mile House
Horse Lake
Dog Creek Road
93 Mile
Sheridan Lake
Bridge Lake
Dog Creek
Lone Butte
24
Canoe Creek
97
Flat Lake Prov. Park
Green Lake Road
Green Lake Prov. Park
Bridge Lake
3200 Road
Fraser River
Meadow Lake Road
Poison Lake Road
Big Bar Prov. Park
70 Mile House
North Bonaparte Road

0   10   20   30   40   50
Kilometres

N
W   E
S

CHAPTER 18

East Cariboo Loop: 100 Mile House – Horsefly – Likely – McLeese Lake

STATISTICS

	Map see page 220.
Distance:	166 km, 100 Mile House to Horsefly.
	Three to four hours driving time.
	50 km, Horsefly to Likely via Ditch Road.
	One to two hours driving time.
	74 km, Likely to McLeese Lake (Hwy 97).
	One to two hours driving time.
Elevation Gain:	Approximately 300 metres.
Condition:	Paved 100 Mile House to Eagle Creek.
	Gravel Eagle Creek to Horsefly.
	Gravel Horsefly to Likely.
	Mixed pavement and gravel, Likely to McLeese Lake.
Season:	Gravel sections may be closed in winter.
Topo Maps:	100 Mile House, BC 92 P/11.
(1:50,000)	Lac La Hache, BC 92 P/14.
	Canim Lake, BC 92 P/15.
	McKinley Creek, BC 93 A/2.
	MacKay River, BC 93 A/7.
	Horsefly, BC 93 A/6.
	Beaver Creek, BC 93 A/5.
	Soda Creek, BC 93 B/8.
Communities:	100 Mile House, Forest Grove, Horsefly, Likely, and 150 Mile House.

"There are several hundred prime fishing lakes east of the Fraser River," said former central Cariboo Fish & Wildlife officer Bill Westover without a hint of exaggeration. Westover's base was Williams Lake before his move to Cranbrook, and his territory covered much of the lake country of the Cariboo.

Canim Lake, Mahood Lake, Horsefly Lake, Quesnel Lake, Williams Lake, and

Fishing is a common sport on the east Cariboo lakes.

Lac La Hache are a few of the major lakes of this region. A 290-kilometre back-roads loop from 100 Mile House, through Forest Grove and Hendrix Lake to Horsefly and Likely, and back to Highway 97 at McLeese Lake can take you through the heart of the historic east Cariboo. It offers fine fishing and a touch of gold rush history that can trigger gold fever in even the toughest old soul. For a diversion from fishing, you can explore historic Quesnel Forks, detour into famous Keithley Creek, or camp at Horsefly Lake Provincial Park.

"The number one sport fish in the region is rainbow trout," added Westover, "although the larger lakes do have significant stocks of Dolly Varden char, koka-nee, freshwater ling *(Lota lota)*, and lake trout. We stock about 50 lakes east of the Fraser River with rainbow trout and all but a few are east of Highway 97. We also stock a small number of lakes with eastern brook trout."

With all the fishing lakes, there are sure to be fishing enthusiasts and facilities to supply their needs. These include provincial and private campgrounds, resorts with rustic housekeeping cabins, and modern lodges. In fact, there are more than 60 fishing resorts and guest ranches in the region.

Resort facilities vary. Some operators require that guests bring their own bedding and food, while others provide almost everything that their guests might need for a fishing vacation. Small fry of the two-legged kind are usually welcome with play areas, recreation lounges, and water skiing often available. But, fishing for rainbow trout is still an important activity in the Cariboo lake country.

"Good fly fishermen can catch fish all year around," said Bill Westover. "The rest of us try our luck with artificial flies then switch to gang troll hardware with worms and lures."

The creeks and rivers harbour resident rainbow trout, but very few people fish them — probably because it takes a little more skill and patience to find the right pools and place the fly or bait where the fish will take it.

Check up-to-date fishing regulations. Most of the creeks are closed to fishing from April 1 to June 30 for spawning. Some lakes are restricted to fishing with artificial flies and fly casting equipment. Other lakes require the use of artificial flies but may allow any kind of fishing equipment.

Canim-Hendrix Lake Road

Canim-Hendrix Lake Road (a.k.a. Forest Grove Road and Canim Lake Road) leaves Cariboo Highway 97 approximately 2.5 kilometres north of the information centre in the heart of 100 Mile House. With the junction with Highway 97 as your km 0 reference, follow Canim Lake Road to the northeast as it follows Bridge Creek downstream. The next major junction is at Forest Grove (km 20.8), where the road to the north continues to Ruth Lake and a network of backroads across the plateau. The Forest Grove Store may be a good spot to stock up on supplies before continuing further into the east Cariboo backcountry. To continue to Horsefly, follow the Hendrix Lake sign and turn right (east) at Forest Grove.

The road (still paved) winds through the Canim Lake First Nations community. The Catholic church on the reserve was built in 1896. Canim is the Chinook word for canoe.

The next major junction is at km 33.5, where the paved Canim Lake South Road to the east parallels the south shore of Canim Lake, providing access to several resorts plus Roserim Creek Park and Mahood Lake in Wells Gray Park. Continue north on Canim-Hendrix Lake Road on the west side of Canim Lake for more resorts and, ultimately, Horsefly.

Hawkins Lake

Another junction at km 46 provides access to more East Cariboo lakes. Hawkins Lake Road winds west up Eagle Creek and Bradley Creek, past Hawkins Lake and Ruth Lake. You can loop back to Forest Grove via Ruth Lake if you are looking for new country to explore. If you are serious about exploring, 4,500-hectare Schoolhouse Lake Provincial Park lies northwest of Hawkins Lake. It is a backcountry wilderness with limited access and no facilities.

At the time of writing, the pavement ended at Eagle Creek and the Canim-

East Cariboo Loop

Hendrix Lake Road (a.k.a. 6000 Road) began a steady climb north from Canim Lake. The dry slopes and grasslands of the Cariboo gradually give way to tall timber, rein orchid, lupine, and Indian paintbrush.

Hendrix Creek Waterfall Trail

The Spanish Creek Forest Road (a.k.a. 7000 Road) near km 63.5 provides access to the Quesnel Highlands and Pendleton Lakes region. The Flourmill Volcano area of Wells Gray Park is also accessible via this route.

If you are interested in a short diversion that includes a hike into a spectacular little waterfall, follow 7000 Road northeast for about 700 metres to 710 Road, then follow 710 Road south for 2.7 kilometres to the Hendrix Falls trailhead parking area. It is an easy three-hundred-metre-hike to a viewpoint just downstream from the falls.

Hendrix Lake

When we first travelled through this area, the community of Hendrix Lake (km 80.5) was virtually a ghost town with the Boss Mountain mining operation closed. Molybdenum was discovered in Boss Mountain as early as 1911, but it wasn't until the 1960s that serious mining began. The Noranda group picked up a long standing option to the mine site early in 1961, and by June of 1965, the mine was employing over two hundred men. A market glut forced closure of the mine in January 1972. In January 1974, it reopened with 185 employees, finally closing in the early 1980s.

The former mining town is now being turned into a recreation community with many of the homes being refurbished. At the time of writing, LandQuest Realty was offering one such home for under $30,000.

LandQuest Realty's website also had a short biography of the lake's namesake: "Named for John 'Slim' Hendrix (1870–1938), who for many years lived at the foot of Canim Lake and had a trapline north of it, in the area of Hendrix Creek. Slim Hendrix was a tall dark gaunt man who wore a blackpatch over one eye. Like a number of men who dwelt in isolated parts of the province, Slim had a 'mail-order' wife — a delightful lady."

The road north of Hendrix Lake is gravel, complete with potholes and washboard. If your vehicle has a stiff suspension, be prepared for a few teeth-chattering sections. Otherwise, it should pose few difficulties in dry weather.

A network of logging roads provides access to several lakes in this region, many of which have Forest Service recreation sites. Keep right at a junction with 5500 Road at km 87.5, passing east of Bosk Lake and Cruiser Lake while following the

Hendrix Creek Waterfall in mid-September.

Crooked Lake from the Crooked Lake South recreation site.

signs to Crooked Lake. This junction also marks the start of a countdown to the Upper Horsefly Road (a.k.a. Black Creek Road or 100 Road).

The 5500 Road joins the 6000 Road south of Bosk Lake (km 87.5). It provides an alternate route to the Black Creek community on Black Creek Road via Tisdall and McKinley Lakes. At 31 kilometres, this route is noticeably shorter than the 51 kilometres via Crooked Lake.

Crooked Lake

Meanwhile, back at the junction south of Bosk Lake, the road to the right continues toward the upper Horsefly River. For the sake of this description, keep right. There is a fairly large, open recreation site on the east shore of 6.5-kilometre-long kidney-shaped Bosk Lake.

The main gravel road continues north for 10 kilometres before beginning a steady descent to Crooked Lake. There is a small recreation site on the southwest shore of the lake (km 105) and another on the north shore. Crooked Lake Resort, to the right at a junction near km 107, offers housekeeping cabins and RV and tenting sites. Crooked Lake is generally a deep lake with some shallows that pro-

Riders traverse the alpine meadows of Eureka Peak.

duce trout to 40 centimetres.

In addition to the lake activities, there is a trail up to the alpine meadows of Eureka Peak that is worth exploring. Stuart Maitland of Eureka Peak Lodge & Outfitters offers guided horseback trips to the alpine. Eureka Peak Lodge is located on Gotchen Lake, southeast of Bosk Lake.

Horsefly River

The gravel road skirts the west end of the lake and continues northwest, paralleling McKuskey Creek to its junction with Horsefly River. Signs of erosion forces of the last ice age are obvious as well as are much more recent forest fires and logging. There is a small open area near the Horsefly River crossing (km 118.5) and a major junction half a kilometre further along. Logging roads continue up the Horsefly River, but the community of Horsefly lies to the west, downstream. The gravel road along the Horsefly River is a considerable improvement from the section south of Crooked Lake. Watch for logging trucks and stay on the main road if Horsefly is your destination.

The McKinley Lake (500) Forest Road, mentioned earlier, joins the Upper

East Cariboo Loop

Horsefly Road at km 138.5, a few minutes east of the Black Creek community. On the downhill run to Horsefly, the Horsefly River appeared to be navigable by rubber raft or canoe — very slow moving and lots of oxbows. If you try it, watch for the rapids at km 158.

Horsefly Lake Park

The last major junction before Horsefly is at km 165. Williams Lake and the village of Horsefly are to the left while Horsefly Lake lies to the right (northeast). The route to Horsefly Lake Provincial Park follows Horsefly Lake Road east for eight kilometres and then swings northeast on Hatchery Road. Houseboats are moored in the channel near where the road bridge crosses the waterway between Little Horsefly Lake and the outlet at the west end of Horsefly Lake.

Twenty-three-campsite Horsefly Lake Park was once the site of a hatchery used to restore the run of sockeye salmon to the Horsefly River. It is one of the prettier campgrounds in the Cariboo, with several of the sites offering direct boat access to the lake. A lake shore trail to the east of the campground offers you the opportunity for a relaxing walk and a chance to see wildlife coming down to the lake for their evening drink.

Sockeye salmon spawn in the Horsefly River in September with the dominant runs in a 2005–2009–2013 sequence. The number of returning spawners has exceeded two million in the past.

Watch out for hungry wildlife along the Cariboo backroads.

Gold Rush Camp

The community of Horsefly, at km 166, was once known as "Harper's Camp." Historians suggest that the first gold in the Cariboo was discovered in the Horsefly River in 1859. Five American gold seekers, headed by Peter Curran Dunlevy, were led to the Horsefly River by a Native guide, Long Baptiste, whom they had met at Lac La Hache. This group panned the first gold in the Horsefly River in the middle of June 1859. Less than a day later, a second group of miners arrived and the rush to the Horsefly was on. Sparked by the finds on the Horsefly, the ever-mobile miners continued north, making rich finds in the Quesnel River, Keithley and Antler creeks, and finally Barkerville on Williams Creek.

Today, Horsefly is a vibrant village, not a ghost town as are so many other communities spawned by the gold rush. Most services are available here and the Jack Lynn Memorial Museum is a welcoming place to visit in the summer to gather historical information on the region. And no trip is complete without mailing a postcard home with a "Horsefly" cancellation stamp.

Horsefly to Likely

The backroads explorer has several options when leaving Horsefly. There is a fairly direct paved route to 150 Mile House and Williams Lake via Miocene and a roundabout route to McLeese Lake via Beaver Creek. Naturally, if you are a serious backroader, your choice could be an even more roundabout route to McLeese Lake via Quesnel Lake and Likely, with optional detours into Quesnel Forks and the world-famous Bullion Pit.

With the Cornerhouse Place Shopping Centre as km 0, turn north on Boswell Street and continue past the Forest Service office, with a stop for additional information on the road, of course. It isn't long before Boswell Street becomes Mitchell Bay Road and the blacktop gives way to gravel.

Use caution because this is an active logging road. The view of the Cariboo Mountains and Horsefly River is excellent, as the road travels through cleared farmland for much of the first half-dozen kilometres. Then the road twists along the Horsefly valley, often offering more views or a place to park and try a little river fishing.

Sea Captain

During the Cariboo gold rush, a sea captain named Mitchell operated a steam ferry on Quesnel Lake. He also ran a pack train via the Lake Trail to Lillooet and later to Harper's Camp (Horsefly) and Keithley. Mitchell Point Landing Road (km 16.5) and Mitchell Bay Landing Road (km 19.2) reflect this heritage. A few minutes before the latter junction, a narrow road to the east leads to Horsefly Bay recreation site, a small site with little to recommend it except a spectacular view of Quesnel Lake and a little privacy.

There is a resort and Forest Service recreation site at Mitchell Bay (km 24). If your destination is Likely, keep to the left on the Horsefly-Likely Forest Road. The giant cedar, tangled undergrowth, devil's club, and thimbleberry alongside the road that now winds high above Quesnel Lake make an impassable jungle — one that the gold seekers of the last century faced with trepidation. This is also a route you should face with caution in all but summer weather.

Major side roads lead to Raft Creek (km 30), Gavin Lake (km 31.5), and Polley Lake (km 36). Unless the urge to wander has taken a firm hold on your steering wheel, keep right at all junctions. However, Polley Lake has a Forest recreations site and can be a pleasant four-kilometre side trip if you are interested in a little fishing.

From the Polley Lake junction, the road follows a surprisingly level course as it winds through thick cedar. Known as the "Ditch Road," it was the route of a 30-kilometre-long ditch used to carry water from Polley Lake and Bootjack Lake to the Bullion Pit near Likely.

The gravel road from Horsefly suddenly emerges at a paved road on a hill

A reconstructed cabin at Quesnel Forks.

(km 48.5). The signpost at this end of the road we had just travelled over was once marked "Polley Lake." On the last visit it was simply marked as an unmaintained forest road. To the west is McLeese Lake on Cariboo Highway 97. To the east is the community of Likely on the Quesnel River.

Quesnel River Bridge

Originally known as Quesnel Dam, Likely (km 51) was renamed in honour of John A. Likely, who was indirectly responsible for the discovery of gold in nearby

Cedar Creek. John Likely was one of a family of six orphans, ranging in age from 5 to 28, who, in 1859, immigrated from Ballyshannon, Ireland, to St. John, New Brunswick.

The Cedar Creek find was so incredibly rich that it became known as the "Nugget Patch." In the last week of October 1922, over 697 ounces of gold was recovered at the Cedar Creek Mine.

Quesnel Forks Side Trip

The 12-kilometre road to Quesnel Forks swings west from the main highway on the hill approximately 1.2 kilometres north of the bridge at Likely and continues to climb until it is out of the town. It then crosses a plateau for about eight kilometres before a steep descent to the junction of the Cariboo and Quesnel rivers.

Quesnel Forks was home to more than 5,000 residents during the early years of the Cariboo gold rush. A number of the original log buildings still stand, and a few pilings from the bridge across the Quesnel River, built by the Royal Engineers in 1862, still jut out of the river. The bridge was destroyed by floods in 1948. In an attempt to let nature take its course without the destructive interference of man, the Forest Service has established a recreation site at Quesnel Forks. Tables have been placed near the original buildings and there is a beach suitable for launching a kayak, whitewater raft, or riverboat.

A labyrinth of narrow roads winds through the various levels of what was once a thriving gold rush town. Wild roses and raspberries grow out of the floor of someone's living room. A hazelnut bush leans against a dilapidated stable — each seeming to support the other.

In 1898, the Quesnel River was dammed near Likely in the belief that down-river areas would prove rich in gold. A few were, but others were found to have been wing-dammed by Chinese miners in earlier years and were already worked out.

Bullion Pit

With the Quesnel River Bridge as km 0, the main road west climbs steadily out of the Quesnel River valley at Likely, passing the Polley Lake Road (Ditch Road to Horsefly) at km 2.4. A "Bullion Pit" rest area and information centre has recently been built on the north side of the road at km 4.2. When we last visited there, the trails were still under construction, but with a little sleuthing, I was able to find the old ditch and the remnants of the diversion gate. An easily missed side road (actually the old highway) dips to the right at km 5.3. Watch for a swampy area and the remains of an old dam within two hundred metres of the main high-

A giant water cannon (monitor) on display at Cedar Point Provincial Park on Quesnel Lake, six kilometres southeast of Likely.

way. Another narrow side road and a creek run downhill to the right. Park here and take the 10 to 15 minute walk to the cliffs overlooking the Bullion Pit. Keep right at the first junction and left at the second, and you should see a trail to the old viewpoint.

In 1892, the Canadian Pacific Railway acquired the rights to Dancing Bill's Gulch and formed the Cariboo Hydraulic Mining Company. In 10 years, the operation produced over a million dollars in gold, using water run through the ditch from the Polley Lake area to wash the glacial till into sluice boxes. From 1897 to 1905, official weather records were kept at the Bullion Mine. In the winter of 1897–1898, the total snowfall was 142 inches — nearly 12 feet or 3.6 metres.

In 1935, the Bullion Pit Mine was the site of the largest monitor ever installed in North America. This giant water cannon created a giant man-made canyon that has seen sporadic activity ever since — in recent years, there has been heavy equipment working in the pit.

Lake Country Options

The Little Lake Road (km 9.2) is the first of many possible detours into the plateau lakes of the area. There is a resort with cabins, a campground, and a restaurant/laundromat at Morehead Lake (km 15) with a side road into Bootjack Lake less than two kilometres earlier. Incidentally, Morehead Lake was created to provide water to feed the hydraulic mining operation at the Bullion Pit. There is a Forest recreation site at Bootjack Lake that could also prove to be a pleasant place to spend a day or two. The Jacobie Lake Forest Road (km 22) offers a similar option a few kilometres off the main road.

The Beaver Valley Road (km 34) provides an alternate route back to Horsefly with fishing opportunities along Beaver Creek. Cattle and log buildings give the Beaver Valley a distinctive western flavour. If your plan is to head west, cross Beaver Creek at km 35.3 and swing west on Beaver Lake Road (a.k.a. Beaver Valley Road) at km 35.9. The paved road to the south at this junction continues to Williams Lake via Big Lake Ranch and 150 Mile House. The shortest route to Cariboo Highway 97 is via Beaver Lake Road to McLeese Lake, 39 kilometres to the west.

The good gravel road quickly climbs out of the Beaver Valley and heads west across the plateau. There are few distractions along the road westward except for Forest recreation sites at Elk (Island) Lake near km 53 and at Jackson Hole, a few minutes farther west and four kilometres south of the main road.

At the time of writing, the pavement began again at the junction of the Beaver Lake Road and Gibraltar Mines Road (km 70). The mine site is about 13 kilometres to the north and McLeese Lake is another four kilometres to the southwest, on Highway 97. Depending on your destination, you can follow Highway 97 south to Williams Lake and, ultimately, the Trans-Canada Highway at Cache Creek. If you are northward bound, Quesnel and Prince George are within easy driving distance.

Note: See the *Information Sources* chapter at the end of the book for contact information on the services mentioned here.

GPS References for major points of interest
Ref: WGS 84 - Lat/Lon hddd.ddddd
Allow +/-100 metres due to data conversions

Wpt	Km	Description	Latitude	Longitude
EC01	0	Hwy 97 and Canim – Hendrix Lake Rd	N51.66462	W121.28885
EC02	20.8	Forest Grove	N51.76676	W121.09834
EC03	33.5	Canim Lakes Rd	N51.77398	W120.93127
EC04	46.0	Hawkins Lake Jct	N51.85567	W120.86373
EC05	46.5	Eagle Creek start 6000 Rd	N51.86222	W120.86326
EC06	49.8	Baldwin Lake to right	N51.88745	W120.82917
EC07	51.2	Succour Lake Rd to left	N51.89275	W120.81036
EC08	52.5	Christmas Lake to right	N51.89993	W120.79602
EC09	56.5	Hoover Bay Rd	N51.92286	W120.75237
EC10	63.5	Jct Spanish Creek FS Road	N51.96532	W120.69429
EC11	80.5	Hendrix Lake Community	N52.09800	W120.79929
EC12	87.5	Jct 5500 Rd – keep right	N52.15256	W120.79062
EC13	90.3	Bosk Lake rec site	N52.16369	W120.76780
EC14	94.3	67–25 Km – Cruiser Lake	N52.19553	W120.76153
EC15	97.7	Jct 500 Rd – keep right	N52.22434	W120.75613
EC16	105.0	Crooked Lake S rec site	N52.27029	W120.73834
EC17	107.0	McKuskey Creek and Resort Jct	N52.28227	W120.73674
EC18	118.5	Horsefly River Bridge	N52.35258	W120.83975
EC19	119.0	67-00 K marker – Black Creek Rd	N52.35357	W120.84512
EC20	138.5	100-26 K marker – Jct 500 Rd	N52.29415	W121.07197
EC21	165.0	Jct to Horsefly Lake Park	N52.33467	W121.40086
EC22	166.0	Jct Horsefly Rd	N52.33312	W121.41694
EC23	0.0	Cornerhouse Place	N52.33461	W121.41489
EC24	13.5	Squaw Flats rec site	N52.42853	W121.43841
EC25	19.0	Jct Horsefly Bay rec site	N52.46734	W121.40989
EC26		Horsefly Bay rec site (3.5 km east)	N52.47266	W121.38991
EC27	21.3	Mitchell Bay Landing Rd	N52.47869	W121.42926
EC28	24.0	Mitchell Bay rec site	N52.48095	W121.46288
EC29	30.0	Raft Creek rec site	N52.50298	W121.50804
EC30	31.5	Gavin Lake Rd	N52.50594	W121.52547
EC31	36.0	Polley Lake Rd	N52.54264	W121.54243
EC32		Polley Lake rec site (4 km west)	N52.53471	W121.58462
EC33	48.0	Jct Ditch Rd and Likely Rd	N52.61576	W121.60600
EC34	51.0	Likely	N52.61658	W121.57124
EC35	0.0	Quesnel River bridge	N52.61559	W121.57248
EC36	4.2	Bullion Pit Rest Area	N52.61962	W121.62745
EC37	35.9	Jct Beaver Valley Rd	N52.47433	W121.85539
EC38	53.0	Elk (Island) Lake rec site	N52.46792	W122.04675
EC39	74.0	McLeese Lake	N52.42580	W122.29842

CHAPTER 19

Backroad to Barkerville: 150 Mile House — Likely — Barkerville

STATISTICS

	Map see page 237.
Distance:	83 km, 150 Mile House to Likely.
	One to two hours driving time.
	147 km, Likely to Barkerville via Cariboo Lake.
	Three to four hours driving time.
Elevation Gain:	Approximately 700 metres.
Condition:	Paved 150 Mile House to Likely.
	Gravel Likely to Barkerville.
Season:	Gravel sections may be closed in winter.
Topo Maps:	150 Mile House, BC 93 A/4.
(1:50,000)	Beaver Creek, BC 93 A/5.
	Hydraulic, BC 93 A/12.
	Spanish Lake, BC 93 A/11.
	Cariboo Lake, BC 93 A/14.
	Mitchell Lake, BC 93 A/15.
	Spectacle Lakes, BC 93 H/3.
	Wells, BC 93 H/4.
Communities:	150 Mile House, Likely, Barkerville, and Wells.

Cariboo Fascination

The Cariboo has attracted explorers since the first humans meandered across the Bering Land Bridge or followed the retreating glaciers northward. These First Nations Peoples did not leave an easily recognizable (to us, anyway) record of their travels and encounters along the way, but more recent travellers have. The journals of Alexander Mackenzie, Simon Fraser, and other fur trade explorers described the land and the people they met in the late 1700s and early 1800s.

As the fur trade waned, the gold rush of the mid-1800s attracted a new type of explorer — one set on discovering riches beneath the surface. While the majority

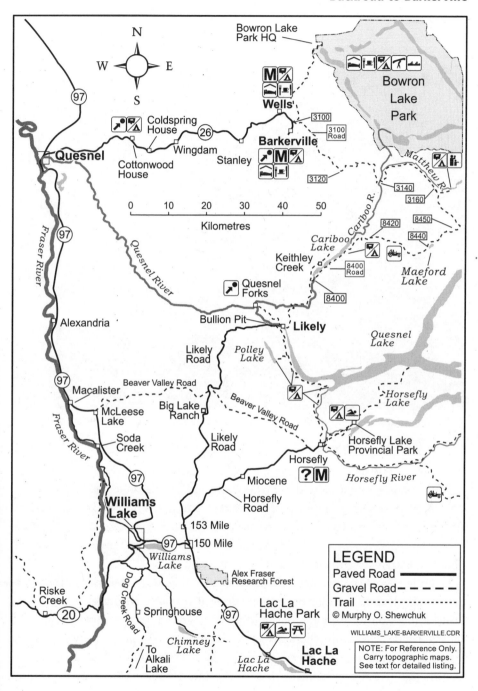

The three-kilometre-long Bullion Pit was created by washing the gravel mountainside with huge monitors.

of the effort was spent on digging for gold or parting it from those who had successfully done so, there were those who wrote about life around them. The results have been recorded in newspapers of the day and in a variety of books, some of which have been reprinted in more recent times. *Cheadle's Journal of Trip Across Canada 1862–1863* by Walter B. Cheadle is one such example of fine writing about an extremely difficult "tourist" adventure.

Historians in the early part of this century paved the way for work by other writers such as the late Art Downs, former editor of *BC Outdoors* magazine, and N.L. "Bill" Barlee, author of numerous gold panning and ghost town books. Branwen C. Patenaude picked up where her predecessors left off and wrote two excellent books on the region. The reason for this preamble is that the space available for this chapter does not permit me to do much more than touch on the opportunities that await you.

While you could drive from 150 Mile House to Barkerville via Likely in a day, if your main reason for travelling is to get there, stay on the blacktop of Highway 97 and Highway 26. If, on the other hand, you are looking for adventure along the way, allow a weekend or a week to make the backroads trip.

150 Mile House Starting Point
The roads across the Cariboo plateau have changed considerably since Peter Curran Dunlevy made "the real strike in the Cariboo" in June 1859. Today, the main access to Likely is an 83-kilometre-long paved highway with several interesting place names along the way — an hour's drive if you are in a rush. If you aren't in a rush, there is a wealth of side roads worth exploring.

Horsefly and Likely Roads
The original Cariboo Waggon Road (then spelled with two "g"s) continued north from 150 Mile House. However, at km 4.5 you have an option to take a scenic tour to Likely via Horsefly, Mitchell Bay on Quesnel Lake and the Ditch Road. It is 46 kilometres east to Horsefly, and then another 48 kilometres to Likely Road via Mitchell Bay. The details are covered in the *East Cariboo Loop* chapter, but it is worth noting that the Ditch Road is rough and only passable in the summer months.

The Likely Road continues north from the junction, detouring around Big Lake and Beaver Lake. You have an option to head west at several locations including Beaver Lake Road at km 46.5. There is also a pleasant backroad to Horsefly via Beaver Valley Road at km 48.5. The Robert Lake recreation site, 21 kilometres to the southeast on Beaver Valley Road, can be an excellent place to spend a summer day birdwatching.

Gavin Lake Road, at km 52.8, provides access to a network of trails and campsites in the UBC Alex Fraser Research Forest.

The Bullion Pit and the Big Ditch
Morehead Lake, at km 67.5, was originally dammed in the 1890s to provide "more head" for the Bullion Pit Mine. According to some sources, the name came from a miner by the name of William Morehead, who lived near the mouth of Morehead Creek (the creek was also named after him).

From Morehead Lake, the Likely Road swings east, passing the new Bullion Pit rest area and lookout at km 79. The remains of a huge excavation can be seen to the north of the viewpoint and from the old viewpoint a kilometre or two to the west.

According to a *Historic Likely* publication, "This huge trough was created over a

50 year period of mining. John Hobson acquired the leases in 1894. During the next 11 years he attracted world class investors, developing one of the biggest hydraulic mines in North America. Water from nearby lakes fed enormous monitors that flushed 1.25 million dollars worth of gold from the sides of this man made gully. Drought caused the first major shutdown but technical innovations made it productive again from 1933 to 1941. The trench is now almost three km (2 miles) long, 122 m (400 feet), 76 m (250 feet) wide at the bottom, and 304 m (1,000 feet) at the top."

Over 64 kilometres of ditches were constructed to carry the water needed to wash the gravel out of the mountainside. In 1935, the pit was the site of the largest monitor ever installed in North America. (For those of you attuned to the computer age, this was no computer screen, but a giant nozzle that spewed more water per day than used by the entire city of Vancouver.)

A junction to the right (south) at km 80.5 can take you up to the road that follows the "Big Ditch" along the mountainside above Quesnel Lake. In dry weather and with a high-clearance vehicle, this could be a scenic backroad drive to Polley Lake or Horsefly. See the *East Cariboo Loop* chapter for details.

Likely

The Quesnel River Bridge at km 83 marks the entrance to the settlement of Likely. While you might rightly suspect that this was a "likely" place to search for gold, the name comes from John A. Likely, the man responsible for the discovery of gold in nearby Cedar Creek. Likely earned his immortality. It is said that Cedar Creek was so incredibly rich that it became known as the "Nugget Patch." In the last week of October 1922, more than 697 troy ounces of gold was recovered at the Cedar Creek Mine.

While there is still "likely" to be gold in the creeks, the Likely "Hilton" is a good spot for pie and coffee and a chance to find out more about the region. Likely is also the last chance to stock up on fuel and supplies before heading out on the 150-kilometre jaunt north to Barkerville.

Quesnel Forks

Although it is a 25-kilometre round-trip detour, no visit to Likely is complete without exploring Quesnel Forks. Better yet, if it suits your schedule, plan to camp at the Forest recreation site at this gold rush ghost town. The junction to Quesnel Forks is about half a kilometre up Keithley Road from the bridge across the mouth of Quesnel Lake. Go left up the hill and left at the Rosette Lake Road sign. Then follow the Quesnel Forks signs as you climb out of the valley and head westward

Members of the Likely Cemetery Society have been restoring the Quesnel Forks Cemetery. Donations can be sent to the Likely Cemetery Society, PO Box 19, Likely, BC V0L 1N0.

across the plateau. The final three kilometres to the ghost town is a steep descent to the confluence of the Quesnel and Cariboo rivers.

Established in 1859, Quesnel Forks was the gateway to the rich Cariboo gold-fields. The Royal Engineers laid out the townsite in 1861, but the Cariboo Waggon Road bypassed Forks City and it was quickly displaced by Barkerville. It didn't die an immediate death, for the bridge across the Quesnel River played an important part in local commerce until it was washed away in the flood of 1948.

There has been considerable local interest in restoring the cemetery as well as stabilizing many of Quesnel Forks' historic buildings.

Cedar Point Park

If spending a night in a ghost town isn't high on your priority list, consider Cedar Point Park, on the north shore of Quesnel Lake. The junction to the park is less than a kilometre farther up Keithley Road (km 84.5), only this time go right. It is about four kilometres to the park where the tall cedars can provide shade in even the hottest Cariboo summer weather. The "star" of the park is a giant steam shovel, originally brought into the area in 1906 to dig a canal from Spanish Lake to the Bullion Mines.

Keithley Road

When you've done about all the detours you can handle, the next step is to follow

Keithley Road north of town. Go left at the Spanish Lake Road junction and continue northwest on Keithley Road to a junction near the 6K marker. Then take the left road down to and across the Cariboo River. Keep right after crossing the river and follow it generally upstream for about 12 kilometres before again crossing to the east side of the Cariboo River (km 106.2). Then head left (northeast) on Cariboo Lake (8400) Road.

Cariboo Lake (8400) Road

8400 Road follows the east side of Cariboo Lake northward for about 16 kilometres before climbing east and then north up to the headwaters of the Little River. There is a

This giant steam shovel, located at Cedar Point Park, was manufactured in 1906 by Vulcan Iron Works, Toledo, Ohio

Forest recreation site on Cariboo Lake just east of

the mouth of Ladies Creek that can be a pleasant place to spend a fall day fishing, kayaking, or canoeing. If you try it in mid-July, be sure to take along plenty of bug repellent. Maeford Lake, near the 8440 marker (40 kilometres up 8400 Rd) is a pleasant break in the climb through the mountain valley.

Cameron Ridge Trail

So far, most of our diversions have been more backroads, but if you are feeling a little tired of seeing the world while shining up the seat of your pants, you could stretch your legs on the Cameron Ridge Trail. The junction is on the right (south) side of the road near the 8445 marker (km 153.5). According to my sources, it is 7.1 kilometres to a lookout that presents an excellent perspective of the Cariboo Mountains. On one mid-September afternoon we followed the old mining roads about 4.3 kilometres southeast to the alpine ridge and an excellent view of Mitchell Lake and the Cariboo Mountains to the east. It took us about 2.5 hours to climb the 260-metre elevation difference and 1.5 hours to return — with allowances for photography, birdwatching, and breathing.

The Cameron Ridge Trail provides access to the alpine of Cariboo Mountains Provincial Park.

Matthew River Road

The road crests near the 8447 marker (at an elevation of approximately 1,400 metres) before swinging northwest and beginning a gradual descent to the Matthew River.

It is always a good idea to look back at the way you came (just in case the road is blocked ahead) and a sign at a junction near km 172 says that we just came off the Cariboo River Forest Road. Ahead, the markers begin a countdown on 3100 Road — 3,160 to be exact — and 60 kilometres to Highway 26 at Barkerville. The junction is worth noting because a few kilometres down a side road to the right (east) is access to Matthew River and a series of spectacular waterfalls, one of which is at the outflow of Ghost Lake.

There is a narrow, rough road to a small campground at Ghost Lake (5.7 kilometres from 3100 Road). There is access to the lake and a network of trails along the embankment above Matthew River. If you are easily distracted by wild huckleberries and blueberries, check out the trail between mid-July and mid-August. This area is part of the new 113,469-hectare Cariboo Mountains Provincial Park, created in 1995 to span the gap between Wells Gray Park and Bowron Lakes Park.

The 150 Mile House to Barkerville backroad now swings west as it follows Matthew River down to the Cariboo River. The bridge over the Cariboo River near the 3140 marker (km 192.5) is, according to one source, a good place to launch a canoe for a leisurely trip to Cariboo Lake. After crossing the Cariboo River, this backroad (good, but dusty gravel throughout) climbs up Cunningham Creek to Cunningham Pass. The Whiskey Flats recreation site (km 217.2) is near the summit of the pass.

Antler Creek

3100 Road then follows Antler Creek northwest for about five kilometres before climbing up Pleasant Valley Creek and the last leg of the backroad to Barkerville. According to N.L. "Bill" Barlee, in *Gold Creeks and Ghost Towns*, John Rose, George Weaver, "Doc" Keithley, and a Canadian named McDonald discovered the riches of Antler Creek in the fall of 1860. After climbing over the mountain from Cariboo Lake, they found a section of a previously undiscovered creek with the bedrock showing through, and began panning the gravel. "Every panful was rich, one contained a staggering quarter pound of gold and even the leaner pans yielded enough metal to pay a day's wages."

When they returned to Keithley Creek to get supplies, the news leaked out and the rush was on. By the next spring, the entire creek was staked and some

There is a spectacular waterfall at the outlet of Ghost Lake plus several more water-falls along Matthew River as it descends to the valley floor.

Brian Blair offers unique yurt-shaped stone cabins, a campsite, and a restaurant at Comet Creek Resort, a few minutes north of the Ghost Lake junction.

of the richest claims were producing ". . . a staggering $1,000 in gold to the square foot." Note that this was at a time when the price of gold was in the $16 per troy ounce range.

Billy Barker's Diggings

The backroad to Barkerville ends at Highway 26 near Barkerville, some 80 kilometres east of Highway 97 at Quesnel, and 231.5 kilometres from 150 Mile House via our circuitous route. The distance is only 14 kilometres longer than the route via Highway 97 and Highway 26, but the travel time is twice as long. And it could be a lot more if you are easily distracted. See the *Cariboo Highway 97* and the *Highway 26: The Barkerville Road* chapters for details.

While we haven't followed the exact route of the gold seekers of the early 1860s, we have had an opportunity to see the terrain they faced in their search for the mother lode. Billy Barker struck paydirt 19 metres down on the bedrock of Williams Creek in 1862, setting off a rush that was to forever change the way of life in British Columbia's Cariboo. Fire destroyed Barkerville in 1868, but it was

A blacksmith demonstrates his trade at Barkerville Historic Town.

quickly rebuilt. Today Barkerville Historic Town is a living museum of life in the latter half of the nineteenth century — a part of our past worth visiting no matter which road you take.

Note: See the *Information Sources* chapter at the end of the book for contact information on the services mentioned here.

Backroad to Barkerville

GPS References for major points of interest
Ref: WGS 84 - Lat/Lon hddd.ddddd
Allow +/-100 metres due to data conversions

Wpt	Km	Description	Latitude	Longitude	Elev.
BV01	0	150 Mile House	N52.11505	W121.93602	752 m
BV02	4.5	Jct Horsefly and Likely Rds	N52.15278	W121.94956	904 m
BV03	46.5	Jct Beaver Valley Rd W	N52.47261	W121.85507	712 m
BV04	48.5	Jct Beaver Valley Rd E	N52.47843	W121.84298	717 m
BV05	52.8	Jct Gavin Lake Rd	N52.48924	W121.80323	947 m
BV06	67.5	Morehead Lake	N52.60222	W121.77890	916 m
BV07	79.0	Bullion Pit Rest Area	N52.61962	W121.62745	874 m
BV08	80.5	Jct Ditch Road	N52.61572	W121.60733	874 m
BV09	83.0	Quesnel River bridge	N52.61559	W121.57248	716 m
BV10	83.5	[0] Jct Rosette Lake Rd	N52.61658	W121.56418	756 m
BV11		[11] Quesnel Forks viewpoint	N52.66293	W121.66921	704 m
BV12		[12] Quesnel Forks	N52.66458	W121.67065	662 m
BV13	84.5	[0] Jct Cedar Creek Rd	N52.61324	W121.55114	796 m
BV14		[4.5] Cedar Point Park	N52.57784	W121.53648	746 m
BV15	93.7	Cariboo River bridge	N52.66290	W121.52827	707 m
BV16	105.5	Jct Cariboo Lake Rd	N52.72240	W121.45064	818 m
BV17	106.2	Cariboo River bridge	N52.71790	W121.44386	793 m
BV18	118.5	Jct Ladies Creek rec site	N52.78401	W121.31573	823 m
BV19	147.5	8440 marker at Maeford Lake	N52.79867	W120.98482	1,215 m
BV20	153.5	[0] Cameron Ridge trailhead	N52.82383	W120.91631	1,367 m
BV21		[4.3] Cameron Ridge views	N52.80973	W120.86909	1,630 m
BV22	172.0	[0] Jct to Ghost Lake	N52.93079	W120.96505	994 m
BV23		[4.2] Mathew River bridge	N52.92643	W120.91193	940 m
BV24		[5.7] Ghost Lake Campground	N52.92480	W120.89746	1,016 m
BV25	176.2	Comet Creek Resort	N52.95991	W121.00464	931 m
BV26	192.5	Cariboo River bridge	N52.94591	W121.17372	833 m
BV27	217.2	Whiskey Flats rec site	N53.00722	W121.39409	1,225 m
BV28	231.0	Start 3100 Rd	N53.08524	W121.50747	1,233 m
BV29	231.5	Jct Highway 26	N53.08354	W121.51043	1,249 m

CHAPTER 20

Cariboo Lake Country Backroad: Clearwater to 100 Mile House

STATISTICS

	Map see page 250.
Distance:	Approx. 117 km, Hwy 5 in Clearwater to Hwy 97 in 100 Mile House.
Travel time:	Three to four hours.
Conditions: ·	Some rough gravel sections; may be closed in winter.
Season:	June through October.
Topo maps:	Clearwater, BC 92 P/9.
(1:50,000)	Deka Lake, BC 92 P/10.
	Mahood Lake, BC 92 P/16.
	Canim Lake, BC 92 P/15.
	100 Mile House, BC 92 P/11.
Communities:	Clearwater and 100 Mile House.

The southeast Cariboo region offers one of the highest concentrations of fine trout lakes and back country campsites in the province. A close look at the Forest Service recreation maps for the Cariboo and the Clearwater area reveals at least 50 recreation sites with at least double that many lakes in the region between Clearwater and 100 Mile House.

Add the campgrounds in nearby Wells Gray Provincial Park and a wide variety of commercial fishing camps and resorts and you have an outdoor recreation paradise.

While we have covered the Bridge Lake area and Highway 24 elsewhere in this book, there is a lesser known backroad across the plateau from Clearwater to 100 Mile House that can keep you exploring and fishing for a week or more.

Camp 2 Road Starting Point

The initial access to the area has changed a bit over the last couple of decades. What was once the Clearwater Timber Products mill yard with an occasionally

Cariboo Lake Country Backroad

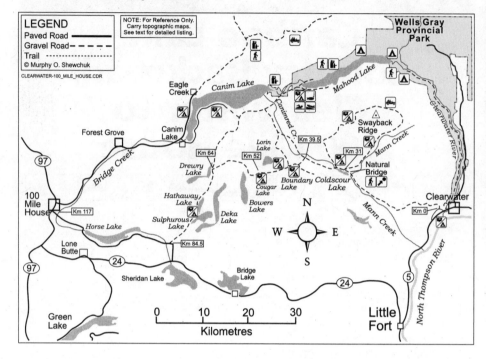

LEGEND
Paved Road ▬▬▬
Gravel Road ▬ ▬ ▬ ▬
Trail ┈┈┈┈┈┈┈┈
© Murphy O. Shewchuk

CLEARWATER-100_MILE_HOUSE.CDR

NOTE: For Reference Only.
Carry topographic maps.
See text for detailed listing.

locked gate is now a large open field with a road across it providing an open access to "them thar hills."

If you are starting off from Yellowhead Highway 5 near the Wells Gray Inn, take the Old North Thompson Highway northwest for about a kilometre to the bridge across the Clearwater River and Camp 2 Road. This will be our reference point for this backroad adventure, but before you head out, double-check your supplies and top up your larder and fuel tank at the nearby Brookfield Shopping Centre.

After you've done your bit to support the local economy, head northwest on Camp 2 Road for under a kilometre to another junction. The road to the right heads to the Clearwater airport and the Clearwater River. Take the road to the left (west) across the old mill yard for kilometre to the km 0 start of the Clearwater – 100 Mile House Forest Service Road. This road seems to go under a variety of names including Road 2, but if the roadside signs also say Star Lake Resort, there is a reasonably good chance you aren't lost yet.

Westward and Upward

The wide, dusty gravel road leads westward and upward, leaving Clearwater, at an elevation of 406 metres, far below. Before long, each switchback in the road offers a newer and better view of the North Thompson Valley and the landmark slopes

At an elevation of about 1,115 metres, Coldscaur Lake remains cool and clear throughout most of the summer.

of Raft Mountain. By km 11 (9 kilometres on the roadside markers), the road reaches 1,070 metres in elevation and the Star Lake Resort junction, and begins heading northwest up Mann Creek, leaving the North Thompson Valley behind.

Natural Bridge Trail

Several side roads beckon, but if you are heading for the plateau, follow Road 2 to the southeast end of Coldscaur Lake (km 29 or 27 kilometres on the roadside markers). There is a small recreation site at this end of the lake, and on the north side of the road a short trail leads to a natural rock bridge across Mann Creek. On one late-summer trip, we picked huckleberries along the trail. On a mid-October trip, we had the privilege of watching a three-toed woodpecker and a Franklin's grouse feeding among the pines.

*Mann Creek has worn a path through the ancient lava layers, creating
a natural rock bridge.*

Recreational Hideaways

Coldscaur Lake has several recreational hideaways, with the largest at the north-west end. This recreation site is far enough off the main road to avoid the dusty fallout from logging truck traffic. It is also equipped with a boat launch site and enough space to offer a little privacy.

Although Mann Creek and the natural stone bridge are only a few minutes walk from Coldscaur Lake, a rocky knoll separates the two, and Coldscaur drains westward through a marsh and into Canimred Creek. The area north of Coldscaur Lake is also a maze of used and disused logging roads. Road 6 loops north from the west end of the lake, tracking a wide oval around 1,800-metre-high Swayback Ridge before returning to Road 2 near the south end of the lake. There are at least a dozen Forest Service recreation sites accessible from this loop — and probably a hundred more places you could safely pull over for the night.

Go West

If 100 Mile House is your destination, cross Canimred Creek at the northwest end of Coldscaur Lake and continue west on an older, slightly less used road. The December 1985 version of the Clearwater Forest Service recreational map shows this as Road 1, but more recent on-site signs called it Road 2. (This is where a good GPS or compass and up-to-date topographic maps help keep you on track.) The next major junction is at km 39.5 (37.5 kilometres on the roadside markers) where Road 2 (formerly Road 271) swings north, following Canimred Creek to the Mahood Lake Road near the community of

A three-toed woodpecker checks out a potential nest cavity.

Muskrats are occasionally seen creating a wake across the small lakes or building their "pushups" in the marshes.

Mahood Falls. It's about 17 kilometres to the Mahood Lake Road via this route, and another 11 kilometres northeast to the Wells Gray Provincial Park campground on Mahood Lake. Aside from being a bit shorter route to Mahood Lake Road than the road to the west, it is a rutted, often muddy route with few other redeeming features.

Boundary Lake

Keep left at km 39.5 and follow Road 7 southwest for a little over three kilometres to another junction; then swing right and down through the trees to Boundary Lake. The boundary here may refer to the dividing line between the Lillooet Land District and the Kamloops Division of the Yale Land District, but it was also the dividing line between the old Clearwater and Cariboo Forest Service recreation site maps. Neither map proved very helpful in this "no man's land" on our first trip through the area so we followed our noses down a narrow road for about two kilometres until we swung left (west) on Bowers Lake – Canim Forest Service Road.

This wider, better maintained road would, as we soon discovered, take us in the correct direction.

Cougar Lake

Bowers Lake – Canim Forest Service Road (also known as 8200 Rd) continues west across the plateau, passing several small lakes, including Cougar Lake (km 51.5), equipped with a camping area and boat launch site. The road then swings north of Bowers Lake, passing the trailhead of the three-kilometre trail into Donnelly Lake. After crossing Jim Creek (km 56.5), continue westward on the forest road, skirting to the north of Rat Lake (km 59). The marshes at either end of this pretty little lake suggest that muskrats may have been the source of the name. Regardless of the source, on one trip the afternoon sun and the beautiful fall colours quickly dispelled any negative connotations and we spent a pleasant hour testing the waters before continuing westward to Mahood Lake Road at km 64.

Mahood Lake or 100 Mile House?

Bowers Lake Road joins Mahood Lake Road at Drewry Lake, and the glimpses of the lake through the aspen can make a pretty picture. It is also decision time.

While off the direct Clearwater – 100 Mile House route, a 32-kilometre detour northeast to Mahood Lake can be well worth your time. On the western leg of Wells Gray Provincial Park, 20-kilometre-long Mahood Lake has a spacious, well-designed park campground with an excellent beach. In addition to water activities, there are hiking trails into nearby Deception Falls on Deception Creek and Canim Falls on the Canim River.

Canim Lake South Road, which joins the Mahood Lake Road about 17 kilometres west of Mahood Lake, offers an alternate and very scenic route to 100 Mile House. It generally parallels the south shore of Canim Lake for 26 kilometres. It then follows Bridge Creek and Canim Lake Road upstream another 40 kilometres to 100 Mile House. There are several seasonal and year-round resorts on Canim Lake that offer cabins and camping facilities.

Lakeside Resorts

If you find the area park campgrounds or forest recreation sites a little too rustic for your liking (or it is time for a warm shower), you may want to time your travels to include a stay at one of the several lakeside resorts in the area. In addition to nearby Hathaway Lake, there are resorts complete with cabins and campgrounds at Sulphurous, Deka, and Horse lakes. Several of these resorts are open year-round to serve the snowmobiler, skier, and ice fishing enthusiast as well.

Mahood Lake Road becomes Horse Lake Road at a junction north of Sheridan Lake. Here you can take a short detour south to Highway 24 and then continue west through Lone Butte to Highway 97 at 93 Mile. Another option is to follow the south shore of Horse Lake and Bridge Creek to Highway 97 at 100 Mile House.

Go Prepared

Back country exploring, such as the east section of this route, requires extensive preparation. Check your vehicle and supplies carefully before heading out. Make sure you are carrying enough fuel to get to your destination *and* back — you may find a locked gate or a bridge out at the most inopportune location. If you are travelling early in the year or after a recent storm, a good saw and axe may also save you a lot of extra driving. Topographic maps and a GPS or compass are also essential. The Forest Service Recreation Site maps are useful if you can find them, but are often incomplete. The BC Ministry of Tourism, Sport and the Arts has taken over administration of the recreation sites and has recently launched an on-line site guide and interactive mapping system (http://www.tsa.gov.bc.ca/sites_trails/) that can help with your preparation.

Note: See the *Information Sources* chapter at the end of the book for contact information on the services mentioned here.

GPS References for major points of interest
Ref: WGS 84 - Lat/Lon hddd.ddddd
Allow +/-100 metres due to data conversions

Wpt	Km	Description	Latitude	Longitude
CL01	0	Camp 2 Rd and Old North Thompson Hwy	N51.64936	W120.06836
CL02	0.8	Former sawmill entrance	N51.65351	W120.07542
CL03	2.0	OK marker – Brookfield Creek	N51.65445	W120.08998
CL04	10.0	Jct Lola Lake to left	N51.65950	W120.16447
CL05	11.0	Jct Star Lake Resort	N51.65644	W120.17165
CL06	29.0	Coldscaur Lake East	N51.71411	W120.37560
CL07	31.5	Coldscaur Lake West	N51.72562	W120.40464
CL08	32.0	Canimred Creek	N51.72569	W120.41083
CL09	39.5	Jct North to Mahood Lake Rd	N51.74808	W120.50961
CL10	42.7	Jct to Boundary Lake	N51.73334	W120.54633
CL11	43.5	Boundary Lake rec site	N51.72937	W120.55580
CL12	44.5	Jct go left	N51.72899	W120.56846
CL13	45.5	Lake and marshes to left	N51.72526	W120.57944
CL14	51.0	Cougar Lake to left	N51.71569	W120.64602
CL15	52.0	Cougar Lake rec site	N51.71378	W120.66042
CL16	52.5	Jct Cougar Creek Rd	N51.71416	W120.67019
CL17	55.0	Donnelly Lake Trail	N51.72989	W120.68572
CL18	57.0	Jim Creek	N51.73738	W120.70747
CL19	59.0	8205 Marker – Rat Lake	N51.73700	W120.73223
CL20	64.0	Jct Mahood Lake Rd	N51.72644	W120.79256
CL21	75.0	Hathaway Lake Resort	N51.64576	W120.84012
CL22	75.5	Suphurous Lake Resort	N51.63926	W120.84066
CL23	84.5	Jct Horse Lake Rd and Mahood Lake Rd	N51.58561	W120.92648
CL24	107.5	Bridge Creek outlet of Horse Lake	N51.60385	W121.19797
CL25	116.5	Jct Horse Lake Rd and Hwy 97	N51.63775	W121.29542

West of the Fraser River: The South Chilcotin Connection

Despite the fact that the Bridge River Valley is less than 200 kilometres from downtown Vancouver, it has only recently come out of isolation, and even then only to a limited extent. The rugged Coast Mountains and the narrow Bridge River canyons have served to create a barrier to all but the most determined traveller.

First Nations Hunting (and Battle) Ground

According to the preamble in *Bridge River Gold*, the First Nations peoples knew the valley as the "Skumakum" or "Land of Plenty." Members of the Fountain,

The Bridge Glacier at the headwaters of the Bridge River.

A 991 troy ounce gold brick at Bralorne, circa 1970.
Photo courtesy of Murphy Shewchuk, Senior.

Fraser River, Lake, and Pemberton bands of the Lillooet Indians hunted in the country of the Upper Bridge River. The area near the headwaters of Tyaughton Creek, a tributary of the Bridge, was also known as the place of "Many Roots" and was noted for its abundance of roots and game. The riches of the region didn't go unnoticed by neighboring First Nations peoples. It was also occasionally the battleground between the Chilcotin and Lillooet peoples.

The challenging terrain, coupled with heavy winter snowfall and limited salmon fishing, discouraged the First Nations peoples from setting up their winter homes or kekuli houses much beyond the mouth of the Yalakom River, some 25 kilometres northwest of the Fraser River and the present community of Lillooet.

Gold in the Lower Bridge River

The Lillooet Native peoples initially resisted the first miners of the 1858 gold rush, but by that November, a report in the Victoria *Gazette* indicated. "There are about two hundred men now on this river working with various results, – a man making $20 or $30 one day and hardly as many cents the next." By the following April, the number of miners were down to one hundred, but the Bridge River made the Victoria *Gazette*'s pages because of a three-ounce gold nugget found in a former river channel.

West of the Fraser River

The placer miners moved north up the Fraser River and into the Cariboo, leaving the Bridge River to a few persistent miners and big game hunters.

Hardrock Miners

As the nineteenth century drew to a close, hardrock miners began to explore the upper Bridge River and uncover traces of gold in the quartz veins that permeated the slopes of Mount Fergusson. This was an entirely different type of mining from panning and sluicing the Cariboo creeks. It required drills and blasting powder and equipment to grind the quartz to a fine dust so that the gold could be released.

The inhospitable terrain resisted the new miners as much as it had the First Nations peoples and placer miners. It took decades to turn the claims into the viable mining communities of Bralorne and Pioneer.

Early Trails and Roads

One of the earliest routes into the upper Bridge River Valley was via a trail from Anderson Lake through McGillivray Pass. In later years a road was built over Mission Mountain from Shalalth on Seton Lake. Both of these routes required a connection to the Pacific Great Eastern Railway to get equipment, supplies, and people into the valley.

It wasn't until the mid-1950s that a direct road connection was made to Lillooet, and several more decades before a summer road was built to Pemberton.

The Adventure Awaits

While the "Moha Road" from Lillooet into the valley has improved significantly since it opened in 1955, there is still a sense of isolation and adventure in visiting the area.

The snow-covered peaks beckon winter adventurers and the clear blue lakes lure fishing enthusiasts. Wilderness backroads and trails are there to explore.

The adventure is awaiting those who plan ahead and go prepared.

CHAPTER 21

Bridge River Gold: Lillooet — Gold Bridge — Bralorne

STATISTICS

	Map see page 262.
Distance:	120 km, Lillooet to Bralorne.
Elev. Gain:	Approximately 880 metres.
Travel Time:	Three to four hours.
Condition:	Approximately 80% paved or seal-coated; remainder good gravel.
Season:	Maintained year-round.
Topo Maps:	Lillooet, BC 92 I/12.
(1:50,000)	Pavilion, BC 92 I/13.
	Bridge River, BC 92 J/16.
	Bralorne, BC 92 J/15.
	Birkenhead Lake, BC 92 J/10.
Communities:	Lillooet, Gold Bridge, and Bralorne.

The Bridge River Valley, west of Lillooet, has lived several lives; in fact, it is well on the way to matching the nine lives of the proverbial cat. Hard rock miners of the first half of the twentieth century remember it for the rich quartz gold mines, with Bralorne and Pioneer being the most notable. Construction workers of the 1950s and 1960s know the Bridge River as the energy source of British Columbia's first giant hydro-electric development. Today, recreationists visit the Bridge River Valley for its fishing, hunting, rockhounding, and rugged mountain beauty. Tomorrow, if the persistent rumors are correct, the hard rock miners could move back in to reactivate the underground gold workings of Bralorne, dormant since 1971.

The once-mighty Bridge River flows out of the foot of the Bridge Glacier in the heart of British Columbia's Coast Mountains about 50 kilometres due west of Gold Bridge and 170 kilometres due north of Vancouver. In its original state, the Bridge River carried its glacial silt two hundred meandering kilometres eastward before emptying into the muddy Fraser River north of Lillooet.

Bridge River Gold

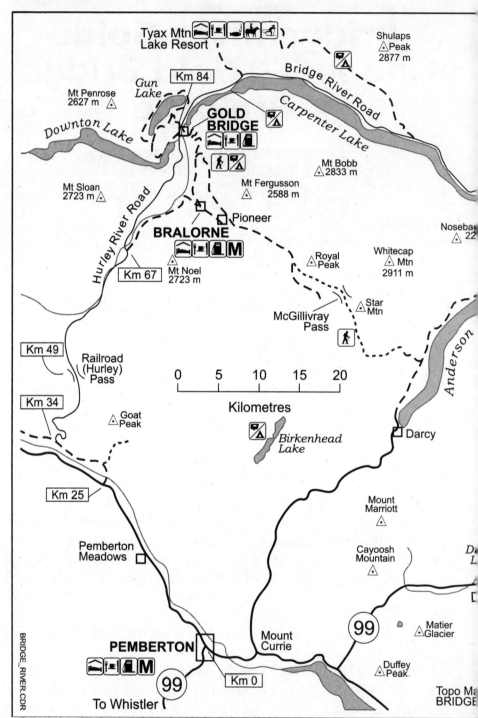

NOTE: For Reference Only.
Carry topographic maps.
See text for detailed listing.

MOHA

Bridge River

Terzaghi
Dam

Mission Ridge

Shalalth

Seton Lake

LILLOOET

12

99

To Cache Creek

To Lytton

N

W — E

S

LEGEND
Paved Road ━━━━━
Gravel Road ─ ─ ─ ─ ─
Trail ·······················
© Murphy O. Shewchuk

Today, much of the Bridge River flows through the turbines of hydroelectric plants at Lajoie (Gold Bridge), Shalalth, and Seton (Lillooet) before emptying into the Fraser River a short distance south of Lillooet. The Terzaghi (Mission) Dam diverted the river through Mission Mountain to Shalalth and British Columbia's first large-scale hydroelectric development. Now the lower Bridge River is a mere trickle compared to its original strength.

However, don't become complacent! BC Hydro can, without warning, open the gates of the Terzaghi Dam and the Bridge River can again become a torrent.

The eastern access into the Bridge River Valley follows the west side of the Fraser River north from Lillooet and then west up the Bridge River. (The valley is also accessible from Shalalth and from Pemberton via the Hurley Road during the summer months.)

Highway 99 Starting Point

While some of the kilometre signs on the Bridge River Road (Road 40) refer to downtown Lillooet, the zero reference for the regular kilometre markers is the junction of Highway 99 near the west end of the Bridge of the 23 Camels. The road quickly climbs up to Lillooet's main level and the BC Railway (CNR) station. After crossing the tracks, the route follows Main Street north to the Mile 0 Cairn and the Lillooet Museum before continuing northeast to the Old Mill Plaza shopping centre on the northern outskirts of Lillooet. (The Old Mill Plaza area was once a sawmill site.)

The Mile 0 Cairn in downtown Lillooet is the symbolic start of the original trail to the Cariboo goldfields.

The original Lillooet-Lytton road crossed the BC Railway tracks near here and wound down the hill to a suspension bridge across the Fraser River. The "Old Bridge" was built in 1913 to replace a winch ferry powered by the river current that had been in use since 1860. While vehicle traffic is no longer permitted on the old suspension bridge, it has been restored and is still well worth a visit.

Historic Bridge

The Bridge River Road (also known as Road 40, Moha Road, or Lillooet-Pioneer Road) winds along the bench for several kilometres before descending to the west bank of the Fraser River and continuing north to km 9 and a narrow wooden bridge across the mouth of the Bridge River gorge. According to Commander R.C. Mayne, R.N., who visited the region in 1859, the Bridge River got its English name from a Native bridge near its mouth. During the gold rush, two enterprising individuals pulled down the old bridge and constructed a new one across the canyon, charging the miners a 25 cent toll.

First Nations fishing enthusiasts consider the confluence of the Bridge and Fraser rivers a favoured salmon fishing location in late summer and fall. The Bridge River cuts a deep, narrow canyon through Bridge River Indian Reserve. The upper boundaries of the reserve and nineteenth century placer gold mining activity end in the Horseshoe Canyon, near where the Yalakom River flows into the bridge, 32 kilometres east of Lillooet.

The West Pavilion Forest Service Road, a hundred metres west of the bridge, provides access to the benches west of the Fraser and north of Lillooet. After the bridge, the road climbs steadily until it reaches the narrow benches high above the Bridge River.

Impervious Clay

The core of the Terzaghi Dam is made up of impervious clay, some of which was hauled 35 kilometres to the dam from a site near km 15.5 in large Euclid trucks. An ordinary car was no match for these machines and during dam construction, more than one vehicle lost its top in a head-on collision with a loaded "Euc."

Although most of the road to Gold Bridge is paved or seal-coated, the pavement initially ends near the 20 km marker. This section of the road has been carved out of the rock bluffs with still more carving needed to be done. The sign "Extreme dust — use headlights" should be ample warning. Slow down and use extreme caution. Logging trucks use this road and driving "blind" can mean a very short trip — straight down.

Horseshoe Canyon

Antoine Creek, near km 30, has always served as a landmark to indicate that the wildest section of the lower Bridge River canyon is almost over and that it is only a few hundred metres to the Horseshoe Canyon viewpoint. Although the mountainside supports more timber than the semi-desert in the vicinity of Lillooet, the roadside growth still consists largely of Saskatoon bushes, scattered ponderosa pine, and a few interior Douglas fir — none of which do much to impede the spectacular view.

Near km 31, the Bridge River cuts a wide bend around a rock outcropping, creating a deep Horseshoe Canyon. There is room to pull off the road and enjoy the

Bridge River Gold

view near the east end of the horseshoe. There is also a rough trail leading down to abandoned gold mining equipment on the canyon floor. Gold panners sometimes try their luck in the canyon stream bed, but a good 4x4 and a shovel are necessary to get back up to the main road.

Yalakom River

The road circles the canyon, joining the Yalakom River Road about two kilometres farther along. The brave (or foolhardy), equipped with a 4x4, winch, lots of fuel, and at least one friend with a similarly equipped vehicle, can follow the Yalakom River upstream, searching for challenging backroads and jade boulders. The route once led over Poison Mountain and China Head Mountain to the Fraser River at the Big Bar Ferry, but the alpine section has recently been closed to vehicles.

The Bridge River Road continues to the left at the junction and descends to the mouth of the Yalakom, just upstream from the Horseshoe Canyon. A search among the roadside brush may reveal a few ancient reminders of the community of Moha, once the site of a few homes and a restaurant, most of which disappeared around 1960, with the widening of what was originally christened the Moha Road.

Moha Road

From the 1920s to the mid 1950s, a flatcar trip from Lillooet to Shalalth and a hair-raising drive over Mission Mountain was the only way to take a vehicle into the Bridge River Valley. In the fall of 1954, local workers began the construction of the "Moha Road" using plenty of blasting powder, perseverance, and equipment borrowed from Bralorne and Pioneer mines. On October 15, 1955, BC MLA Phil Gaglardi officially opened the road, ending dependency on the PGE Railway (now BC Rail/CNR) for passenger and freight transportation.

Rockhounds and river rats still find the occasional gold flake or pebble of jade in the river gravel near the Bridge and Yalakom confluence. Don't be a claim jumper as there are several small placer operations working the gravel of the Bridge River.

Hell Creek

Upstream from the Yalakom, the Bridge River becomes a mere trickle. The reason will be obvious 17 kilometres farther along, when the massive earth-fill Terzaghi Dam becomes visible.

The clear, ice cold water of Hell Creek, near km 39, makes it an excellent spot

The Terzaghi Dam, completed in the early 1960s, was part of British Columbia's first major hydroelectric development. Originally known as the Mission Dam, it was renamed the Terzaghi Dam in 1965 to honor Karl von Terzaghi, the civil engineer whose knowledge of the science of soil mechanics contributed to the design of the dam.

to stop and fill the water jug. A short scramble up the creek bed reveals the remains of a narrow bridge that was once part of the packhorse trail into the valley. Beyond Hell Creek, a section of the road resembles a tunnel with one side missing.

Erosion at Work

The canyon walls are scoured by spring waterfalls, most of which leave little more than a dry, white scar by midsummer. One such scar is far more visible. A few years after the construction of the Terzaghi Dam was completed, a creek on the slopes of Mission Mountain, near km 45, ran wild during a rainstorm, sluicing thousands of tonnes of gravel and debris down into the valley. Had it happened earlier, it would have buried men and equipment in the construction camp near the base of the dam.

Terzaghi Dam

A gravel road across the crest of the Terzaghi Dam (km 50) leads over Mission Mountain to Shalalth and Seton Portage. Access to Carpenter Lake is provided at several locations on the south shore near the dam. In the summer, fishing enthusiasts troll for kokanee, rainbow trout, and Dolly Varden char. Upstream of the 55-metre-high, 365-metre-wide dam, concrete towers mark the gates of two four-kilometre-long tunnels that divert the Bridge River through Mission Mountain to turbines at Shalalth on Seton Lake.

500,000 Horsepower

The vast hydroelectric potential of the Bridge River was first recognized in 1912. Work began in 1927, and by 1960 dams were completed at Lajoie, near Gold Bridge, and at the foot of Mission Mountain. Powerhouses were built at Lajoie, Shalalth on Seton Lake, and Lillooet at the Fraser River. The water of the Bridge River was used three times to generate a total of 500 megawatts of electricity. In the process, two new lakes were created. Lake Downton, behind Lajoie Dam, is 26 kilometres long. During high water, Carpenter Lake, behind Terzaghi Dam, stretches 55 kilometres to Gold Bridge.

The road into the Bridge River Valley continues west along the north shore of Carpenter Lake. Up until the completion of the Terzaghi Dam in the early 1960s, the road was located on the valley floor and the vale of cedars at Cedarvale Creek (km 65) and waterfall at Fall Creek (km 66.6) were significant landmarks. The cedars are gone and the waterfall is hidden by a bridge.

Marshall Lake

Marshall Lake Road West, a good gravel forest access road, climbs to the northwest at km 70.5, providing access to Carol Lake, Marshall Lake, and the Shulaps Mountain Range. There are Forest Service recreation sites on Carol Lake and Marshall Lake. Numerous backroads and trails lead northwest of Marshall Lake into the South Chilcotin Mountains. Unfortunately detailed descriptions are beyond the scope of this book, but Trail Ventures BC has produced an excellent GPS based map of the area. See the *Information Sources* section at the end of the book for details.

One kilometre farther up the Bridge River Valley, Marshall Creek Falls cascades off the Shulaps Range, making its final plunge into a pool before flowing into Carpenter Lake. In low water, a rough trail leads to the foot of the falls. When the reservoir is full, the falls drops directly into the lake.

The Bridge River Road continues along the lakeshore, crossing several creeks

Marshall Creek Falls.

BC Hydro maintains a recreation site near Gun Creek.

with limited access for self-contained camping before reaching Tyaughton Lake Road (km 94). From the junction, there is a good gravel road to Tyaughton Lake (locally known as "Tyax") and the Tyax Mountain Lake Resort. If good food, accommodations and fishing in a spectacular mountain setting is on the agenda, it's well worth the 10-kilometre detour.

Minto Gold Mine

If self-contained camping fits your plans better, a small, accessible BC Hydro recreation site near the mouth of Gun Creek (km 98) could serve as a place to relax and try a little stream fishing. The mining community of Minto was also once near here. It began in 1933 and became the third-largest-producing gold mine in the valley, after Pioneer and Bralorne. The vein petered out and Minto City declined until it was briefly revived in 1942 as a centre for Japanese displaced from the coastal cities and towns during World War II.

Gun Creek flooded in 1950, inundating part of the town. By 1960, all of the buildings had been removed or demolished prior to the flooding of Carpenter Lake Reservoir.

Gold Bridge Bridge

A bridge across the Bridge River at Gold Bridge (try saying that one fast) near km 105 serves as a landmark for a major junction. The road following Carpenter Lake has been gradually swinging from a westerly direction to a southerly direction. Now, at the bridge, there is a choice of three directions. Straight ahead and to the left at the crest of the first short hill is the start of the summer-access Hurley River Road to Pemberton. Keep straight ahead and to the right at the crest, and the Lajoie Dam and powerhouse looms ahead.

Just before the dam, the road forks again. The road to the right climbs steadily for eight kilometres until it reaches Lajoie (Little Gun) Lake and Gun Lake, another kilometre farther. These two lakes, the latter 6.6 kilometres long, have been the local water playground for decades. There are private cabins on Little Gun Lake plus cabins and camping on Gun Lake.

The road to the left crosses the Bridge River just downstream from the confluence of the Bridge and Hurley rivers and leads into the community of Gold Bridge. Although the mines have closed, Gold Bridge is still the valley, commercial centre, with accommodations, supplies, and fuel available. Liquor and beer are also available through the grocery store. There are also several guide/outfitters in the area that can take you off the beaten track, winter or summer. It's best to contact the Bridge River Valley Economic Development Society for up-to-date information.

With Gold Bridge as a new km 0 reference, the winding road climbs steeply, passing the tiny settlement of Brexton at four kilometres and leveling off a kilometre or so later near the Kingdom Lake Forest Road after having climbed over 350 metres.

Bridge River Gold

The "Bridge River Gold" stop-of-interest sign, on a wide spot in the narrow road near km 6, gives a fleeting glimpse of the value of the valley's minerals to the British Columbia economy. Gold was once the lifeblood of the Bridge River Valley. The mining towns of Bralorne and Pioneer produced four million troy ounces of gold before shutting down in the early 1970s. Although Bralorne Gold Mines Ltd. continues mining exploration with the intent to re-open the mines, at the time of writing, Bralorne (km 12) was still a recreation community, relying on logging, mining exploration, and the attractions of the Coast Mountains for its life.

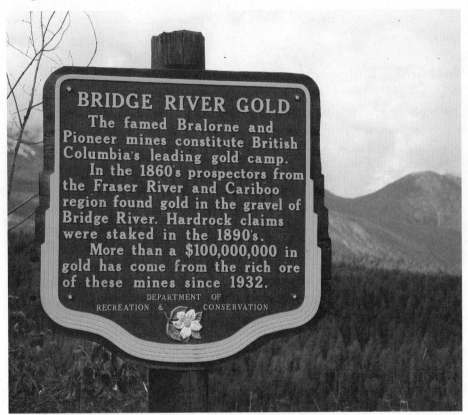

Prospectors first discovered gold in the gravel of the Bridge River, but by 1900, their interest had shifted to the underground quartz veins.

Disappearing Townsites

The narrow road winds through Bralorne, past the old mine office (now a motel) and many refurbished homes. If you are interested in a glimpse of Bridge River Valley history, turn right on Lorne Street to the community ballpark and Bralorne Pioneer Museum. The museum, open from late May until late September, is housed in what was once Bralorne Consolidated High School's industrial arts shop. (I have fond memories of my late 1950s woodworking classes in that shop.)

In addition to the displays at the museum, Lewis Green's book, *The Great Years: Gold Mining in the Bridge River Valley*, published in 2000, provides a wealth of information on the valley history.

A short drive past Bralorne is the townsite of Bradian. While a number of the homes have been refurbished, several rows of once-neat homes stand among the weeds, waiting for the miners to return or a heavy winter snowfall to bring them crashing to the ground. It's another couple of kilometres to the end of the road at

Pioneer Mine, once a major gold producer and now a jumbled wreckage of corrugated steel sheets and timber.

Pioneer Mine was my home from 1955 to 1961. I lived in several of the townsites that have now reverted to nature, delivered the *Vancouver Province* newspaper to the miners who lived in the homes and bunkhouses, and spent my last school summer holidays working in the mill that lies in ruins. Many pleasant weekends were spent hiking in the nearby mountains, fishing in the lakes, and following the old mining roads up Cadwallader Creek to McGillivray Pass.

The remnants of a mine road winds through the mill debris to a dead end at a decaying bridge across Cadwallader Creek. Straight ahead was the Circle Townsite, with the remains of a few foundations, including the mine manager's house. Although my parent's house is gone, my sister's "fort" — a small outbuilding — still stands against the mountainside on the northeast side of the Circle Townsite. Across the bridge was the Pioneer cookhouse, bunkhouses, church, and

Pioneer Mine in 1964. Little remains of the buildings that made up the core of the surface operation. © *1964 Murphy Shewchuk.*

Noel Lake, known as Fairy Lake in the 1950s, was later named after Arthur and Delina Noel, key Bridge River Valley prospectors and promoters in the late 1890s and early 1900s.

hospital. Farther south, the old road along the valley floor continued past several more townsites. At last check, it was virtually impassable due to mud slides and washouts.

Kingdom Lake Forest Road

The old road along the valley floor is now closed due to mud slides and washouts, but a newer 25-kilometre-long logging road, the Kingdom Lake Forest Road, continues past several fine fishing lakes to within a kilometre or two of 1880-metre McGillivray Pass.

With the junction north of the "Bridge River Gold" stop-of-interest sign as km 0, look for a junction to the Kingdom Lake recreation site near km 5. The campground and lake are a short drive off the road. At the time of writing, it was a free, user-maintained site adjacent to the lake. Campers are encouraged to be responsible and respect the environment by keeping the sites in an unspoiled condition for others to enjoy. There is also a one-kilometre trail from the main campsite to a small picnic site at nearby Noel Lake.

There are several narrow side roads beyond the turnoff to the Kingdom Lake recreation site. With a little perseverance and a narrow 4x4 vehicle, you may be able to find Mead Lake to the east or the backroad down to Bradian Townsite. There are also old, overgrown roads to the Pioneer Mine "Top Townsite" between km 9 and km 10. The former PE Mine townsite, marked by encroaching timber and decaying bunkhouses, is near the 11 K marker.

There is a rough recreation site at Hawthorne Creek (km 15) and a covered footbridge across Cadwallader Creek just past the Hawthorne Creek Bridge. The footbridge marks the start of the Chism Creek Trail into what we knew as the Paymaster Peaks when I was a teenager.

McGillivray Pass Trail

A difficult-to-find trail starts near Piebiter Creek (19 km) and winds up Standard Creek to the pass before continuing down McGillivray Creek to Anderson Lake,

Kingdom Lake Forest Road ends near the foot of Mount Weinhold.

Bridge River Gold

a short distance northeast of D'Arcy on the BC Rail (CNR) line. The historic McGillivray Pass Trail was an important route into the valley in the late 1800s and early 1900s. It is now used as an access route to a fine, open ski area in the vicinity of the pass. Note that the trail north of the Piebiter Creek bridge climbs up to what was once Mrs. Delina Noel's tungsten mining claim.

End of the Road
In late 2006, the passable logging road ended near km 24 in a log landing at the foot of Mount Weinhold. Skid roads continued up some of the side valleys, and the open slopes had an abundance of huckleberry bushes. There were also signs that bears were enjoying the berries.

GPS References for major points of interest
Ref: WGS 84 - Lat/Lon hddd.ddddd
Allow +/-100 metres due to data conversions

Wpt	Km	Description	Latitude	Longitude	Elev.
BR01	0	Hwy 99 Jct to Lillooet	N50.68067	W121.93346	204 m
BR02	1.5	Lillooet Mile 0 Cairn	N50.69126	W121.93754	253 m
BR03	2.8	Old Mill Plaza	N50.70212	W121.92567	252 m
BR04	8.7	Bridge River bridge	N50.75257	W121.93579	218 m
BR05	30	Antoine Creek	N50.85160	W122.14124	420 m
BR06	31	Horseshoe Bend viewpoint	N50.85836	W122.15268	490 m
BR07	33	Yalakom Rd	N50.86424	W122.16339	531 m
BR08	34.6	Yalakom River bridge	N50.86418	W122.17124	437 m
BR09	50	Terzaghi Dam and Mission Mtn Rd	N50.78987	W122.22416	637 m
BR10	66.6	Falls Creek	N50.80486	W122.39019	700 m
BR11	70	Jones Creek	N50.84202	W122.44108	670 m
BR12	72	Marshall Creek Falls	N50.84159	W122.46041	656 m
BR13	94	Tyaughton Lake Rd	N50.90740	W122.73221	661 m
BR15	98	BC Hydro Gun Creek rec area	N50.89551	W122.77331	662 m
BR16	105	Gold Bridge Jct	N50.85157	W122.84736	664 m
BR17	106	Gold Bridge	N50.85113	W122.83744	704 m
BR18	110	Brexton	N50.83566	W122.82497	976 m
BR19	112	Kingdom Lake FS Rd	N50.82261	W122.82526	1,061 m
BR20	112.5	Bridge River gold plaque	N50.81652	W122.82369	1,063 m
BR21	117	Bralorne	N50.77854	W122.81964	1,001 m
BR22	118	Bralorne Museum	N50.77144	W122.80696	1,065 m
BR23	119	Bradian	N50.77042	W122.80115	1,128 m
BR24	121	Pioneer Mine	N50.75877	W122.77773	1,159 m

Note: See the *Information Sources* chapter at the end of the book for contact information on the services mentioned here.

Wpt	Km	Description	Latitude	Longitude	Elev.
		GPS References for major points of interest **Ref: WGS 84 - Lat/Lon hddd.ddddd** **Allow +/-100 metres due to data conversions**			
BR25	0	Kingdom Lake FS Rd	N50.82261	W122.82526	1,061 m
BR26	4.7	Jct to Kingdom Lake	N50.80095	W122.80217	1,309 m
BR27		Kingdom Lake rec site	N50.80293	W122.79919	1,310 m
BR28		Noel Lake rec site	N50.80903	W122.79707	1,300 m
BR29	5.1	Trail to Mead Lake	N50.79593	W122.80155	1,322 m
BR30	9.0	Trails to Holland Mine and Pioneer	N50.76518	W122.77845	1,341 m
BR31	10.0	10K marker – Trail to Pioneer	N50.75881	W122.76823	1,273 m
BR32	11	P.E. Townsite	N50.75359	W122.75784	1,235 m
BR33	11.5	Kingdom – Crazy Creek Branch Rd	N50.75236	W122.75289	1,230 m
BR34	15	15K marker – Chism Creek Trail	N50.74138	W122.70749	1,277 m
BR35	16.5	Kingdom – Chism Bridge Rd	N50.73445	W122.69121	1,289 m
BR36	19	19K marker – Piebiter Creek Rd	N50.71832	W122.65896	1,313 m
BR37	23.5	End of road	N50.67993	W122.64018	1,453 m

*The overflow area of BC Hydro recreation site near the outlet of Seton Lake.
It can be a busy place on a summer evening.*

CHAPTER 22

Coast Mountain Circle Tour: Lillooet — Pemberton — Gold Bridge — Lillooet

STATISTICS

	Map see page 262.
Distance:	100 km, Lillooet to Pemberton.
	85 km, Pemberton to Gold Bridge.
	105 km, Gold Bridge to Lillooet.
Travel Time:	One to two days.
Condition:	Paved Lillooet to Pemberton.
	Mostly gravel, Pemberton to Lillooet.
Season:	Hurley (Railroad) Pass may be closed in winter.
Topo Maps:	Lillooet, BC 92 I/12.
(1:50,000)	Shalalth, BC 92 J/9.
	Duffey Lake, BC 92 J/8.
	Pemberton, BC 92 J/7.
	Birkenhead Lake, BC 92 J/10.
	North Creek, BC 92 J/11.
	Bralorne, BC 92 J/15.
	Bridge River, BC 92 J/16.
	Pavilion, BC 92 I/13.
Communities:	Lillooet, Pemberton, Gold Bridge, Bralorne.

If you are looking for a backroad adventure that you can do as a circle tour starting in a couple of different locations, or do in sections depending on your other travel plans, this loop trip through the Coast Mountains should certainly fit the bill.

You can start in Lillooet and do the Duffey Lake section to Pemberton, then north and east to Gold Bridge, and then back via the Bridge River Valley to Lillooet. Or you can start in Pemberton and head north through the Hurley (Railroad) Pass to Gold Bridge and then east to Lillooet and then return via Duffey Lake Road to Pemberton. Or you can start by reading the *Bridge River*

Gold chapter and doing the circuit in a counter-clockwise direction — you get the picture.

Lillooet Starting Point

While Lillooet was the starting point of the Fraser River Trail to the Cariboo goldfields and the reference for many of the place names along Highway 97, the "backroad" route to Pemberton via Duffey Lake didn't see much activity until long after the gold rush had died.

The Lillooet-Pemberton section of the loop follows Highway 99 southwest with the junction near the west end of the Bridge of the 23 Camels as the starting point. While hardly a backroad, this scenic route follows Cayoosh Creek and Seton River upstream to Seton Lake before beginning a spectacular climb up the Cayoosh Creek canyon to Duffey Lake. There is a viewpoint above Seton Lake and a side road down to a lovely beach about five kilometres west of the Bridge of the 23 Camels.

Military Surveyor

Sapper James Duffy was one of the British military surveyors who arrived in British Columbia in 1858, under Captain R.M. Parsons, R.E., as part of the Columbia detachment of Royal Engineers. In September 1860, Duffy (also spelled Duffey and Duffie) was part of a group of Royal Engineers surveying the townsite of Cayoosh (Lillooet) when Governor James Douglas asked for a volunteer to check out the Native trail from Cayoosh to Lillooet Lake.

According to Beth Hill in *Sappers: The RE in BC*, "On the 10th September, 1860, Duffy was on his way with a party of Indians, following an Indian trail at a steady 13 kilometres (8 miles) per day, reaching Lillooet Lake on the 16th September and returning by a different route. He sent his report to Lt. Palmer at Pemberton. He submitted notes and sketch maps and his opinion that a wagon road was feasible, the greatest obstacle being the rapid drop of 300 metres (1,000 feet) to Lillooet Lake, which could be descended by zigzagging."

Recreation Sites

While the drive from Lillooet to Pemberton now takes an hour and a half compared to Sapper Duffy's six days, you could easily spend six days exploring the area from base camps at half a dozen Forest recreation sites as well as Duffey Lake Provincial Park and Joffre Lake Provincial Park. Side roads up Blowdown Creek and Van Horlick Creek lead south into more spectacular mountain terrain and the Stein Wilderness Area.

The Duffey Lake Road is definitely part of a scenic route from the Interior to the Coast.

Coast Mountain Circle Tour

Two-thousand-hectare Duffey Lake Provincial Park, 50 kilometres south-west of Lillooet, was established in 1993 to protect the wilderness and recreation values of the lake and the alpine slopes to the north. Unlike nearby Joffre Lake Provincial Park, it does not have any organized campgrounds or marked hiking trails.

Joffre Lake Park, on the west side of Cayoosh Pass, has a picnic site near Highway 99. Camping is permitted at Upper Joffre Lake, a 5.5 kilometre-hike from the parking lot.

Zigzag Descent

The Joffre Lake parking lot marks the start of Sapper Duffy's brake-burning zigzag descent to Lillooet Lake. The steep grade and sharp corners are definitely a challenge for big RVs and motorhomes. Once down at lake level the winding road through the Mount Currie Reserve is a tame but slow chance to let the brakes cool down.

The last few kilometres of the one-hundred-kilometre trip to Pemberton are along the floor of the broad Pemberton Valley. Then it's time to decide: Do you head back into the mountains for another adventure or take the "Sea to Sky Highway" back to the Lower Mainland?

Pemberton Is an Alternate Starting Point

Whether you have just made the trip from Lillooet, or you have driven up from North Vancouver, the entrance to Pemberton, approximately 135 kilometres north of Horseshoe Bay, is a good reference point for a Coast Mountains tour through the Bridge River Valley. Pemberton is an excellent place to top up the cooler and the fuel tank, because there is little in the way of services between here and Gold Bridge or Bralorne.

After doing your bit for the local economy, continue northwest on the Pemberton Valley Road. For the next 25 kilometres, the paved road winds through farmland and small settlements. Extensive flood control has tamed the once-wild Lillooet River and created a haven for potato farmers. For decades, the world knew this valley for its prime seed potatoes.

While potato fields still line the road, recreationists have found other distractions in the Pemberton Valley and surrounding mountains. This is the western Canada headquarters for Outward Bound and home to the Coast Mountain Outdoor School. The Tenquille Lake trail and numerous other trails in the area attract hikers and campers.

The road through the Hurley (Railroad) Pass reaches an altitude of 1,400 metres. Because of the heavy snowfall, it is usually closed in winter.

Hurley River Forest Road

Your route to the Bridge River leaves the banks of the Lillooet River near km 34 (the 9K marker) and begins a switchback climb to Railroad (Hurley) Pass. The Howe Sound and Northern Railway studied the pass in the early 1900s as a possible route to the Bridge River Mining District. The railway never materialized, but work began as early as the 1950s for a vehicle road through the pass. (In the 1950s, my Dad, a Bralorne hardrock miner, contributed to a fund to pay the cat skinner's wages and fuel.) However, it wasn't until the 1970s that a passable link was made between logging operations on both sides of the 1,400-metre pass.

While the 15-kilometre climb from the Lillooet River to the pass is steep, averaging over six percent, the 35-kilometre descent to Gold Bridge is gradual, though no less spectacular. The road first follows Donnelly Creek, then the Hurley River before crossing the Hurley River. A lesser-used road to the right just before the bridge parallels the Hurley for about 10 kilometres before climbing over a low divide into the Cadwallader Creek valley, reaching the Bralorne Store about four kilometres later. Although this route is the shortest way to Bralorne, it is narrow and rough and not really practical for a large RV.

The main route crosses the Hurley and continues northeast to La Joie Dam and the junction with the Bridge River Road near Gold Bridge. For the rest of this discussion, I will assume that you chose to continue to Gold Bridge before exploring the mining communities.

Harnessed for the Cities

The once-mighty Bridge River flows out of the foot of the Bridge Glacier about 50 kilometres west of Gold Bridge. In its original state, the Bridge River carried its glacial silt 150 kilometres eastward before emptying into the muddy Fraser River north of Lillooet.

Geoffrey Downton, an engineer visiting the goldfield towns in the area, first recognized the vast hydroelectric potential of the Bridge River in 1912. Work began on the first tunnel through Mission Mountain in 1927, and by 1960 dams were completed on the Bridge River at La Joie and at the foot of Mission Mountain. In the process, 26 kilometre-long Downton Lake and 55-kilometre long Carpenter Lake were created. Powerhouses were built at La Joie, Shalalth on Seton Lake, and at Lillooet. The generators create a total of 500 million watts of electricity.

Gold Bridge

A bridge across the Bridge River near Gold Bridge serves as a landmark for a major junction. Here there is a choice of three directions. To the northeast, the road follows Carpenter Lake to Lillooet. Just before the bridge, the road to the left climbs steadily for eight kilometres until it reaches La Joie (Little Gun) Lake and Gun Lake, another kilometre farther. These two lakes, the latter seven kilometres long, have been the local water playground for decades.

The road to the right crosses the Bridge River just downstream from the confluence of the Bridge and Hurley rivers and leads into Gold Bridge. Although the mines have closed, Gold Bridge is still the valley commercial centre, with accommodations, supplies, and fuel. There are also several guides/outfitters in the

Downton Lake from the Hurley Road.

area. It's best to contact the Bridge River Valley Economic Development Society for up-to-date information.

Bridge River Gold

The history of the mines and the recreation opportunities in the Bralorne-Pioneer area are described in the *Bridge River Gold* chapter, so I won't repeat them here. Suffice it to say that there is plenty to explore from both perspectives.

Carpenter Lake Road

After you've satisfied your curiosity about the mining communities, you can return to Gold Bridge and follow the north shore of Carpenter Lake eastward to Lillooet. The mining community of Minto was once just east of Gun Creek. It began in 1933 and became the third largest gold producer in the valley, after Pioneer and Bralorne. The vein petered out and Minto City declined until it was briefly revived during World War II as a centre for Japanese displaced from the Coast. Gun Creek flooded in 1950, inundating the town. By 1960, all of the buildings had been removed prior to the flooding of Carpenter Lake reservoir. Today the Gun Creek floodplain downstream from the road is the site of an excellent BC Hydro campground.

Tyax Mountain Lake Resort

The Bridge River Road continues along the lake shore, passing Tyaughton Lake Road. From the junction, there is a good gravel road north to Tyaughton Lake (locally known as "Tyax") and the Tyax Mountain Lake Resort. If good food,

Carpenter Lake at the mouth of Tyaughton Creek.

The Bridge River is diverted through tunnels to hydroelectric generators on Seton Lake.

accommodations, horseback riding, and fishing in a spectacular mountain setting are on your agenda, it's well worth the eight-kilometre detour.

Marshall Creek Falls, a favourite stop 23 kilometres farther down Carpenter Lake, cascades off the Shulaps Range, making its final plunge into a pool before flowing into the lake. In low water, a rough trail leads to the foot of the falls. When the reservoir is full, the waterfall drops directly into Carpenter Lake. Marshall Lake Road West, just east of the falls, climbs to the northwest. It provides access to Carol Lake, Marshall Lake, and the Shulaps Mountain Range. There are Forest recreation sites on Carol Lake and Marshall Lake.

Terzaghi Dam

A gravel road across the crest of the Terzaghi Dam leads over Mission Mountain to Shalalth and Seton Portage. Access to Carpenter Lake is provided at several locations on the south shore near the dam. In the summer, fishing enthusiasts troll for kokanee, rainbow trout, and Dolly Varden char. Upstream of the 55-metre-high, 365-metre-wide dam, concrete towers mark the gates of two four-

Salmon drying near Lillooet.

kilometre-long tunnels that divert the Bridge River through Mission Mountain to turbines at Shalalth on Seton Lake.

The Bridge River Road continues straight ahead at the junction and follows the foot of the canyon wall for about 15 kilometres to the mouth of the Yalakom River, just upstream from the Horseshoe Canyon. From the 1920s to the mid-1950s, a flatcar trip from Lillooet to Shalalth and a hair-raising drive over Mission Mountain was the only way to take a vehicle into the valley. In the fall of 1954, local workers began the construction of the "Moha Road" using plenty of blasting powder, perseverance, and equipment borrowed from Bralorne and Pioneer mines. On October 15, 1955, BC MLA Phil Gaglardi officially opened the road, ending dependency on the PGE Railway (now B.C. Railway/CN Rail) for passenger and freight transportation.

After a switchback climb up the hill, you have the option of exploring the Yalakom River into the heart of the Shulaps Range or continuing east to Lillooet. The Yalakom River route once led over Poison Mountain and China Head Mountain to the Fraser River at the Big Bar Ferry, but the route through the alpine has been closed to vehicles.

Downstream from the Yalakom, the Bridge River cuts a wide bend around a rock outcropping, creating Horseshoe Canyon. There is room to pull off the road and enjoy the view near the east end of the horseshoe. There is also a rough trail leading down to the canyon floor. Rockhounds still find the occasional gold flake or jade pebble in the river gravel near the Bridge and Yalakom confluence. From the Horseshoe Canyon to the mouth of the Bridge River, the road has been carved out of the rock bluffs with still more carving to be done. Slow down and use extreme caution.

Historic Bridge

According to Commander R.C. Mayne, R.N., who visited the region in 1859, the Bridge River got its English name from a Native bridge near its mouth. During the gold rush, two enterprising individuals pulled down the old bridge and constructed a new one across the canyon, charging the miners a 25 cent toll.

Native fishing enthusiasts consider the confluence of the Bridge and Fraser rivers a favourite salmon fishing location. If you stop at a handy pullout on the Lillooet side of the bridge in late summer or fall, you can see the colourful array of tarpaulins used to protect the drying salmon. You can even get a snack at the roadside restaurant.

Lillooet Destination

The Old Mill Plaza shopping centre on the northern outskirts of Lillooet was once a sawmill site. The original Lillooet – Lytton road crossed the B.C. Railway tracks near here and wound down the hill to a suspension bridge across the Fraser. Today, you can continue through Lillooet, past the museum and Mile 0 Cairn, to Highway 99 and the Bridge of the 23 Camels that spans the Fraser River near the site of the original gold rush ferry, completing this Coast Mountains Circle Tour.

Note: See the *Information Sources* chapter at the end of the book for contact information on the services mentioned here.

GPS References for major points of interest
Ref: WGS 84 - Lat/Lon hddd.ddddd
Allow +/-100 metres due to data conversions

Wpt	Km	Description	Latitude	Longitude	Elev.
		Lillooet to Pemberton			
CM01	0	Lillooet Mile 0 Cairn	N50.69170	W121.93691	244 m
CM02	1.5	Jct Hwy 99 – Bridge of the 23 Camels	N50.68476	W121.91899	222 m
CM03	5.3	Seton River spawning channel	N50.66915	W121.97338	229 m
CM04	6.3	Seton Lake viewpoint and beach	N50.66817	W121.98642	299 m
CM05	14.2	Cross Cayoosh Creek	N50.64367	W122.05376	501 m
CM06	51.4	Duffey Lake – 40K marker	N50.40884	W122.29965	1,154 m
CM07	67.6	Joffre Lakes Prov Park	N50.36999	W122.50047	1,199 m
CM08	81.3	Cross Birkenhead River	N50.30730	W122.60678	201 m
CM09	92.3	Mount Currie	N50.31626	W122.71717	203 m
CM10	97.3	Jct Hwy 99 to Pemberton	N50.31664	W122.79685	211 m
		Pemberton to Gold Bridge			
CM10	0	Jct Hwy 99 to Pemberton	N50.31664	W122.79685	211 m
CM11	1	Pemberton Town Centre	N50.32257	W122.80768	224 m
CM12	26	pavement ends	N50.50266	W122.96747	257 m
CM13	33.5	start Hurley River Forest Service Rd	N50.53280	W123.04982	287 m
CM14	49	Railway pass	N50.60040	W123.02026	1,370 m
CM15	67	Cross Hurley River	N50.73094	W122.94200	997 m
CM16	84	Hurley Road – Gold Bridge Jct	N50.85154	W122.84716	670 m
		Gold Bridge to Lillooet			
CM17	0	Gold Bridge Bridge	N50.85113	W122.83744	704 m
CM18	7	Gun Creek rec area	N50.89551	W122.77331	662 m
CM19	11	Tyaughton Lake Rd	N50.90740	W122.73221	661 m
CM20	33	Marshall Creek Falls	N50.84159	W122.46041	656 m
CM21	55	Terzaghi Dam	N50.78987	W122.22416	637 m
CM22	72	Yalakom Rd	N50.86424	W122.16339	531 m
CM23	96	Bridge River bridge	N50.75257	W121.93579	218 m
CM24	102	Old Mill Plaza – Lillooet	N50.70212	W121.92567	252 m
CM25	103.5	Lillooet Mile 0 Cairn	N50.69126	W121.93754	253 m
CM26	105	Jct Bridge of the 23 Camels	N50.68067	W121.93346	204 m

The Chilcotin Plateau: The Connection to the Pacific

While the Cariboo Regional District takes in most of the land between the summits of the Cariboo Mountains and the Coast Mountains, the land west of the Fraser River is known by all as the Chilcotin.

It is a vast plateau stretching some 250 kilometres from the Fraser River to Heckman Pass at the crest of the "Big Hill" – half again as much by road. The elevation ranges from about 350 metres at the Fraser to 1,524 metres at Heckman Pass, but much of that climb takes place in the first 50 kilometres of the westward drive.

Whitewater rafters drift under the Chimney Creek Bridge over the Fraser River on Highway 20, the gateway to the Chilcotin.

The Farwell Canyon section of the Chilcotin River, south of Riske Creek.

First Nations Communities

A close look at a map of the region reveals a wide variety of decidedly non-British place names. Riske Creek was named after L.W. Riskie, "a Polish gentleman." Hanceville got its name from Tom Hance, an early settler that came north from Oregon. Alexis Creek was named after Chief Alexis, a noted leader of the Chilcotin peoples. The list continues as you travel west: Chilanko Forks, Tatla Lake, Kleena Kleene, Towdystan, Nimpo Lake, and Anahim Lake.

A close look at many of the residents also reveals a decidedly non-British population. The Chilcotin First Nations peoples, phonetically pronounced Tsilkotin, meaning "people of young man's river," belong to the Athapascan linguistic group. The "young man's river" reference aptly describes the wild nature of the Chilcotin River. A good place to view it is at the Farwell Canyon, a short drive south of Riske Creek.

Cattle Ranches and Wide Open Spaces

The communities are small with limited services and the vast land between is punctuated by the occasional ranch house and hayfield. It is not uncommon to see cattle on the roadways, particularly the side roads. It is also not uncommon to see deer, moose, and other wildlife.

Humongous Parks

Ts'is?os (pronounced "sigh-loss") Provincial Park takes in 233,000 hectares surrounding Chilko Lake. Itcha Ilgachuz Provincial Park protects almost 112,000 hectares of unique landscape in the West Chilcotin Uplands. Tweedsmuir Park, on the western edge of the Chilcotin Plateau, covers approximately 981,000 hectares of the Coast Mountain peaks. Scattered across the plateau are another half-dozen parks and protected areas.

Plenty of Diversions

Time doesn't move very fast in the Chilcotin. To make the most of any visit to the region, put your watch in your pocket and drag out your calendar. It will prevent ulcers if you plan your trip in days or weeks rather than hours or minutes.

Horses graze in an upland meadow in Itcha Ilgachuz Park, north of Anahim Lake.

CHAPTER 23

Chilcotin Country Highway 20: Williams Lake to Bella Coola

STATISTICS

Map see page 295.

Distance: 456 km, Williams Lake to Bella Coola.
Travel Time: Eight to ten hours.
Condition: Mostly paved or seal-coated with gravel sections west of Anahim Lake.
Season: Maintained year-round.
Heckman Pass could be closed temporarily in winter.
Map: British Columbia Highway Map.
Communities: Williams Lake, Tatla Lake, Anahim Lake, and Bella Coola.

The Chilcotin is a living legend — a land with a mystical aura of giant cattle spreads and weathered cowhands, of wood smoke and wilderness, and of towering peaks that rise out of the Pacific Ocean.

The word *Chilcotin* triggers a cinematic image of a proud Native cowhand riding into the sunset, the criss-cross shadows of a Russell fence licking at his horse's hooves. It smells of lodgepole pine, giant cedar, and spawned-out salmon tossed ashore by a majestic grizzly. It sounds like the clap of thunder echoing down through a rocky canyon.

Strong individuals — *characters* might be a better term — the likes of Cliff Kopas (Bella Coola), Ralph Edwards (*Crusoe of Lonesome Lake*), and Paul St. Pierre (*Breaking Smith's Quarter Horse*) have created and maintained the Chilcotin legend through their action and writing.

Civilization Hasn't Changed the Chilcotin

The 456-kilometre drive from Williams Lake to Bella Coola, across the full width of the Chilcotin, does little to detract from the image. This road has character. Although millions of dollars are being spent to remove the bumps, fill the sand-

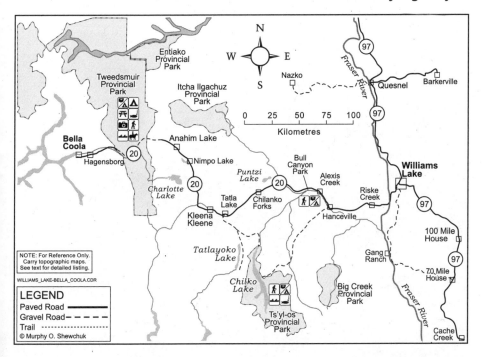

trap potholes, and straighten the curves, it will always be remembered as a way to get nowhere very slowly. The shortage of service centres are only small inconveniences that add to the mystique.

As if to lull the first-time traveller into a false sense of security, Highway 20 is paved when it leaves Williams Lake. The pavement does not end until the traveller finds himself west of Anahim Lake and facing the snow-capped Coast Mountains. By this time it's too late to resist the lure of the Pacific.

Beneath the Chimney Creek Bridge that carries the highway over the Fraser River, First Nations fishing enthusiasts can be seen each autumn dipping their nets into the perpetually muddy waters in search of the invisible, migrating sockeye salmon. The salmon that fail to escape the deft swing of the long-handled nets are cleaned, split, and hung to dry in a manner that has changed little over the ages.

Bighorn Country

To the west of the river lies California bighorn country. A roughly triangular chunk of inhospitable plateau bounded by the Fraser and Chilcotin rivers has been set aside as a protected area for these sure-footed mountain sheep. Although they avoid contact with humans, herds of bighorn can often be seen by whitewater rafting enthusiasts and visitors to the famous Gang Ranch.

California bighorn sheep live on the plateau near the Fraser and Chilcotin rivers.

The viewpoint overlooking the Chilcotin River near Hanceville, some 85 kilo-metres west of Williams Lake, is an unmarked time change. Not an hour or even a day as might occur when travelling across the province or around the world, but almost half a century — back! The true character of the Chilcotin begins to unfold as you descend to Lee's Corner: great expanses of grasslands, rail fences built in the time-honoured tradition without the use of nails, and people who go out of their way to be friendly. These are all part of the life style that has survived the hustle of the twentieth century. The image is occasionally broken by a loaded logging truck heading east, but is quickly reinforced when one looks for a cellular phone signal, a cash machine, or a Tim Horton's coffee shop.

Lee's Corner is also the departure point from Highway 20 for a side trip to Chilko Lake covered in a separate chapter. Chilko Lake, 120 kilometres to the southwest, is the central gem in 233,000-hectare Ts'il?os Provincial Park. Pronounced "sigh-loss," this undeveloped wilderness park is one of the Cariboo-Chilcotin region's newest parks.

Undulating Passage Westward

Beyond Lee's Corner, Highway 20 continues its undulating passage westward across the plateau. The undulations are three-dimensional. In addition to the north-south ripple that is obvious on the road map, there is an up-down ripple that can be a little deceiving as it bounces along about a kilometre above sea level.

The posted speed limit is 90 kilometres per hour. However, the speeding traveller who tries to wrap his tongue around such Chilcotin names as Choelquoit, Tatlayoko, Kleena Kleene, or Punkutlaenkut may wonder if he has bounced off one bump too many.

Bull Canyon Provincial Park

Beyond Alexis Creek — named after a proud Chilcotin Native chief — lies Bull Canyon Provincial Park. Note that Bull Canyon is the only provincial campsite along Highway 20 between Williams Lake and Tweedsmuir Provincial Park. Here circular depressions mark the sites of long-abandoned First Nations winter homes, or kikulis.

This 20-unit campground takes its name from more recent events in Chilcotin history. According to the late Kathleen Telford, in *Chilcotin: Preserving Pioneer*

Fishing boats on Puntzi Lake at sunrise.

Memories, "Bull Canyon got its name from the first ranchers in the district who used it as a bull pasture. It was a natural pasture; all they had to do was put in a fence at each end of the canyon." The sheer rock faces to the north and the glacial silt-laden Chilcotin River to the south would likely deter even the biggest bull from escaping.

Beyond Bull Canyon the road begins its gradual climb to the Coast Mountains, paralleling the Chilanko River. To the south lies some of the most challenging wilderness white water in British Columbia. Rafting outfitters offer week-long vacation adventures drifting down the glacial green waters of the Taseko, Chilko, and Chilcotin rivers to the muddy Fraser.

Puntzi Lake near Chilanko Forks, like many other local lakes, offers commercial campgrounds, resort accommodations, and excellent fishing for travellers who would rather wet a fly than dunk themselves.

Chilcotin Blue

The Chilcotin sky is a clear blue, the likes of which is seldom seen closer to BC's Lower Mainland. However, one of the best examples of Chilcotin blue lies in the

Chilcotin fence near Choelquoit Lake.

form of Choelquoit Lake near the road to the north end of Chilko Lake, some 40 kilometres south east of Tatla Lake. With the square top mountains of the Chilcotin Range to the south and the sawtooth Niut Range to the west, it is a photograph that begs to be taken. Incidentally, while in the area, consider camping at the Forest Service recreation site at nearby Tatlayoko Lake.

Chilcotin War

Near Nimpo Lake and the Dean River Forest Service recreation site, a roadside stop-of-interest plaque once stood as a reminder of the Chilcotin War. In 1864, a small band of distraught Native people killed a road construction party about 100 kilometres to the south, effectively halting the Coast-to-Cariboo road for almost a century. (It was not until 1953 that the Bella Coola Road was finally completed through the Coast Mountains.) The resulting arrest, trial, and hangings are becoming increasingly recognized as a truly black mark on BC's history.

Anahim Lake Stampede

The community of Anahim Lake is the service centre of the west Chilcotin and the host, the second week of July, of the wildest rodeo in the west. The Anahim Lake Stampede gathers people from all over the Chilcotin to try their skills at wild cow milking, calf roping, bronco riding, and the many other events. They take their turns at the chute, heckle and cheer their friends and, most of all, have a damn good time. "We don't run no circus out here," says one old-timer. "This is a working man's rodeo and everybody else had better stand back!"

Anahim Lake is also excellent fishing country and the last service stop before Tweedsmuir Park and the long hill down to Bella Coola. Although Tweedsmuir Park has government campsites at the Atnarko River and at Burnt Bridge, it is still a one-million-hectare wilderness that should be treated with the utmost respect.

South of the highway lies the rugged lake country of Ralph Edwards, made famous in *Crusoe of Lonesome Lake*. This is also where Hunlen Falls, near the outlet of Turner Lake, drops 335 metres, making it one of the tallest waterfalls in British Columbia.

The Hill

At 1,524-metre-high Heckman Pass, Highway 20 begins the brake-burning descent to Stuie at the head of the Bella Coola Valley. With 18 percent grades, one-lane cuts across vertical cliffs, and sharp hairpin turns, it is no road for the weak-hearted. It can be wicked in winter, but in mid-summer residents, tourists,

Katharine Shewchuk on an alpine ridge in 112,000-hectare Itcha Ilgachuz Provincial Park, north of Anahim Lake.

and commercial truckers wave at each other as they gingerly round the corners. West of Stuie the road levels off as the Bella Coola valley gradually opens up until it is almost four kilometres wide at the head of North Bentinck Arm. It is boxed in by almost-vertical mountain walls that reach 3,000 metres toward the sky.

Norwegian Settlers

The rough-and-tumble image of the Chilcotin begins to develop cracks as the traveller approaches lush farmland carved out of the cedars by the Norwegian settlers. Firvale is the first settlement of the valley, followed by Hagensborg and then, at the end of a long Pacific fjord, Highway 20 ends at the docks of Bella Coola. This strip of communities, with an area population of 2,200, is the largest west of Williams Lake. Here the "cowboy" rides a tiny tug, sorting logs for the mill. The rubber rafts of the Chilko and Chilcotin have given way to fishing boats and deep-sea freighters.

The Bella Coola Valley Museum, located in a historic log cabin near the end of the road, is well worth a visit.

The mountains hem in the Bella Coola Valley near Hagensborg.

Stone Faces

Totems stand in the Native village, and hidden in a forest glade near Thorsen Creek are petroglyphs — faces and figures carved into solid stone — mute reminders of British Columbia's unknown past.

Alexander Mackenzie's rock still stands in the Dean Channel, 60 kilometres from Bella Coola, marking the end of his historic journey across the continent. The Chilcotin has seen considerable change since he left his mark there on July 22, 1793, but I think Mackenzie would be pleased with the results.

Note: See the *Information Sources* chapter at the end of the book for contact information on the services mentioned here.

The petroglyphs at Thorsen Creek, near Bella Coola, may be thousands of years old. They number more than 40 in all and are located just outside the village. You can arrange for a guided tour with the Nuxalk First Nation band office or the local tourism office.

CHAPTER 24

The Dome Trail

STATISTICS

	Map see page 303.
Distance:	20 km, Highway 20 to The Dome Lookout.
	Trail length: 2 to 6 km, depending on access vehicle.
Travel Time:	Allow a day for travel and hiking.
Condition:	Gravel road plus mountain trail.
Season:	June through September.
	Note: The area may be closed in mid-summer
	due to military exercises.
Topo Maps:	Riske Creek, BC 92 O/15.
(1:50,000)	Drummond Lake, BC 93 B/2.
Communities:	Williams Lake and Riske Creek.

Riske Creek Roadhouse

Stack Valley Road, the access road to "The Dome," leaves Highway 20 approximately one kilometre west of the Riske Creek Roadhouse or 47.5 kilometres

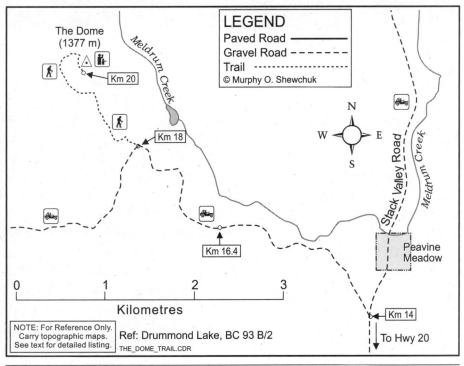

The Dome is an eroded volcanic outcrop of the Pleistocene era — the volcanic activity took place during or prior to the last ice age.

west of downtown Williams Lake. Riske Creek is the site of one of the earliest ranches in the area. It was established in 1859 by a Polish gentleman, L.W. Riskie. The first post office in the Chilcotin region was set up at Riske Creek on May 1, 1886, and was called the Chilcoten Post Office. On May 1, 1911, the spelling was changed to Chilcotin. On November 1, 1912, the name was changed to Riske Creek.

Chilcotin Lodge

The Chilcotin Lodge, to the east of Stack Valley Road and a few hundred metres north of Highway 20, was built in 1940 by George Christensen. It has had a variety of owners and presently serves as a country inn. Those with a good memory for early CBC TV programming may remember the lodge as the filming site for the *Cariboo Country* programs, a summer replacement show from 1960 to 1967. The star was Chief Dan George, and the series was based on the books by Paul St. Pierre. Several scenes were shot in the living and dining rooms

Curious horses inspect the photographer near Stack Valley Road.

of the lodge. The lodge was also mentioned in the book *Three Against the Wilderness* by Eric Collier, who with his wife and son, homesteaded in the Meldrum Creek area to the north.

Stack Valley Road

Stack Valley Road initially climbs north of Highway 20 before levelling off near a meadow at km 3. On a late-August trip into the area, we stopped for lunch here and enjoyed the company of a curious band of horses.

We continued north after our lunch, stopping near Drummond Lake to let a small herd of cattle meander off the road. We kept left at the major junctions and followed the main road north to a junction at the 14 K marker. We then headed northwest on a narrow gravel road, keeping right at a junction at km 16.4 and parking at a junction at km 18. The road was dry and somewhat rutted to this point, but a downed tree blocked the road ahead.

In retrospect, the decision to park here was a good one as the remainder of the

The Dome Trail

The wooden lookout tower doesn't prompt a lot of confidence. Despite the guy wires, it may be a crumpled heap by the time you reach the summit of The Dome.

old road to the Forest Fire Lookout got steeper and progressively more rutted. While it may be possible to drive a Jeep or Hummer to the top — the latter may have problems with encroaching brush — the two-kilometre climb to the summit is best done on foot.

Chilcotin Panorama

It took us less than an hour to climb to the Lookout — with a few stops to breathe and photograph a grouse. The climb was worth the effort as the 360-degree panorama from the summit of this 1,377-metre-high volcanic plug covers much of the eastern Chilcotin.

Chilcotin Military Reserve

SPECIAL NOTE: *The area surrounding The Dome is part of the Chilcotin Military Reserve, established in 1924, and may occasionally be closed for military exercises.*

GPS References for major points of interest
Ref: WGS 84 - Lat/Lon hddd.ddddd
Allow +/-100 metres due to data conversions

Wpt	Km	Description	Latitude	Longitude	Elev.
TD01	0	Jct Hwy 20 and Stack Valley Rd	N51.96861	W122.53345	900 m
TD02	3.2	Cariboo pond and horses	N51.99337	W122.53621	986 m
TD03	7.7	Drummond Lake	N52.03190	W122.53092	1,005 m
TD04	13.5	13K marker	N52.06992	W122.57223	1,044 m
TD05	14.1	Jct 14K marker – go left	N52.07547	W122.57219	1,045 m
TD06	16.4	Keep right	N52.08422	W122.59667	1,159 m
TD07	18.0	Jct – Hike from here	N52.09227	W122.60934	1,200 m
TD08	18.9	Jct – Keep left (west)	N52.09765	W122.61718	1,290 m
TD09	19.3	Jct – Climb hill to north	N52.09878	W122.62172	1,286 m
TD10	20.0	The Dome Lookout	N52.09991	W122.61913	1,382 m

CHAPTER 25

Ts'il?os Provincial Park: Exploring Chilko Lake Country

STATISTICS

	Map see page 309.
Distance:	117 km, Lee's Corner to Chilko Lake.
	63 km, Tatla Lake to Chilko Lake.
Travel Time:	Two to four hours.
Condition:	Gravel road with some rough sections.
Season:	Open year-round; best in dry weather.
Topo Maps:	Hanceville, BC 92 O/14.
(1:50,000)	Scum Lake, BC 92 O/13.
	Elkin Creek, BC 92 O/12
	Mount Tatlow, BC 92 O/5.
	Tatlayoko Lake, BC 92 N/9.
Communities:	Williams Lake, Lee's Corner (Hanceville), and Tatla Lake.

The Taseko and Chilko Lakes region has had a special interest to me since my school days in the Bridge River Valley. As a teenager, I envied the hunters and cowboys who rode north through Warner Pass into the Chilcotin. Many years later, in 1984, a poster promoting a south Chilcotin park piqued our curiosity, and my wife and I made our first foray into the area. Up to that point, Chilko Lake was one lone photograph and a 65-kilometre-long strip of blue on a topographic map. However, such scanty information hadn't stopped us before.

We have returned to Chilko Lake a number of times since that first foray. Each time there are incremental improvements to the road — except for the final half-dozen kilometres to the Ts'il?os Provincial Park Nu Chugh Beniz campground on Chilko Lake.

Lee's Corner Starting Point

A common reference for most non-Chilcotin travellers would be Williams Lake, at the junction of Highway 97 and Highway 20. We will start 90 kilometres west.

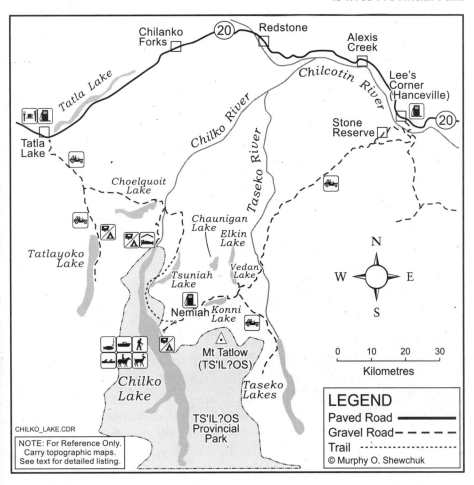

With Lee's Corner (Hanceville) as your km 0 starting point, turn south off of Highway 20. The pavement soon ends as you begin a switchback descent to the Chilcotin River and a switchback climb up to the bench on the south side.

Your first major decision is at a junction about 5.4 kilometres south of Hanceville. To the left (east) is Fletcher Lake, Big Creek, and the Gang Ranch country. To the right, the signs mark the way to Elkin Creek Guest Ranch and Chilko Lake. This route winds through the Stone Indian Reserve and into the timber-covered plateau on the way to Taseko and Chilko lakes. What the signs don't say is that if you continue south on the Fletcher Lake Road (700 Road) for another three kilometres, you have a second option. The newer Minton Creek Forest Road (also known as Nemaiah Valley Road or 900 Road) bypasses the Stone Reserve and rejoins the other route about 22 kilometres from Highway 20.

A logging feller-buncher works near the Nemaiah Valley Road.

Cattle and Timber

To make it easier for travellers who may have come to this point via Farwell Canyon, I will restart the kilometre references at the junction of Fletcher Lake Road and Minton Creek Road. Your first major junction will be near the 13 km marker where the road crosses Minton Creek. To the right is the Stone Reserve and to the left (west) is Chilko Lake.

There is certainly a sense of isolation as you wind southwest. It's as though you are going nowhere with nothing at the end of the road. Then fences and hay meadows bring back a tenuous link with people and civilization.

Decision time arrives again at a junction about 18 kilometres from Fletcher Lake Road. The logging roads (4400 Road and 4500 Road) look well used, but the Nemaiah Valley Road has an appearance of permanence unusual in BC's backcountry. In addition to being two lanes wide, it has a wide right of way cleared through the lodgepole pine.

Hereford cattle meandering down the centre of the road break up the washboard drive down the pine corridor.

Coast Mountains Come into View

A straight stretch near the 23 K marker offers the first glimpse of Mount Tatlow (Ts'il?os) on the southwestern horizon. Then the relatively flat route across the plateau is broken near the 51.5 km point by a switchback descent to Tete Angela Creek. The climb out of the valley is straighter, and the roadside clearings soon reveal more sawtooth spires on the western horizon.

Taseko Crossing

Ten kilometres later, you will again make a switchback descent. This time it's to the banks of the grey-green Taseko River. Laden with glacial silt brought down from the ever more prominent peaks, it was once known as the Whitewater River. Rough campsites are nestled among the trees between the road and the river, including a large, spacious Forest recreation site near the Davidson Bridge at km 67.

A rough road heads up the east side of the Taseko River while the main road crosses the bridge and begins a steady climb to the southwest.

The gravel road, still wide and in good condition, crests near Big Lake and the Ts'il?os Park information signs, offering an even better panoramic view of the Coast Mountains. Mount Tatlow, at 3,061 metre stabs its spire into the sky, often attracting a shroud of rain clouds while the sun shines all around it.

Guest Ranches and Fishing Camps to the North

A few minutes beyond the crest the road forks, with the right fork swinging north to Vedan Lake, Elkin Lake, and Chaunigan Lake. A second nearby intersection

Mount Tatlow, at 3,061 metres, can be seen from 50 kilometres away.

Chilko Lake at the Nu Chugh Beniz Campground.

leads right to Elkin Creek Guest Ranch. If you continue following the main road southwest into the Nemaiah Valley, you should reach the remnants of a village at the east end of Konni Lake near km 85.

The lodgepole pine gradually give way to grasslands as you descend into the valley. As you follow the north shore of Konni Lake westward, you will find the slope of 2,207-metre Konni Mountain almost barren of timber.

Beyond the west end of Konni Lake, continue through the Nemaiah village at km 92.5. Then follow the south shore of Nemaia Lake for a short distance before descending westward through ranchland.

Watch for the Longhorn Wilderness Ranch sign about 10 kilometres past the Nemaiah village. One kilometre beyond the ranch gate (still on the main road) is a junction with a rough road marked "Ts'yl-os Provincial Park" to the left.

The rutted five-kilometre-long road to Nu Chugh Beniz Campground has changed little since our first mid-summer visit in 1984. Unless it is improved, it obviously could be difficult in wet weather. But that doesn't seem to stop a variety of cars, vans, and campers from winding around the bumps and ruts down to the shore of Chilko Lake. While there are always those that can prove otherwise, I would suggest that high clearance and four-wheel-drive is an asset.

Nu Chugh Beniz Campground: Worth the Trip

The campground is near the mouth of Robertson Creek, opposite Duff Island. To the north, trails lead along dry, wind-swept cliffs — a stark contrast to the solid green of the timber-covered mountains across the lake. Glaciers grip the peaks to the south with icy fingers. Squalls whip down the mountains and pound the driftwood against the shore despite the shelter of Duff Island.

Chilko Lake often acts more like a stormy Pacific fjord than an inland plateau lake, creating a deadly mix that has taken more than one life. According to BC Parks, only experienced boaters and kayakers should attempt Chilko Lake due to the unpredictable winds and other challenges, such as high waves, icy waters, and a shortage of safe landing areas. Canoeing on Chilko Lake is not recommended.

Tatla Lake to Chilko Lake

An alternate route to Chilko Lake begins at Highway 20, just east of the community of Tatla Lake. It generally winds through the pine on the eastern approach to the Coast Mountains with some open grasslands near Choelquoit Lake.

Twenty-three-kilometre-long Tatlayoko Lake drains south into the Homathko River and Bute Inlet.

Ts'il?os Provincial Park

With Highway 20 as your km 0 starting point, keep left at the junctions at km 4.0 and km 20.7. The road to the right at km 20.7 leads south to Tatlayoko Lake with an excellent lake shore Forest recreation site about 16 kilometres from the junction.

There is also a recreation site in the meadows near Choelquoit Lake. Side roads lead in from the lower Chilko River and the Tsuniah Lake area at Henry's Crossing. Older maps show a road to the Nemaiah Valley via Tsuniah Lake, but the information we received from several sources is that it is not being maintained and is virtually impassable.

The main road ends at km 63 at the Chilko Lake Resort Hotel. An alternate route to the right just before the air strip leads south to a Forest Service recreation site nestled in the pines near the lake and a 6.2-kilometre hiking trail up Tullin Mountain.

Cowboy Vacations

There are several guest ranches and adventure vacation lodges along both routes into Chilko Lake. They offer everything from ranch vacations to whitewater rafting and heli-hiking. We don't have the space here to list them all, so it's best to check with the Tourism BC publications and your travel agent.

Note: There are various spellings for Ts'il?os (pronounced "sigh-loss"). The one used here is the BC Parks version. The version used in *Nemiah: The Unconquered Country*, co-authored by Terry Glavin and the people of the Nemiah Band, adds a "^" over the first "s." There are also various spellings for the word "Nemaiah." The accepted spellings seem to vary depending on whether the reference is to the lake (Nemaia), the valley (Nemaiah), or the First Nations wilderness preserve (Nemiah).

Note: See the *Information Sources* chapter at the end of the book for contact information on the services mentioned here

GPS References for major points of interest
Ref: WGS 84 - Lat/Lon hddd.ddddd
Allow +/-100 metres due to data conversions

Wpt	Km	Description	Latitude	Longitude	Elev.
W01	0	Hwy 20 at Lee's Corner	N51.94195	W123.09836	720 m
W02	3.4	Chilcotin River bridge	N51.92025	W123.08122	626 m
W03	5.4	Jct Taseko Lake Rd	N51.91041	W123.09249	711 m
W04	8.5	Jct Big Creek Rd and Minton Creek FS Rd	N51.88943	W123.07654	875 m
		Fletcher Lake Road to Chilko Lake			
W04	0.0	Minton Creek FS Rd (900 Road)	N51.88943	W123.07654	875 m
W05	13.0	13K marker – Cross Minton Creek – go left	N51.88447	W123.24128	979 m
W06	16.9	Tsuh Lake to left	N51.87135	W123.29222	1,113 m
W07	23.0	First glimpse of Mount Tatlow	N51.84401	W123.36261	1,165 m
W08	51.5	Cross Tete Angela Creek	N51.68651	W123.65418	1,210 m
W09	59.5	Jct keep right to Nemaiah Valley	N51.61889	W123.68561	1,329 m
W10	64.5	Taseko River access	N51.58149	W123.70474	1,177 m
W11	67.0	Cross Taseko River at Davidson bridge	N51.56288	W123.69742	1,192 m
W12	72.5	Big Lake and Tsylos Info	N51.52158	W123.73142	1,294 m
W13	78.0	Jct Elkin – Taseko FS Rd	N51.50818	W123.78329	1,365 m
W14	79.0	Jct to Elkin Creek Guest Ranch	N51.49963	W123.79463	1,271 m
W15	80.5	Cross Elkin Creek	N51.48828	W123.80166	1,243 m
W16	85.0	Konni Lake at Church	N51.47756	W123.84414	1,209 m
W17	92.2	Jct Keep left – west end of Konni Lake	N51.46832	W123.93899	1,223 m
W18	92.5	Nemaiah Valley Service Centre	N51.46681	W123.94445	1,224 m
W19	95.0	Nemaia Lake	N51.45552	W123.96837	1,202 m
W20	101.0	Cross Robertson Creek	N51.42070	W124.03360	1,201 m
W21	103.5	Jct to Ts'yl?os Park to left	N51.41407	W124.06523	1,180 m
W22	107.0	Jct to Ts'yl?os Park to right	N51.39868	W124.10274	1,213 m
W23	108.5	Chilko Lake Nu Chugh Beniz Campground	N51.38999	W124.11519	1,179 m

Wells Gray Provincial Park: Wilderness, Waterfalls, and Volcanoes

At 540,000 hectares, Wells Gray Provincial Park is certainly one of the largest in the Cariboo Region. From Clearwater, on the North Thompson River, it extends north approximately 140 kilometres to Mount Winder, taking in a large chunk of the Cariboo Mountains. Add Bowron Lake Provincial Park at 149,207 hectares and the relatively new Cariboo Mountains Provincial Park at 113,469 hectares, and the protected wilderness area covers over 800,000 hectares or nearly 1.5 times the area of the province of Prince Edward Island.

Together the three parks make up a 200-kilometre-long boundary on the eastern edge of the Cariboo. Bowron Lake Park is noted for its wilderness

Canoeists near the east end of Azure Lake.

canoe circuit and Cariboo Mountains Park is noted primarily for its limited-access wilderness.

Wilderness, Waterfalls, and Lakes

Wells Gray Provincial Park, one of the oldest wilderness parks in British Columbia, was initially established in 1939; to protect the wild rivers, waterfalls, and lakes drained by the Clearwater River.

William E. Noble, then Clearwater area Forest Ranger, wrote a letter to the District Forest Ranger in Kamloops on May, 15 1939:

> I am herewith suggesting that a considerable area of the Clearwater Valley be set aside as a Park; from a protection viewpoint also, I believe this area would benefit by being so administered, as with its natural attractions for Tourists it is sure to be well peopled during the dry weather, and if in a park people are naturally more careful with fire...
>
> The area I would recommend would include the whole of the watershed of the Clearwater River north of the Murtle River, and include the Murtle Lake, Mahood Lake, Clearwater Lake, Blue Lake and Hobson Lake, as well as numerous smaller lakes...

A "Clearwater Park" had been previously discussed for nearly a decade without action. It would be difficult to gauge how much Noble's letter contributed to the decision, but he had his wish before the year ended.

Big Lakes

The lakes Bill Noble wrote about make up the core of the park. Hobson Lake is nearly 30 kilometres long. Azure Lake (Noble's "Blue Lake") and Clearwater Lake are both 24 kilometres long. Murtle Lake, a favourite for canoeists, is over 30 kilometres from its northern input to Diamond Lagoon on the Murtle River. Mahood Lake, on the western edge of the park, is 20 kilometres long. The "numerous smaller lakes" Noble mentions range from beautiful roadside ponds such as Shadow Lake and Alice Lake to alpine tarns.

The waterfalls can also compete with the best in Canada. Helmcken Falls, at 142 metres, is considered to be the fourth-highest in Canada. The dozens of other waterfalls and rapids contribute to the wild (and unnavigable) reputation of the park.

And Volcanoes

The roadless wilderness, lakes, rivers, and waterfalls are obvious on the maps of the

Alice Lake, near the Ray Farm, is a short walk from the Clearwater Valley Road.

region, but what isn't quite as obvious is the underlying foundation of Wells Gray Provincial Park and the Clearwater valley and the volcanic icing on top.

A slow drive north of Clearwater, with frequent stops, will gradually reveal a foundation that has been in turmoil. Deeply sculpted valleys carved by glacial ice into metamorphic and granitic rock hundreds of thousands of eons old, form the foundation of the park. On top of these rocks, countless volcanic eruptions over the past three million years have poured forth, modifying the landscape even further.

Stop at Spahats Falls and you can see where the force of water at the end of the last ice age (ten thousand years ago) has cut a 122-metre-deep canyon in the lava beds that underlay the valley. A few minutes farther north, at the Shadden Viewpoint, you can stand on the edge of the lava cliffs and look down on the rubble that breaks away with each winter's frost. Straight up the mountainside to the east of the Shadden is Buck Hill, a volcano that was erupted during the waning stages of the last glaciation period.

These lava flows are just a prelude to the multiplicity of volcanic rocks that await investigation by the visitor. Home to more than two dozen volcanoes formed in a variety of ways, Wells Gray has a volcanic heritage virtually unique in the world. Here in Wells Gray, volcanoes formed under large lakes dammed by glaciers, under the glaciers themselves, and by erupting into the air such as those seen in Hawaii.

As you continue northward, Pyramid Mountain comes into view. Although it initially looks like a volcanic cinder cone (one that erupted into the air), it

Third Canyon Creek cuts through the ancient lava beds adjacent to Clearwater Valley Road, 16 kilometres north of Clearwater.

The Murtle River in winter, with the snow-covered volcanic dome of Pyramid Mountain in the background.

actually formed under two thousand metres of glacial ice. Its sub-peak formed when the ice surrounding it melted away, leaving the cone unsupported, and it slumped valleyward.

The Clearwater Valley Road continues northward to Clearwater Lake, occasionally revealing its once-molten icing to those who venture off the paved roadway. A hike down to the foot of Dawson Falls reveals more of the lava foundation. There is also an access trail to Pyramid Mountain near the Helmcken Falls junction; north of Dawson Falls. And for those with plenty of determination and stamina, there is a rough trail down to the foot of the canyon carved through the lava beds by Helmcken Falls.

Clearwater Lake owes approximately three metres of its depth to a dam across its outlet that was created when the 7,600-year-old Dragon's Tongue lava flow travelled 15 kilometres from its vent near the Goat Peaks.

One of the youngest and least accessible volcanoes in this part of the park is the Kostal Volcano on the east shore of Kostal Lake, approximately 17 kilometres east

Osprey Falls, at the outlet of Clearwater Lake, flows over a dam created by the Dragon's Tongue lava flow.

of Clearwater Lake. There is a rough trail (route might be a better description) to Kostal Lake, but you should allow three or four days for the round-trip. According to Dr. Catherine Hickson, a volcanologist with Natural Resources Canada, the latest eruption took place about four hundred years ago.

The Flourmill Volcano on the western boundary of the park, once accessible via the Clearwater River Road, is now only accessible from the Spanish Creek area northeast of 100 Mile House. The Flourmill eruptions took place since the last ice age. The cinder cone is visible from Spanish Creek Forest Road (7000 Rd) and is accessible via a rapidly in-growing trail that starts off near the outlet of Spanish Lake.

Wells Gray Provincial Park

The twin cones of the Flourmill Volcano are visible from near the 30K marker on Spanish Creek (7000) Forest Road.

Note: Special thanks to Trevor Goward and Catherine Hickson, co-authors of *Nature Wells Gray*, for information on the volcanoes of Wells Gray Provincial Park and the Clearwater region.

The Flourmill Lava Flow shows little sign of significant weathering.

CHAPTER 26

Wells Gray Provincial Park West: 100 Mile House to Mahood Lake

STATISTICS

	Map see page 324.
Distance:	85 km, 100 Mile House to Mahood Lake.
	Five km, Mahood Lake Park to Deception Falls Trailhead.
Elev. Descent:	Approximately 300 metres.
Travel Time:	Two to three hours to Mahood Lake.
Condition:	Partly paved; remainder good gravel road.
Season:	Dry weather road.
Topo Maps:	100 Mile House, BC 92 P/11.
(1:50,000)	Deka Lake, BC 92 P/10.
	Canim Lake, BC 92 P/15.
	Mahood Lake, BC 92 P/16.
Communities:	100 Mile House, Lone Butte, Interlakes, and Bridge Lake.

Mahood Lake, at the western end of Wells Gray Provincial Park, is the lesser known of the park's destinations. It doesn't have the spectacular mountain scenery of the Trophy Mountains or the continuous string of wild rapids and spectacular waterfalls of the Clearwater and Murtle rivers. However, if you take the time to explore the area, you'll soon discover that the Canim Lake – Mahood Lake region has its fair share of spectacular waterfalls.

If you venture into the west end of the park in mid-summer, you may also discover that Mahood Lake is much warmer and much more kid-friendly than the other lakes of Wells Gray Provincial Park.

Access from 100 Mile House

There are numerous ways to access the campground and beach at the west end of Mahood Lake. We've previously mentioned links from the Clearwater – 100 Mile House backroad as well as from Bridge Lake Road (Highway 20) and Lone Butte

Wells Gray Provincial Park West

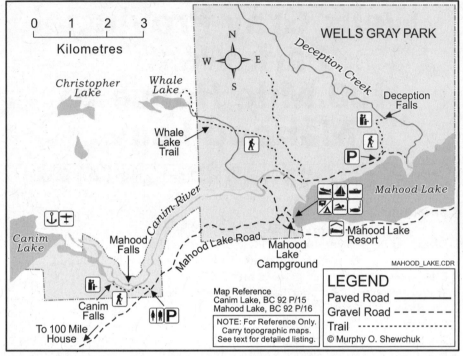

The east end of Canim Lake and the west end of Mahood Lake make up the western section of Wells Gray Provincial Park. The waterfalls, campground, and beach are easily accessible via a backroad from 100 Mile House.

– Horse Lake Road. There is also access from the Canim Lake Road, and if you are a really determined hiker, from the Clearwater River Road and the Mahood River Trail.

However, if you are interested in a family-camping adventure without the inconvenience of two or three days of serious backpacking, consider the scenic route from 100 Mile House via the south shore of Horse Lake and the string of lakes to the east.

With the junction of Horse Lake Road and Highway 97 near the heart of 100 Mile House as your km 0 reference point, head southeast for nine kilometres to Horse Lake and then follow the south shore of Horse Lake east for another 23 kilometres to Mahood Lake Road.

You'll have the opportunity for a few diversions along the way, including stops at resorts along Horse Lake or side trips to Lone Butte or Fawn Lake, but stay focused and continue northeast on Mahood Lake Road.

An old boat slowly sinks into the rushes on the shore of Dragonfly Lake.

Interlakes District

Sulphurous Lake, at km 39.5, presents the first of a whole new set of diversions that make up the northern part of the Interlakes District. Mahood Lake Road

Canim Falls during the spring runoff.

follows the north shores of Sulphurous Lake, Hathaway Lake, and Dragonfly Lake and the east shores of Drewry Lake and McNeil Lake. If you have a week to spare, you can detour off the main road on your return trip and try a little angling at Deka Lake, Bowers Lake, or more than half a dozen prime fishing lakes. The *Bridge Lake Road* and *Clearwater to 100 Mile House* chapters will help you get started on your way to more backroads adventures. The Clearwater – 100 Mile House backroad joins Mahood Lake Road as Bowers Lake – Canim Forest Road near km 52.3.

A junction at km 69 presents the last chance for a visit to Canim Lake and a big lake diversion before the final eastward run to Mahood Lake. It may not be obvious unless you've been studying your maps, but you've driven through a pass between Hathaway Lake and Dragonfly Lake. The water from Hathaway and the surrounding lakes drains west into Horse Lake and Bridge Creek before winding through 100 Mile House and northeast to Canim Lake and east to Mahood Lake.

If you are still looking for return-trip diversions, make note of the Bowers Road junction at km 74.5. If you follow your nose, GPS, or compass southward for about

Mahood Lake looking east just before a summer sunset.

17 kilometres, there is a good chance you will link up with the backroad to Clearwater.

Canim Falls Trail

The roundabout water circuit takes an estimated 150 kilometres including hundreds of oxbows and marshes. Along the way the water has plenty of time to warm up before tumbling over Canim and Mahood falls and making the last dash to Mahood Lake.

There is plenty of room to park at the trailhead next to the main road (km 79.5) and it's barely more than a kilometre to the viewpoint at the lip of 20-metre-high Canim Falls. There is also a viewpoint for Mahood Falls about one-third of the way along the easy trail. Both viewpoints are fenced and the trail is wide enough for a baby stroller if the junior members of your family still aren't self-propelled.

Mahood Lake Campground

It is another five kilometres to the campground and beach at Mahood Lake. If it is getting late on your inward journey, you can return to the falls in the morning when the light will turn the mist into a series of rainbows.

The beach and 34-unit campsite is open from May to September with the gates closed and locked in the off-season. There are no lifeguards on the 220-metre-long beach, but the gradual slope makes it a popular swimming area for kids of all ages.

Deception Falls Trail

This backroad heads north to the Canim River and then continues east along the north shore of Mahood Lake to the Deception Falls trailhead (km 88.7) and the end of the public road at Deception Point. It is about a kilometre north to 40-metre-high Deception Falls with a 150-metre difference in elevation. Not quite as easy a walk as to Canim Falls, but still well worth the effort.

According to Muriel Dunford in her book *North River*, "River Deception" was given its name in 1874 by a Scottish engineer, Joseph Hunter, who was surveying a potential route for the Canadian Pacific Railway. They had climbed up to the plateau from the Blackpool area, south of the mouth of the Clearwater River. After building a raft to carry their horses and equipment across Mahood Lake, they continued north up the creek that a previous surveyor, E.W. Jarvis, had mistaken for the Clearwater River — thus the "Deception."

Mahood Lake's name is also linked to the search for a route for the CPR. James Adams Mahood led a survey party through the area in 1872.

Forty-metre-high Deception Falls tumbles over the ancient lava cliffs.

A cluster of ground dogwood (Cornus canadensis) seeks shelter at the base of a tree near the Deception Falls Trail.

Whale Lake Trail

In this case, it's not the size that counts, but the shape. A bit of imagination and a close look at a map could explain why a lake 4.5 kilometres northwest of the Mahood Lake was given that moniker. We have yet to sample its waters to see if there are any whales, but the BC Parks website reports that Whale Lake offers good fishing at the end of a four-kilometre hiking trail (about a 1.5 hour walk). The trailhead is on the east side of the Canim River bridge on the road to Deception Point.

GPS References for major points of interest
Ref: WGS 84 - Lat/Lon hddd.ddddd
Allow +/-100 metres due to data conversions

Wpt	Km	Description	Latitude	Longitude
ML01	0	100 Mile House	N51.63801	W121.29790
ML02	8.8	Horse Lake Outflow	N51.60511	W121.19780
ML03	14.1	Lone Butte – Horse Lake Rd	N51.57663	W121.14397
ML04	31.6	Jct Mahood Lake Rd	N51.58428	W120.92647
ML05	39.5	Sulphurous Lake Resort	N51.63019	W120.85301
ML06	41.5	Hathaway Lake Resort	N51.64467	W120.84029
ML07	46.7	Dragonfly Lake	N51.68256	W120.81587
ML08	51.4	Bower – Deka FS Rd	N51.71990	W120.79420
ML09	52.3	Bowers Lake – Canim FS Rd	N51.72644	W120.79263
ML10	53.0	Drewry Lake E rec site	N51.73172	W120.79308
ML11	69.0	Canim Lake S Rd	N51.83144	W120.70791
ML12	74.5	Bowers Lake Rd to Clearwater	N51.84105	W120.63843
ML13	77.0	Canimred Creek	N51.84919	W120.60733
ML14	79.5	Canim Falls Trail	N51.86522	W120.58069
ML15	83.8	Jct Mahood Lake Resort	N51.88110	W120.53028
ML16	84.0	Mahood Park Entrance	N51.88172	W120.52910
ML17	84.7	Canim River trailhead	N51.88752	W120.53243
ML18	85.7	Canim River Bridge	N51.89065	W120.52599
ML19	88.7	Deception Falls trailhead	N51.89602	W120.48735
ML20	90.0	Deception Falls	N51.90358	W120.48697

Wells Gray Provincial Park East

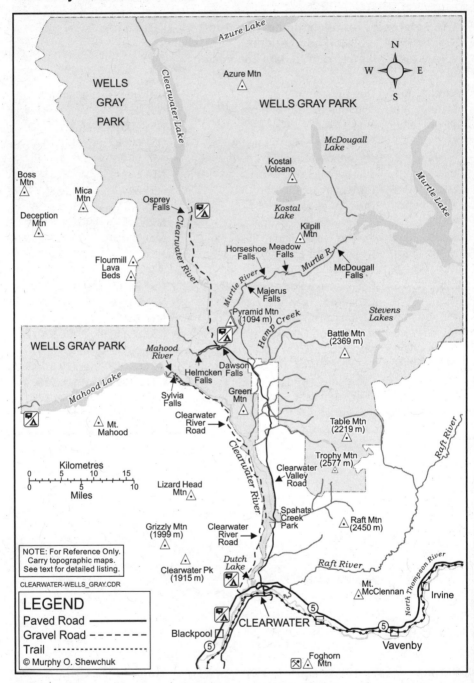

Southeast Wells Gray Provincial Park, accessible from Clearwater on Yellowhead Highway 5, is undoubtedly the busiest section of the park.

CHAPTER 27

Wells Gray Provincial Park East: Clearwater to Clearwater Lake

STATISTICS

	Map see page 332.
Distance:	68 km, Yellowhead Highway 5 to Clearwater Lake boat launch.
Travel Time:	One to two hours.
Condition:	Paved to Helmcken Falls, remainder gravel.
Season:	Year-round to Helmcken Falls.
	Remainder summer and early fall.
Topo Maps:	Clearwater, BC 92 P/9.
(1:50,000)	Vavenby, BC 82 M/12.
	Mahood Lake, BC 92 P/16.
	West Raft River, BC 82 M/13.
	Clearwater Lake, BC 93 A/1.
	Murtle Lake, BC 83 D/4.
Communities:	Clearwater.

Wells Gray Provincial Park, with its southern boundary approximately 125 kilometres north of Kamloops, is one of British Columbia's most accessible wilderness parks. At 540,000 hectares, it is also one of the province's largest parks.

It also boasts many other distinguishing features, including not-so-ancient lava beds, clear cold lakes, snow-capped peaks, and beautiful alpine meadows. However, the park's most spectacular feature is the numerous waterfalls and rapids that turn its wild rivers into beautiful yet deadly waterways.

The summer months are the busiest season for park visitors, yet while much of the park is inaccessible in winter, the road is maintained to 141-metre-high Helmcken Falls, providing year-round access to what one author considers to be the world's fifth largest waterfall. Winter activities also include backcountry skiing and snowshoeing in the Trophy Mountains as well as on the trails in the Majerus Farm area.

Spahats Falls, at 75 metres high, is the first major waterfall on the road from Clearwater to Clearwater Lake in the heart of Wells Gray Provincial Park.

Clearwater Start

No trip into the Wells Gray area is complete without a stop at the Clearwater Information Centre at the junction of Yellowhead Highway 5 and Clearwater Valley Road (a.k.a. Wells Gray Road). This could be your last chance to get up-to-date information and maps on the park and the attractions and accommodations along the way. Your reading material should include Trevor Goward and Cathie Hickson's *Nature Wells Gray* book. It provides far more details on the park's volcanoes, waterfalls, wildlife, and trails than I am able to present here.

A service station across Clearwater Valley Road from the Information Centre is also your last chance to top up the fuel tank before venturing into the wilderness.

Spahats Falls

With the junction of Clearwater Valley Road and Yellowhead Highway 5 as km 0, the first major stop-of-interest is Spahats Creek Park at km 10.2. Spahats Creek, once known as Bear Creek, rises in the alpine north of Raft Mountain and flows west to the Clearwater River. It is a wild creek throughout most of its length, making one final 75-metre plunge in the heart of the park before cascading into the Clearwater River.

Although Spahats Creek Park previously had a campground, the day-use area and parking lot has been expanded, with many of the campsites gradually reverting to their natural state. A nature trail through the interior rainforest begins near the parking lot with plenty of opportunity to observe numerous unusual wildflowers. A well-marked trail follows the creek downstream to the edge of the 75-metre falls. Over the centuries, the creek has cut a deep trench through the ancient lava beds. Then, where it spills out into a giant cauldron, the erosion reveals the layers of multi-coloured lava that serve as the foundation for much of the park. While the waterfall is particularly spectacular in May and June, a winter jaunt down to the lip could reveal a 20-metre-high ice cone at its base. Use caution when proceeding beyond the guard rails because the trail to Clearwater River can be extremely dangerous.

Trophy Mountain Meadows Trail

Spahats Creek Road, one kilometre past the Spahats Falls access road, provides access to the Trophy Mountain alpine trails. The Trophy Mountain meadows are spectacular with some of the Interior's best wildflower fields in mid-summer and some of the best ski-touring snow in mid-winter. See the *Trophy Mountain Trail* chapter for additional information.

First, Second, and Third Canyons

Meanwhile, back on Clearwater Valley Road, the paved road crosses three major canyons between km 13 and km 16. The steep canyon walls, unstable lava and glacial soils, and frequent high runoffs have made this an "interesting" section of road ever since the first settlers moved into the area in the early 1900s. Although major improvements have been made as recently as 2006, it was not uncommon during the last century to arrive at one of the bridges only to discover that it had been carried away by a flash flood.

Clearwater Valley Road winds along the lava benches, occasionally offering a view of the roadside attractions such as Third Canyon Creek Falls.

Clearwater Community Hall

After clinging to the mountainside near Third Canyon, the road descends to the broader Clearwater Valley — still well above the roaring river. It passes the old Community Hall, built in the 1930s, and several newer guest ranches and bed-and-breakfast establishments. Battle Mountain, with an access road near km 26, is one of the reasons for the growing tourism industry in the Clearwater Valley. The hiking trails accessible along the route as well as the attractions in Wells Gray Provincial Park are receiving increasing attention from European travellers who are also interested in the peripheral activities.

Pyramid Mountain, from the Green Mountain lookout tower. According to the Geological Survey of Canada, "Pyramid Mountain, once mistaken for a cinder cone, is now known to have formed below several thousand metres of glacial ice ... Although it had a vigorous start, the eruption that formed Pyramid Mountain was not sufficiently sustained to form a larger edifice that could break through the surrounding ice and water to form a tuya."

Pyramid Mountain

While there is a trail from the Dawson Falls area that leads to a closer look at the twin volcanic cones of Pyramid Mountain, the first view of this imposing interruption of the otherwise "mellow" landscape is from the road near km 32. Clearwater Valley Road then descends to Hemp Creek before beginning a steady climb past the last of the resorts and into the park at km 35.5.

Green Mountain and Placid Lake Trail

The first opportunity to detour off the main road for a little exploring and a real "overview" of the park presents itself five hundred metres past the park entrance. If the weather is dry and the snow is gone from the park, Green Mountain Road should be an easy 3.5 kilometre drive to the 1,085-metre summit. A lookout tower at the top, complete with information panels, is a bit more of an incentive to make the drive. And if it is a cool morning, you may recognize the mist rising from Helmcken Falls, eight kilometres to the west-north-west (293°).

At Dawson Falls there is ample room to park and follow the short trails to several excellent views of this 20-metre-high cascade.

The Placid Lake Trail, an eight-kilometre round trip with minimal elevation gain, could be an excellent birdwatching and nature photography route, especially in June. In winter you could consider testing your snowshoes for some great ice fishing.

Majerus Farm Trailhead

My first adventure into the park was with the Kamloops Outdoor Club more than three decades ago. It was February of a record snowfall year and our snowshoes and skinny skis were no match for what Nature had left us. However, we did trek from the park entrance to Dawson Falls with a short detour into the then aged Majerus Farm cabin. Michael Majerus first built a cabin in the area prior to World War I. After several jaunts to the outside world, he returned to the Murtle River and later set up a homestead, building the existing cabin in the 1930s.

I've taken family and friends back to the cabin on numerous occasions since then and noticed how the access has gradually changed from a tree-lined narrow path to a well-developed parking lot at km 39.7 and a 32-kilometre loop trail used by cross-country skiers in winter and hikers and cyclists in summer.

Dawson Falls

The original Dawson Falls trailhead, at km 40.1, is now reserved for tour buses. The present trailhead and parking area is now at km 40.7 at what was a campground. (The nearest place to camp is now the Pyramid Campground at km 41.9.) It's an easy 300-metre walk along

Columbian lily on the Alice Lake Loop Trail.

the wide trail to an excellent viewpoint. You can continue upstream another three hundred or four hundred metres to a viewpoint at the brink of the falls. In low water (around October), you can scramble down to the riverbed and get a close look at the rock formations that have helped form this 90-metre-wide, 20-metre-high miniature Niagara Falls. In high water (May and June), there is nothing "miniature" about the deadly force of the Murtle River. If you survive a fall into the river at the base of Dawson Falls, the Mushbowl, five hundred metres downstream, could turn you into "mush." Helmcken Falls, another four kilometres downstream, will pulverize that mush into trout feed.

Helmcken Falls Trail

The Helmcken Canyon Trail begins across the road from the Dawson Falls parking area and follows the Murtle River four kilometres downstream to Helmcken Falls. We've "done" this trail on touring skis and found it a bit of a challenge, but the winter view of Wells Gray Provincial Park's star attraction was well worth the effort. If you are not into hiking or skiing, continue along Wells Gray Road to km 42.3, where a four-kilometre side road leads to the brink of the falls on the north

Helmcken Falls is Canada's fourth-highest waterfall; at 141 metres it is about three times higher than Niagara Falls.

side of Murtle River. Note that in the past, the road has been maintained to Helmcken Falls in winter, but it is not open in winter from the junction north to Clearwater Lake.

Surveyor R.H. Lee discovered the world-famous falls in 1913 and suggested that it be named after then BC Premier Richard McBride. McBride insisted that the honour go to Dr. J.S. Helmcken who had come west as a Hudson's Bay Company employee in 1850 and stayed to become an active politician in the infant colony of British Columbia.

Helmcken Falls, at 141 metres, is the fourth-highest falls in Canada and one of the most impressive in North America. A second 15-metre falls, a short distance downstream, contributes to the Murtle River's reputation as a wild waterway. It rises in the glaciers of the Cariboo Mountains and tumbles down a long, narrow valley before emptying into Murtle Lake. After leaving Murtle Lake, the river flows more than 30 kilometres across the plateau. Along this route, the water tumbles over McDougall, Horseshoe, Meadow, Majerus, Dawson, and Helmcken falls before joining the Clearwater River.

John Bunyan Ray

The Ray Farm, at km 54.5, marks a long-abandoned homestead. John Bunyan Ray first came to the upper Clearwater in 1910 as a trapper. He married Clearwater Valley girl Alice Ludtke in 1932 and lived in the area until his death in 1947.

Ray Farm – Alice Lake Loop Trail

Cold mineral springs bubble out of the ground near the farm buildings and a 4.4-kilometre loop trail continues northwest, joining the Ray Mineral Spring Trail about a kilometre from the farm buildings. Although the loop trail is well marked and easy to follow, allow a couple of hours to enjoy the wildflowers and wildlife in the forest as well as the views along Alice Lake, named after Mrs. Alice Ray (nee Ludtke).

Bailey's Chute

A 15-minute walk from the road at km 56.9, Bailey's Chute is one of the wildest rapids on the Clearwater River. During high water in early June, the roar of the chute can be heard a hundred metres away. This spectacular rapid was named after Jim Bailey, an engineer who lost his life to the river while scouting a potential bridge site.

Falls Creek

Falls Creek (km 65.3) drains Ray Lake and empties into the Clearwater River a few hundred metres from the outlet of Clearwater Lake. Forty-one-unit Falls Creek Campground and the 39-unit campground at Clearwater Lake can serve as a base for boating on the lake or hiking the local trails. Just north of the Falls Creek Bridge is a parking area and the trailhead for a network of trails to the east. See the *Sticta Falls Trail* chapter for details.

Clearwater Lake

Osprey Falls, at the outlet of the lake, can make launching a boat here a deadly pastime. To increase the safety factor, the public boat launch is another three kilometres up the lake at km 68.2. The boat launch is the end of the road, but even if you don't have a boat of your own, it need not be the end of your trip as a private company offers boat tours of Clearwater and Azure lakes during the summer. They will also transport you and your kayak or canoe up Clearwater Lake and into Azure Lake where you can enjoy lake shore camping at the wilderness campsites.

Clearwater Lake is about 24 kilometres long, lying in a north-south direction.

Bailey's Chute is one of the wildest rapids on the Clearwater River.

Canoeists near the east end of 24-kilometre-long Azure Lake.

A short portage links Clearwater with Azure Lake, approximately the same length but lying in an east-west direction. Hobson Lake, to the north, is a 35-kilometre-long lake that rarely feels the intrusion of man. In the late 1890s and the early twentieth century, the area was the subject of a minor gold rush with placer miners coming from the Cariboo via Quesnel Lake.

Note: See the *Information Sources* chapter at the end of the book for contact information on the services mentioned here.

Wells Gray Provincial Park East

GPS References for major points of interest
Ref: WGS 84 - Lat/Lon hddd.ddddd
Allow +/-100 metres due to data conversions

Wpt	Km	Description	Latitude	Longitude	Elev.
WE01	0	Jct Wells Gray Rd and Hwy 5	N51.65249	W120.03849	453 m
WE02	9.5	W.G. Park boundary	N51.72963	W120.00790	742 m
WE03	10.2	Spahats Creek	N51.73418	W120.00703	745 m
WE04	11.2	Spahats Creek FS Rd	N51.74447	W120.00642	776 m
WE05	12.8	Clearwater River trailhead	N51.75798	W120.00780	761 m
WE06	13.5	First Canyon Creek	N51.76441	W120.00739	770 m
WE07	14.1	Second Canyon Creek	N51.76976	W120.00795	755 m
WE08	16.0	Third Canyon Creek	N51.78674	W120.01235	721 m
WE09	28.5	Nakiska Ranch	N51.89299	W120.02293	703 m
WE10	29.3	Flat Iron rrailhead	N51.89594	W120.03413	761 m
WE11	34.4	Helmcken Falls Lodge	N51.93652	W120.05654	650 m
WE12	35.5	Wells Gray Park entrance	N51.94348	W120.06967	734 m
WE13	36.0	Green Mountain Rd	N51.94425	W120.07602	729 m
WE14	39.7	Majerus Farm trailhead	N51.96440	W120.11828	805 m
WE15	40.1	Dawson Falls bus parking	N51.96406	W120.12336	803 m
WE16	40.7	Dawson Falls parking	N51.96256	W120.13101	806 m
WE17	41.2	Murtle River Mushbowl	N51.96383	W120.13050	780 m
WE18	41.9	Pyramid Campground	N51.96673	W120.13473	809 m
WE19	42.3	Jct to Helmcken Falls	N51.96905	W120.13744	792 m
WE20	46.3	Helmcken Falls parking	N51.95801	W120.18255	746 m
WE21	48.9	Redspring	N52.00877	W120.15103	617 m
WE22	52.0	Deer Creek	N52.03575	W120.14740	618 m
WE23	54.5	Ray Farm	N52.05600	W120.16013	654 m
WE24	55.7	Alice Lake	N52.06241	W120.17203	646 m
WE25	56.1	Lone Spoon Creek	N52.06559	W120.17593	626 m
WE26	56.9	Bailey's Chute trailhead	N52.06965	W120.18354	637 m
WE27	60.5	Shadow Lake	N52.10024	W120.18701	703 m
WE28	63.8	Norman's Eddy trailhead	N52.12678	W120.19199	677 m
WE29	64.9	Falls Creek Campground	N52.13614	W120.19055	686 m
WE30	65.2	Chain Meadows trailhead	N52.13841	W120.18923	684 m
WE31	65.3	Clearwater Lake Campground	N52.14002	W120.19005	684 m
WE32	68.2	Clearwater Lake boat launch	N52.16210	W120.20691	701 m

CHAPTER 28

Trophy Mountain Trail

STATISTICS

	Map see page 346.
Distance:	13 km, Clearwater Valley Road to Trophy Meadows Trailhead. Trail length: 5 to 7 km, depending on destination.
Travel Time:	Allow a day for travel and hiking.
Condition:	Gravel road plus mountain trails.
Season:	July through September.
Topo Maps:	Clearwater, BC 92 P/9.
(1:50,000)	Vavenby, BC 82 M/12.
	Mahood Lake, BC 92 P/16.
	West Raft River, BC 82 M/13.
Communities:	Clearwater.

Trophy Mountain Meadows Trail

Spahats Creek Road, one kilometre past the Spahats Falls turnoff, provides access to the Trophy Mountain alpine trails. The Trophy Mountain meadows are spectacular with some of the Interior's best wildflower fields in mid-summer and some of the best ski-touring snow in mid-winter.

If you are interested in a closer view of the meadows, follow Spahats Creek Road east for 4 kilometres and then turn left (north) for 3.5 kilometres before turning right (northeast). This last leg of the route soon begins a switchback climb up through a large logged area. The road reaches the Trophy Mountain trailhead approximately 5.5 kilometres from the last major junction or 13 kilometres from Clearwater Valley Road.

The trail to the meadows begins to the left of the parking area. It winds northeast

The glacier lily (Erythronium grandiflorum) is among the earliest of two dozen wildflower species to grace the slopes of Trophy Mountain.

Trophy Mountain Trail

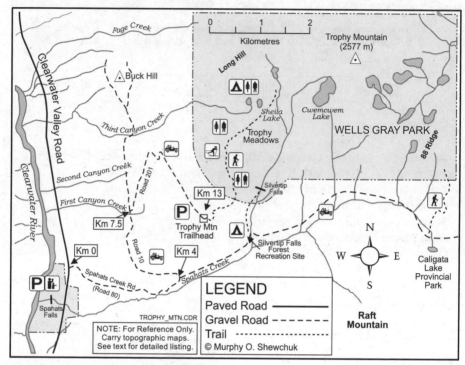

The Trophy Mountains rise 2,575 metres, with nine peaks towering over southern Wells Gray Provincial Park. Wildflowers attract photographers from late June to early August. The deep powder snow attracts touring skiers and snowshoers in winter.

through the harvested area and the old growth forest before reaching the meadows. It is a distance of about five kilometres to Sheila Lake and the headwaters of Third Canyon Creek. There is a designated wilderness campsite at Sheila Lake. The trail also has an elevation gain of about 430 metres from the trailhead to the alpine plateau overlooking Sheila Lake.

A memorial plaque at the summit honours Sheila Leonard (1939–1977). Sheila was a regular visitor to the Trophy meadows. After her death her ashes were scattered here.

Plan an early start and allow a full day if you hope to enjoy an early-August wildflower photography excursion to the meadows. Take along plenty of water and/or a water purifying kit.

It is another three to four kilometres to the summit of 2,577-metre Trophy Mountain. If that is your destination, it may be wise to plan an overnight camp at Sheila Lake.

Buck Hill

Approximately 4.5 kilometres north of the road junction at km 7.5 is Clearwater's closest volcanic cone. Buck Hill is outside the boundaries of Wells Gray Provincial Park, but the "Friends of Buck Hill" are working hard to have this unique feature preserved and protected as part of the park.

To quote their website (http://www.buckhill.ca):

Clearwater's mascot, Buck Hill, is one of a small handful of cinder cones in the Clearwater – Wells Gray area ... It is thought that the ridge of Buck Hill is actually the surviving uphill side of its crater whereas the other side has either collapsed or eroded. Buck Hill erupted when the valley of the Clearwater River was still brimming with ice

Telemark skiing in the Trophy Mountains.

from the last ("Fraser") glaciation. The hot lava fountaining from Buck Hill melted some of this ice creating a weak western flank that ultimately collapsed, tumbling into the Clearwater Valley.

Buck Hill is an easy hike for young or old. It's an unexploited educational resource and its park-like environment encourages thought and meditation. Clearwater is the only Canadian town that can boast having its own pet volcano.

Note: See the *Information Sources* chapter at the end of the book for contact information on the services mentioned here.

Trophy Mountain Trail

GPS References for major points of interest
Ref: WGS 84 - Lat/Lon hddd.ddddd
Allow +/-100 metres due to data conversions

Wpt	Km	Description	Latitude	Longitude
TR01	0	Jct Clearwater Valley Rd	N51.74456	W120.00608
TR02	0.7	Bear Creek Correction Centre	N51.74258	W119.99899
TR03	2.4	Log landing and side road	N51.73846	W119.97550
TR04	4.0	Jct Spahats Creek Rd and Rd 10	N51.74229	W119.95356
TR05	7.5	Jct Rd 10 and Rd 201	N51.76095	W119.97763
TR06		Buck Hill	N51.79866	W119.98117
TR07	13.0	Trophy trailhead parking	N51.75853	W119.94294
		Trophy Mountain Trail		
TR07	0.0	Trophy trailhead parking	N51.75853	W119.94294
TR08	0.6	Enter old growth forest	N51.75995	W119.93769
TR09	3.5	Rest area	N51.77930	W119.93158
TR10	5.0	Alpine plateau	N51.78529	W119.91858
TR11	5.5	Cliff-top viewpoint	N51.78511	W119.91519
TR12	6.0	Sheila Lake	N51.78999	W119.91720

CHAPTER 29

Sticta Falls Trail

STATISTICS

	Map see page 351.
Distance:	600 metres, Chain Meadows Lake Trailhead to Sticta Falls.
	1.5 km, Trailhead to Osprey Falls Lookout.
Elevation Gain:	Approx. 200 metres, Trailhead to Osprey Falls Lookout.
Travel Time:	Allow half a day for hiking, birdwatching, and photography.
Condition:	Mountain trails.
Season:	June through September.
Topo Maps:	Clearwater Lake, BC 93 A/1.
(1:50,000)	Murtle Lake, BC 83 D/4.
Communities:	Clearwater.

Sticta Falls, Dragon's Tongue, and Osprey Falls Lookout Trails

If you are looking for a break from driving or an interesting hike for the younger or older members of the family, consider the 600-metre-long trail to Sticta Falls. And if the hiking mood persists, it's less than a kilometre walk around the Dragon's Tongue Loop or an 800-metre walk north to the Osprey Falls Lookout.

Falls Creek has eroded a section of the Dragon's Tongue lava flow.

Sticta Falls is about a 45-minute walk from the Clearwater Lake Campground.

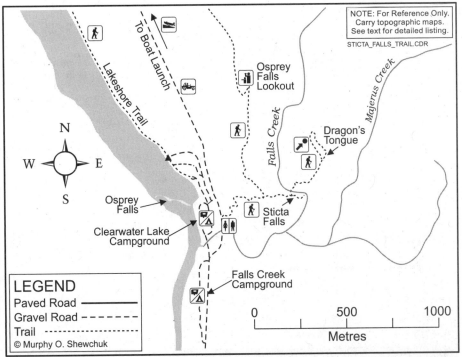

NOTE: For Reference Only.
Carry topographic maps.
See text for detailed listing.

STICTA_FALLS_TRAIL.CDR

To Boat Launch

Lakeshore Trail

Osprey
Falls
Lookout

N

W — E

S

Falls Creek

Dragon's
Tongue

Majerus Creek

Osprey
Falls

Clearwater Lake
Campground

Sticta
Falls

Falls Creek
Campground

LEGEND
Paved Road ————
Gravel Road ––––––
Trail ················
© Murphy O. Shewchuk

0   500   1000

Metres

If you are really energetic, you can continue north of the lookout on a trail that will eventually loop around to the Clearwater Lake boat launch and back along the lake shore. Check the park maps for the details on this 16.5-kilometre loop excursion and the 14-kilometre (one-way) wilderness route to Kostal Lake.

The Chain Meadows Lake trailhead is on the east side of the main road, just south of the Clearwater Lake Campground. Good boots and drinking water will be an asset. Take along your camera and be prepared to do a little scrambling to get that prize-winning shot of Sticta Falls or the Dragon's Tongue lava caves.

GPS References for major points of interest
Ref: WGS 84 - Lat/Lon hddd.ddddd
Allow +/-100 metres due to data conversions

Wpt	Km	Description	Latitude	Longitude	Elev.
SF01	0	Chain Meadows trailhead	N52.13842	W120.18921	673 m
SF02	0.4	Jct Lookout Trail	N52.13934	W120.18592	745 m
SF03	0.6	Sticta Falls	N52.13947	W120.18366	730 m
SF04	0.9	Dragon's Tongue loop	N52.14117	W120.18110	748 m
SF05	1.2	Osprey Falls Lookout	N52.14443	W120.18776	881 m

CHAPTER 30

Clearwater River Road and Mahood River Trail

STATISTICS

	Map see page 353.
Distance:	38 km, Clearwater to Mahood River.
	3 km, Mahood River Trailhead to Sylvia Falls.
Elevation Gain:	Approximately 170 metres.
Travel Time:	One hour to the Mahood River.
	One to two hours via the trail to Sylvia Falls.
Condition:	Gravel road; narrow and rough in places.
Season:	Dry weather road.
Topo Maps:	Clearwater, BC 92 P/9.
(1:50,000)	Mahood Lake, BC 92 P/16.
Communities:	Clearwater.

Rafting the Clearwater River near km 9.

One of the wildest of British Columbia's many wild rivers, the sparkling Clearwater River drains Clearwater Lake in the heart of Wells Gray Provincial Park. The Clearwater River is not recommended for river travel by canoe or kayak. The rapids and waterfalls make it extremely dangerous. Many people have drowned in the river.

Previously known also as the Mahood River Road, the Clearwater River Road follows the west side of the Clearwater River upstream to the Mahood River. The road was built by Clearwater Timber Products Ltd., but when logging ended in the area in 1975, the bridge across the Mahood was removed.

Camp 2 Road Start

This trip begins at the junction of Camp 2 Road and the old North Thompson Highway at the south side of the Clearwater River Bridge, near the Brookfield Shopping Centre. Follow the road northwest about 1 kilometres and then follow the gravel road branching right near the entrance to the old saw mill yard and past the Clearwater airport.

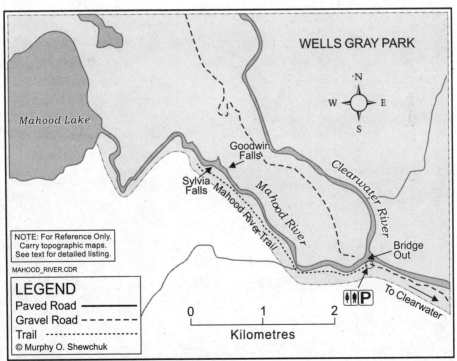

The three-kilometre-long trail to Sylvia Falls starts at the site of the former Mahood River Bridge, 38 kilometres from Clearwater.

Kettle Rapids

There are five major lakes and a number of smaller ones within Wells Gray Provincial Park. They are all drained by the Clearwater and its tributaries, making up what is probably the largest concentration of waterfalls, rapids, and chutes in British Columbia. Dawson Falls and 142-metre-high Helmcken Falls, both on the Murtle River, attract 70,000 visitors to Wells Gray Provincial Park each year. However, it is only recently that the wild Clearwater has attracted commercial rafting outfitters. Experienced outfitters, including Interior Whitewater Expeditions, run approximately 25 kilometres of the lower Clearwater River.

A short hike down to the wild Kettle Rapids, near km 8, will confirm why they are the exception. Rafts are transported around the Kettle Rapids and put back into the Clearwater River for a run to Clearwater, disembarking near the Brookfield Shopping Centre.

A walking trail has been cut to the Kettle, but it is unmarked and will require some sleuthing to find. Watch for the road cut down to the river pullout, and then backtrack for less than a kilometre.

A view of the rapids from a rock bluff at km 21.4.

Natural Bridge

Wells Gray Provincial Park, a giant wilderness area exceeding 540,000 hectares, is well known for its striking cliffs and canyons carved out of ancient lava beds. Extinct volcanoes, some considered to be as little as three thousand years old, are a dominant feature.

Erosion in the lava cliffs across the river has created a natural bridge partially hidden by the timber. Look for it near km 8.7 and the rafting pullout road.

Batholith Rapids

The road descends to river level near a set of particularly wild rapids near km 21. There is an excellent viewpoint with a little bit of space to pull off the road near km 21.4. At one time several sections of the road were

A fisherman tries his luck near the mouth of the Mahood River.

in danger of becoming impassable when it was no longer being maintained by the logging company. However, in October 2007, it was easily passable to the Mahood River. A shovel and a pair of gloves could be useful items in your toolkit if you happen to make the trip after a rain or wind storm.

White Horse Bluff

Forest Service picnic tables mark a trail to the river's edge and an excellent view of White Horse Bluff, a giant volcanic outcropping near km 33. Fishing is a favourite activity in the Clearwater drainage area, and rainbow trout and Dolly Varden char inhabit most of the region's lakes, rivers, and streams.

Mahood River

The Lower Clearwater River Road ends at km 38 where the Mahood River empties into the Clearwater. The bridge spanning the Mahood has been removed, preventing further access to the north. There is room to park a few vehicles and a pit toilet at the end of the road.

Mahood River Trail and Sylvia Falls Trail

A well-marked trail leads three kilometres up the Mahood River to two spectacular waterfalls and then continues another three to four kilometres farther to Mahood Lake. The trail initially follows the banks of the Mahood River, then shifts away from the river as it winds through a stand of cedar and other evergreens — some as much as two metres across. It then climbs well above the river. While it is not a particularly difficult trail, good boots and a hiking pole might save a slip or two. It is not suitable for bicycles.

Goodwin Falls is initially visible through the trees from a high point in the trail at km 2.4. A short side trail, marked by survey ribbons, leads north to the lip of the falls at km 2.8 of the trail. The unmistakeable roar of Sylvia Falls can be heard as the trail winds through the evergreens and around the rock outcrops and boulders near km 3. Sylvia Falls, named after the wife of the well-known BC writer and filmmaker, C.P. Lyons, is about 20 metres high and one hundred metres wide.

In late summer, the sun warms Mahood Lake and the river level drops, enabling a knee-deep hike into the river at the foot of Sylvia Falls. The current is strong and there are a few deep "kettles," so be cautious.

There are rumours that the trail continues to Mahood Lake; however some sources suggest that it is steep and overgrown in places. I've never hiked beyond the falls, *Watch out for wildlife along the Mahood River Trail.*

The "kettles" in the flat area downstream from Sylvia Falls can be a welcome respite from a hot August day. Use caution because the current could carry you downstream to Goodwin Falls and disaster.

but it is worth noting that Mahood Lake is also easily reached by a backroad from 100 Mile House and Cariboo Highway 97. See the *Wells Gray Provincial Park West* chapter for details.

Note: See the *Information Sources* chapter at the end of the book for contact information on the services mentioned here.

Clearwater River Road and Mahood River Trail

GPS References for major points of interest
Ref: WGS 84 - Lat/Lon hddd.ddddd
Allow +/-100 metres due to data conversions

Wpt	Km	Description	Latitude	Longitude	Elev.
		Clearwater River Road			
CR01	0	Camp 2 Rd	N51.64923	W120.06810	412 m
CR02	0.7	Start Clearwater River Rd	N51.65348	W120.07514	452 m
CR03	8.0	Trail to Clearwater River	N51.71012	W120.03259	478 m
CR04	9.0	Gate and river access	N51.71811	W120.02722	460 m
CR05	11.3	Spahats Creek	N51.73732	W120.02619	476 m
CR06	13.9	Picnic table and river access	N51.75805	W120.02017	479 m
CR07	18.8	Rafting rest area	N51.79891	W120.03762	495 m
CR08	20.0	Narrow Rd	N51.80547	W120.04879	505 m
CR09	21.4	Viewpoint of rapids	N51.81659	W120.05429	521 m
CR10	25.0	Campsite	N51.84381	W120.07466	516 m
CR11	29.0	River access	N51.87029	W120.10659	515 m
CR12	38.0	Mahood River	N51.91574	W120.19434	524 m
		Mahood River Trail			
CR12	0.0	Mahood River trailhead	N51.91574	W120.19434	524 m
CR13	1.9	Boulder field	N51.92056	W120.21455	565 m
CR14	2.4	View of Goodwin Falls	N51.92341	W120.21905	615 m
CR15	2.8	Trail to Goodwin Falls	N51.92571	W120.22268	600 m
CR16		Goodwin Falls	N51.92593	W120.22259	597 m
CR17	2.9	Sylvia Falls viewpoint	N51.92668	W120.22341	592 m
CR18	3.0	Sylvia Falls	N51.92688	W120.22400	596 m

CHAPTER 31

A Jewel in a Snowy Setting: Creating the Landscape

Some of the landforms in Itcha Ilgachuz Provincial Park in the west Chilcotin are clearly the result of volcanic action.

The Coast Range to the west, the Cariboo Mountains to the north, and the Monashee Mountains to the east form a snowcapped setting that almost encloses the southern portion of the Fraser Plateau and the Thompson Plateau. This land, now drained in large part by the Fraser and Thompson rivers and their tributaries, spent many millions of years under the sea. The sea was shallow and adjacent to slowly eroding landscapes that deposited fine layers of silt and sand upon its floor. Through time the weight of these sediments and the heat they generated gradually solidified them into sedimentary rocks.

About 135 million years ago, in early Jurassic to early Cretaceous times, the underlying mass of igneous rocks began to rise due to pressures elsewhere on the earth's crust. As it rose it lifted up much of what are now the Coast Mountains

A Jewel in a Snowy Setting

The Fraser River has carved a 400-kilometre-long canyon through the Interior Plateau. This fine example of the river's artistry is Pulpit Rock, south of the Gang Ranch Bridge.

and the Interior Plateau. As time passed, the sedimentary rocks of the higher points of land were alternately pushed up by land shifts and eroded by glaciation periods. The igneous rocks that were under the softer sedimentary material began to show through, and as the erosion continued, these rocks became the area's highest peaks.

The buckling and pushing that took place in the earth's crust released layer upon layer of volcanic lava that blanketed much of the high plateau, covering both the igneous and the sedimentary rocks. Passing glaciers and the rivers cut deeply into the lava beds, creating deep canyons and vertical cliffs with the characteristic columnar pillars and, in some locations, the building-block appearance of lava flows.

The foundation of the Interior Plateau was laid many millions of years ago, but it wasn't until the recent past, geologically speaking, that the valleys began to take on the shape that we now see. The intricate and unusual shapes that the walls of the main valleys have assumed are not just a chance happening or an overnight occurrence but are the results of a slowly retreating glacier and a dry climate.

As the ice slowly melted, some ten thousand years ago, the last glacier retreated northward in a broad crescent. Many years passed and each new season's rains and melting snows brought more clay and gravel out of the surrounding hills, creating deltas where the rivers flowed into the lake and benches along the shoreline.

As the glacier continued to retreat northward, the slow process of erosion carried on its work. Steep cliffs and deep canyons were formed as the rivers cut new channels through the layers of glacial drift and the silt deposited in the ancient lake beds. Rushing waters of spring melts and sudden summer thunderstorms carved the edges of the ancient terraces into picturesque hoodoos — columns of a rock-hard gravel-sand-clay mixture. Dry weather limited the further destruction of these oddities by frost or plant life and many of them can still be seen in the Cariboo region.

When the last of the giant glaciers retreated, the Interior Plateau began to go through slow climatic change. At first the area had a cool, wet climate, and then about six thousand years ago, the climate became warmer and drier. Ponderosa pine and bunch grass thrived, even in the more northerly portions of the region.

The climate has since become cooler and wetter. In the higher and more northerly regions, the ponderosa pine has been slowly replaced by the interior Douglas fir and hemlock. At still higher altitudes, alpine fir and white spruce dominate the land up to timberline.

With more recent indications of global warming, the movement of plants and animals may repeat the cycle of six thousand years ago.

The results of millions of years of erosion are clearly visible throughout the grasslands and canyons of the land we call the Cariboo. The never-ending grinding and polishing of nature has created a jewel a richly variegated jewel in a snowy setting.

CHAPTER 32

The Interior Salish First Nations Peoples: The First Known Human Inhabitants

The first known human inhabitants to enter the Cariboo Region came as the glaciers retreated northward seven thousand to nine thousand years ago. These people, the forefathers of the Interior Salish Native peoples, led a generally nomadic life until about three thousand years ago. At that time, possibly due to climatic changes and other factors, they began wintering in the pit-house communities that have proven to be the prime source of archaeological information about their way of life.

The Kekuli or Pit-House

The kekuli, or keekwilly, as these pit-houses are often called, was the winter home of the Interior Salish peoples. Though little remains to indicate the style and size of these homes except the circular depressions that are left where they were constructed, very old photographs and the written descriptions of early fur traders give some idea of the nature of these winter dwellings.

The kekuli was built on a well-drained site near a good supply of fresh water. The women were given the back-breaking task of scooping out the sandy earth and carrying it in baskets to the perimeter of the proposed pit. The men gathered the posts and rafters that were needed to complete the construction. Great quantities of earth were excavated in this manner to create a circular pit that reached as much as two metres deep and 10 metres in diameter. Set well into the floor were four stout posts which were either forked or notched at the top to support the main rafters.

The main rafters were footed well outside the edge of the pit and sloped to within a metre of the centre. Side braces were added to the main rafters, and all of the timbers were lashed together with rope made from willow bark, sagebrush bark, or the green shoots of the willow.

Hundreds of poles, five to ten centimetres in diameter, were cut and lashed to the main framework in concentric rings about a metre apart. The uppermost row

A fine example of a kekuli house is located at the Hat Creek Ranch Historic Site, north of Cache Creek.

formed the neck of the kekuli entrance, and to these heavier logs, the log notched to serve as a ladder was firmly tied. More poles and a quantity of brush, grass, and bark were added to make this framework as dirt-proof as possible.

Over this whole structure, the previously excavated soil was built up to a depth of a foot or more. The result was a warm, though often dusty shelter in which the smoke from the cooking and heating fire exited through the same hole as the inhabitants entered. The layer of soil served as an excellent barrier against sub-zero temperatures of the winter months. The dwellings were generally inhabited from December until February or March before the heat, smoke, and constantly falling dust became more unbearable than the outside temperatures.

Several different sizes of kekuli depressions can be found in the area of the habitations. The larger of these were used by the males and the married family members, while some of the smaller dwellings were occupied by the unmarried women or used as storehouses or sweathouses.

The depressions left by the collapsed kekulis can be found along the banks of most of the rivers in the Fraser and Thompson system.

Summer Nomads

During the summer months the early First Nations peoples moved about in small nomadic groups. They had no cultivated crops and, until the arrival of the horse, their only domesticated animal was the dog. Taking along their worldly possessions, they left the winter home sites and travelled up into the higher valleys and onto the plateau in search of game and the numerous wild roots and berries available. During their summer travels they lived in lean-to or teepee-style tents made of long strips of pine bark, rush mats, or animal skins. They preserved the roots and berries they found by cooking or drying them and storing them in birch bark containers or in intricately woven cedar or spruce baskets like the ones few Native women still make today.

Woven Baskets

The Interior Salish peoples expertly crafted baskets for many uses from the best roots that they gathered in June. They peeled and split the roots into long thin strands and then left them to soak in water until they were pliable. Working with the materials still under water, the basket-makers gathered the coarser strands of

Native women expertly crafted baskets for a wide variety of purposes. This basket may have been made primarily for trade.

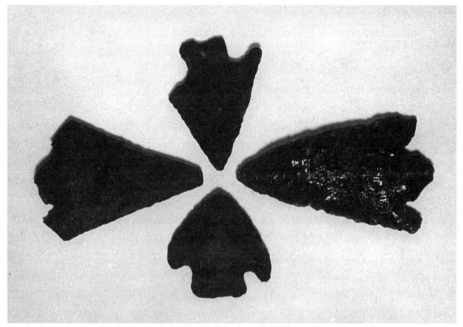

A selection of points that were very likely arrowheads.

the roots into small rope-like bundles and wrapped them with the finer root strips. A bone awl served as the main tool for splitting the roots and sewing the rope-like bundles together as the weaving progressed.

In addition to the woven baskets needed to carry and store the winter's supply of berries, roots, and nuts, others were made to use as bathtubs and papoose bags. Because they were assembled underwater, the baskets shrank when they dried, becoming watertight and rigid. The people, who did not have metal or pottery cooking pots, used the woven baskets to cook in by filling them with water and dropping in stones heated in the fire.

Along with the best cedar and spruce roots for their baskets, the early Aboriginal peoples valued the pliable roots and inner bark of the willow and the roots of the sagebrush to make their ropes.

Stone Weapons and Tools

The stone weapons and tools used by British Columbia's first known inhabitants are the most common and lasting reminder that they once passed through the Thompson Valley. Their travel routes, battlefields, summer campsites, and winter kekuli sites are all littered with the remnants of the tool-makers trade.

To make their tools, they sought out local stones such as opalite, obsidian, flint, chert, basalt, and agate because all of these rocks could be worked to a sharp edge. With careful pressure, all these materials could be shaped because they broke with a conchoidal or glassy-type fracture. They did not split easily and, because of their hardness, they held an edge.

With careful choice of the size and shape of the original material, the skilled craftsperson, through steady chipping, could produce a tool or weapon to suit the need. Sharpened on one end, it may have been used as a chisel or wedge. Tapered and sharpened on both sides, it may have been used as a knife, drill, arrowhead, or spearhead. Sharpened on one side only, it may have been used as a scraper. Left unsharpened, it may have been used as a pestle to grind dried berries or a club to drive wedges or influence enemies.

In addition to the weapons and tools, archaeologists have also uncovered stone and antler carvings, some of which have been dated as far back as 300 A.D. A few of the carvings were of interesting figurines, the meaning or purpose of which remains unclear. A comb and a few Native copper beads, along with a miniature mortar and pestle, have been added to the growing collection of artifacts. Bone and stone counters, used to keep score in various gambling games, help us to gain an insight into life in the early First Nations communities.

Pictographs

Kekuli depressions and stone artifacts mark the camps of the Interior Salish, but another reminder of the past, the pictographs or rock paintings, mark the routes of their travels in a most intriguing manner.

Those who have studied the pictographs believe that many of them were made by young boys and girls during ceremonies of puberty. It also appears that such ceremonies usually took place during the summer months, for the majority of the pictograph sites are located near well-travelled trails and migration routes. Many of these pieces of artwork have been discovered at sheltered campsite locations along the rivers and lakes of the Thompson and through the lower passes interconnecting the main valleys. Other pictograph sites show little sign of the debris of overnight camps, and these locations may have had special significance as ceremonial sites.

John Corner, in his book *Pictographs in the Interior of British Columbia*, lists at least 20 separate pictograph locations in the Thompson and Fraser drainage area. Some of these sites require considerable canoeing or hiking to reach; others are closer to current transportation routes. Many of the rock paintings are on Native Reserve or private land and permission should be obtained before visiting them. A few pictographs, such as those in the North Thompson Valley, south of the town

Aboriginal art is generally divided into categories: carvings (petroglyphs) and paintings (pictographs). The majority of First Nations rock art in the Cariboo region are pictographs that were made by applying a mixture of red ochre and animal fat to the rock surface.

The Interior Salish First Nations Peoples

of Avola, are adjacent to busy highways and, as a result, are more likely to be the subject of vandalism.

In the autumn the people left the summer hunting grounds and returned to the main rivers to prepare for the migrating salmon. Traps were prepared and set into the river beds, and nets were built from rope made of roots, bark, strips of hide, and Native hemp. As the salmon were caught, they were immediately split and cured. The Aboriginal peoples had several methods of curing the body of the salmon: by drying in the sun, by drying in a shaded, windy location, by drying in special smokehouses, and by drying near the cooking fires. The salmon roe and oil were stored in sealed baskets and skins, for use during the winter months.

After the salmon run had ended and before the winter snows forced them into the kekulis, the hunters made their final trip into the hills in search of big game. Deer were hunted by encircling them and driving them over high cliffs or into specially built compounds where they were killed with arrows, spears, or clubs. The animals were then butchered and the meat cured in much the same manner as the salmon.

The warm weather ended, and with it ended another year in the calendar of the Interior Salish. The first moon of the New Year was "Going-in Time," the time when the people entered their winter homes. It was a time for indoor games and outdoor winter sports. It was a time for renewing old tools and clothing and replacing those lost in the previous season's activities.

And, at day's end, it was time for tales of great wars, hunting, and heroes, and, as the children drifted off to sleep, it was time for the stories of First Nations mythology.

CHAPTER 33

Fur and Gold: Before the Rush

It was mid-June and the year was 1808. Simon Fraser, John Stuart, and their crew, members of the North West Company, were searching for a trade route to the Pacific Ocean and, ultimately, to the riches of the Orient. They wanted a route that would allow easy passage of fur-laden canoes to transfer the wealth of the mountains to ocean-going ships, which would then satisfy the vanities of the China trade.

Wild, foaming canyons and hostile Native peoples at what is now Vancouver persuaded Simon Fraser that the Fraser River was not a viable trade route to the Pacific. It was not until several years later that the fur traders would return to these waters.

In the summer of 1811, David Stuart, a cousin of John Stuart and a member of the rival American-owned Pacific Fur Company, left Fort Astoria at the mouth of

Native fishermen at the Bridge River Rapids on the Fraser River. This is one of the many rapids that persuaded Simon Fraser to abandon any hope of using the Fraser as a fur trade canoe route.

Fur and Gold

the Columbia and proceeded upriver. At the junction of the Okanagan and Columbia rivers, Stuart established Fort Okanagan and then set off northward through the grassy Okanagan Valley. Late in 1811, he crossed over the divide and into the Fraser watershed and became the first white man to set eyes on what is now known as the South Thompson River. Stuart found friendly Native peoples in the form of the Shuswaps, who wintered near the confluence of the North and South Thompson rivers. The Shuswaps were eager to trade for the white man's tobacco and cotton, and Stuart spent a profitable winter trading before leaving in the spring. Later in 1812, Stuart returned to "Cumcloups" to build a more permanent trading post — and the first permanent European settlement in southern British Columbia.

In the meantime, the fur trade was being expanded in what is now northern British Columbia with North West Company bases at Fort St. James and other locations. A rivalry developed between the Pacific Fur Company and the North West Company, and later with the Hudson's Bay Company. In 1821, they combined forces under the name of the Hudson's Bay Company.

The northern furs were transported west to the Pacific by water routes. The furs of the Cariboo region were transported overland by horse brigades to Kamloops and then on to Hope where water transport could be used to get them to the ships.

Prior to the Cariboo gold rush, the life of the Native peoples and fur traders may not have been easy, but it was predictable and relatively uncomplicated.

The discovery of gold in the rivers and streams that flow into the Fraser River was soon to change all that. Like many of the pages of British Columbia's early history, this one has become faded, and the stories surrounding that first discovery are difficult to verify. M.S. Wade, in his book *The Thompson Country* (1907), suggests that "the presence of gold in the streams and rivers became known and Chief Trader McLean, then in charge of Fort Kamloops, in 1852 purchased gold from the Indians who had obtained it from the Thompson River." It was at Nicoamen, between Spence's Bridge and Lytton, that gold in paying quantities was first discovered.

The private papers of Sir James Douglas, Governor of British Columbia during the gold rush, seem to verify Wade's account as he says that the first gold on the Thompson River was found just below Nicoamen: "The Indian was taking a drink out of the river. Having no vessel he was quaffing from the stream when he perceived a shiny pebble which he picked up and it proved to be gold. The whole tribe forthwith began to collect the glittering metal."

Wade's account is suspect on one detail, which is that Paul Fraser, a son of the famous Simon Fraser, was in charge of the fort at Kamloops from 1850 to 1855

Sandra Teegee at Fort St. James. This fur trade post was established by Simon Fraser for the North West Company in 1806.

and Donald McLean did not become Chief Trader there until 1855. The explanation could be that McLean was in charge of Alexandria House near Quesnel, some distance up the Fraser River, during this period and the Native peoples may have brought the gold to him. Rivalry between the two forts could have induced the Native peoples, who were trading outside their designated area, to keep the discovery a secret. McLean, fearing that an influx of miners would destroy the fur trade, may also have wanted to keep the transactions quiet.

Judge F.W. Howay, an early British Columbia historian, believed differently. *Many persons claim the honor and many places are named as the site; but the contemporary records all favour the view that, in 1855, the first gold on the mainland was discovered on the Columbia River, just north of the boundary line. Letters of Governor Douglas and John Work to that effect, written in 1856, are still extant. James Cooper affirmed this view before the select committee in 1857. The exact spot, according to Angus McDonald, then in charge of the Hudson's Bay Company's Fort Colville, was at 'the mouth of the Pend d'Oreille, where it leaps with a bound of about ten feet into the Columbia.' In the fall of 1856 he sent seventeen pounds of Pend d'Oreille gold to Victoria, by way of Fort Hope. The Journal of Nanaimo shows the effects of the great news, for, in 1856, some of the coal miners left to seek fortune in the Columbia River diggings. The chase for gold widened: it was found, in 1856, on the Thompson River, and on the Fraser near Fort Hope.*

Fur and Gold

The *Victoria Times*, dated July 26, 1907, reports Gavin Hamilton, a Chief Factor of the Hudson's Bay Company, as saying that it "is absolutely certain that gold was discovered in the Thompson River during the season of 1856, because Mr. McLean at Kamloops had two pint pickle bottles half full of gold taken from the river that year."

It was also claimed that Chief Trader McLean sent to Victoria for iron spoons to be used in extracting the nuggets from the crevices in the bedrock.

James Houston of Langley claimed 1854 as the date of the first discovery of gold on the mainland. His story was that he was travelling from the Columbia River via Fort Okanagan and had stopped at the Hudson's Bay Company's Thompson's River Post. In the following month he spent some time prospecting and discovered coarse gold near the point where Tranquille Creek empties into Kamloops Lake.

Regardless of the finer details, which will probably always remain clouded, Hudson's Bay Company records indicate that three hundred ounces of gold had been received by their agents at the Thompson and Fraser rivers between October 6, 1857, and the end of the year. It must generally be conceded that discoveries on the Thompson and its tributaries were the most significant factor leading to the Fraser River gold rush of 1858.

The trading post at Fort Langley played an integral part in the later years of the fur trade and the beginning years of the colony of British Columbia.

CHAPTER 34

Cattle Ranches

Cowboys, horses, and dogs have been an essential part of the Cariboo cattle industry since the 1860s.

The flood of men into the British Columbia Interior brought with it a requirement for a considerable amount of meat. The wild game soon became wary of the gold-seekers, and other sources of meat were needed to fill the cooking pots. During the period of 1859 to 1870, records indicate that 22,000 head of cattle from Oregon and Washington were driven across the border at Osoyoos, en route to supply the Cariboo gold fields. Some of the early cattle drovers saw opportunities in ranching and many stayed to become settlers. Most notable among the early settlers and drovers were the Harper brothers, who started the Harper Ranch east of Kamloops in 1861, and in succeeding years acquired the Perry Ranch, Cache Creek; the Kelly Ranch, Clinton; and, around 1880, the present Gang Ranch. Breeding stock was purchased from the cattle drives for the establishment of the early ranches.

As the gold rush subsided, the pattern of settlement shifted away from the travel routes toward the more choice grazing lands. These were associated with a favourable climate, adequate water supply, meadows, and open grassland. Winter feeding was often a problem due to the climate and the terrain. Then, as now, the limited arable land was required to grow hay and other forage crops for winter supplies.

Cattle Ranches

Railways Improved Access to Markets

Marketing of livestock was difficult until the advent of the railways in the period of 1885 to 1917. There was a good market at the coast but this was more easily supplied by boat from California. However, cattle drives were attempted from the Nicola Valley over the Hope-Princeton trail, and one attempt was made from Pavilion to North Vancouver. Another famous cattle drive was attempted from the Chilcotin to the Klondike gold rush. These attempts meant drives of three hundred to five hundred kilometres over mountainous terrain. The completion of the Canadian Pacific Railway and the Canadian National Railway, the Columbia & Western Railway and the Kettle Valley Railway in southern British Columbia, and the Pacific Great Eastern Railway (later known as the British Columbia Railway and now part of the Canadian National Railway) from Quesnel to Squamish put most areas of the Cariboo district within easy access of transportation and markets. Cattle became a fluid commodity, while the old markets for hay and produce dwindled as the stopping places for the stage-lines and wagon trains disappeared.

In recent years, highways have further eased the transportation problems, and growing interior communities have moved the markets closer to the producer, making cattle ranching the largest agricultural business in the Cariboo.

Hereford cattle are a common sight on Cariboo ranches.

CHAPTER 35

Rockhound Paradise

ritish Columbia is a rockhound's paradise. It has everything needed to make the life of a rockhound, regardless of his or her personal preferences, a series of exciting challenges and discoveries. Discoveries that may seem small or insignificant to the uninitiated only serve to whet the appetite of the enthusiasts and slowly hook them on the sight and touch of nature's mineral bounty.

British Columbia has had rockhounds of one type or another ever since people first moved into the province. The arrowheads and spearheads that wash up on our sand bars and beaches meant a great deal more to the health and well being of the original inhabitants than they do to the present day collector. Stone hand tools made from jade, obsidian, flint, and many other materials have been found in many parts of the province. The early First Nations migrants, who may have come by way of a land bridge between Asia and Alaska more than 11,000 years ago, placed a high value on their stone tools. To them it was a matter of survival.

First Nations Sites are Protected

Collecting First Nations artifacts or historical relics can be a touchy subject. In British Columbia certain types of archaeological sites are protected by provincial legislation. These sites are protected whether they occur on public or private land. Protected sites include graves, ship wrecks, plane wrecks, First Nation Rock Art (petroglyphs and pictographs), sites which have been designated protected by the provincial government, and sites that predate 1846.

The majority of the province has not been surveyed for archaeological sites, and thus most archaeological sites have not been recorded. *The Heritage Conservation Act* provides substantial penalties for destruction or unauthorized disturbance of archaeological sites including imprisonment for up to two years and fines of up to $1,000,000. The BC Archaeology Branch (Ministry of Tourism,

Stone artefacts, such as these arrowheads, can occasionally be found in river sandbars near historical First Nations settlements. Note that disturbance of archaeological sites is prohibited.

Rockhound Paradise

Recreational gold panning is permitted in a number of locations near Lillooet.

Sport and the Arts) is responsible for issuing permits to conduct archaeological studies.

Not all artifact hunting is banned or restricted. Sandbars, stream beds, and freshly plowed fields often yield an arrowhead or two, but when you come across any signs of a major settlement, the colleges and museums want to be informed so that a proper systematic study can be undertaken.

Jade Amongst the Rubble

Civilization has reduced the present day rockhounds life or death dependency on stone weapons and implements. In its place has come a recreational, and in some cases financial, dependency on nature's storehouse of rocks and minerals. The ancient alchemist's persistent search for ways to turn lead into gold was nothing compared to the modern rockhound's search for ways to turn serpentine (or any green stone) into jade. No one has succeeded in either transformation, but many have succeeded in finding a genuine jade boulder or two amongst the tons of green rubble they pack home.

Jade is the gem that is most commonly linked with British Columbia, and "Ma Murray's" Lillooet claims, with some justification, to be the jade capital of the world. According to the BC Ministry of Energy, Mines and Petroleum Resources, all of the known jade deposits in BC are of the nephrite variety, as compared to jadeite, found primarily in Burma.

British Columbia has a jade reserve for rockhounds on the Fraser River between the bridge at Lillooet and the bridge at Hope. Anyone may hunt for jade in this reserve on the gravel bars, keeping in mind that you should not trespass on First Nations and private property to access the river. (Please note that many of the Fraser River gravel bars have placer gold claims, so don't bring your gold pan.)

Gold Panning Reserves

The BC Ministry of Energy, Mines and Petroleum Resources has created a number of recreational panning reserves around the province that are open to the general public for recreational gold panning. Recreational panning is restricted to hand pans, hand shovels, and metal detectors. The use of sluice or shaker boxes, suction dredges, and other mechanical devices are not permitted.

PDF maps of the various sites are available online at the Ministry website at http://www.em.gov.bc.ca/mining/titles/Panning/Rec_Panning.htm or Google "recreational panning reserves."

Agate Addicts

Jade is somewhat hard to find throughout the province, but the same is not the case with the common agate. Many different varieties of agate can be found all through the west, or so I have been told by one of British Columbia's worst agate addicts (name withheld to protect his relatives). The true agate addict can be spotted a mile away. There are the stooped shoulders and hung head of a man that society has kicked once too often. He has eyes that always appear to stare at the ground a yard or two in front. It is these eyes though, that set him apart from other addicts. The eyes of an agate addict shine with an inquisitive gleam, continually searching for the glint of light reflected through the rough stone.

The agate addict's beat is an odd one. Wave-washed seashores, gravel-strewn stream beds, rough road shoulders, railway beds, and gravel pits are typical haunts, expecially in the rain. You can always tell the mark of a true addict. He is the man whose unwavering search doesn't even let up when walking the concrete pathways of the city.

I've walked the path of the agate addict and I know the feeling. I've walked the railway tracks near McBride as a summer shower, complete with rainbow, slowly drifted toward the horizon. I searched for riches at the end of that rainbow.

Thoughts of riches as great as those that Pierre Berton found in the laying of the CPR tracks crossed my mind. This, unfortunately, was the CNR and gold

A rockhound searches for agate in a rock bluff south of Kamloops.

would not be what I stepped on if I didn't watch where I was walking. I found agates on the railway bed — not many, nor were they very good — but they were enough to steady my trembling hands and tide me over till another day.

Other Rocks Attract the Boulder Basher

Agate is only one of the hundreds of rocks and minerals that attract the attention of the educated boulder basher. Common opal, rhodonite, petrified and opalized wood, jaspers, amethyst, garnet, plus fossils and other stones too numerous to mention here are to be found by the sharp-eyed hunter. Diamonds are not yet being mined in British Columbia, but I know that nearly every rockhound secretly carries a claim stake in his back pocket waiting for that lucky day.

On the subject of claims, the Lapidary, Rock & Mineral Society of British Columbia have several claims that are kept active by local clubs and their members. The general rule with respect to these claims is that any rockhound may remove material for personal use providing it is non-commercial and he or she does not blast or use power tools. Cleaning up after oneself is mandatory. These are the general rules and they may change at any time. Most of the local rock shops or rock clubs can be contacted for up-to-date information on material and location.

Respect Private Property

With the resurgence in mining interests in British Columbia, those other rockhounds — the mining companies — have also staked a lot of claims, which should, with all due respect for the law and industry, be treated as private property.

Private property is a bone of contention among all outdoor enthusiasts, rockhounds included, and common sense, etiquette, and respect for the rights of others must be given top priority. Ask permission before entering. In most cases it will be granted, but if it is refused, move to another location. When permission is granted, treat the area as though you want to come back again. Clean up after yourself, fill any holes that could injure livestock, and leave no garbage behind.

Yesterday's Garbage

Speaking of garbage, the refuse of the past has developed into one of the hottest hobbies of the present. Bottles, discarded or lost by our ancestors, are being recovered in record numbers and traded by collectors for record prices. How would your great-grandfather feel if he knew that his discarded empties are now worth more than they were before he emptied them?

Pioneer antiques are still to be found in some of the old abandoned settlements. Hand-made horseshoes may prove to be your lucky find. Pottery, china dolls, fruit jars, and telegraph insulators all fit into the collector's knapsack.

Physical Mobility

To become a rockhound you need physical mobility and reasonable eyesight. Age is not a factor; one need only adjust one's activity to suit one's ability. I've seen three generations of one

The refuse of the past has become the treasure of the present.

Rockhound Paradise

family strolling along the gravel bars together in search of colourful rocks. The joint satisfaction of discovery soon overcomes the age barrier.

The basic tools and clothing are not expensive, particularly when compared to many of our other recreational pursuits. You'll need a few tools: a rock hammer or pick, a pack sack for your lunch and your treasure, and two or three chisels — a heavy flat chisel, a lighter one, and a gadpoint chisel for separating agates from the surrounding rock. A three pound sledge is handy for driving chisels and busting boulders.

Strong clothing, hiking boots, mosquito repellant, sun screen, muscles, patience, maps, and good eyesight are also basic necessities.

Equipment

Converting that newly found gemstone into a brooch for m'lady takes a little more time and equipment. To find out whether you like rock work, a good beginner tumbler can be purchased for about $100 to get you started. To go into it seriously, you're going to have to spend $500 to $1,000 for equipment. A diamond saw, a grinder, a belt sander, a disc buffer with various pads, and assorted other odds and ends are part of the equipment required to turn that boulder into a brooch. Kits and combination units can save some money. When buying any type of equipment, pay careful attention to the bearings, a weak point in a very dusty atmosphere.

Rockhound Clubs

Rockhounds generally work alone or with their families but, when the time comes to show that new piece of jewelry or to exchange ideas and tales, they join clubs. The first of these, the Lapidary Club of Vancouver, was formed in 1952. From that point on they grew like the proverbial beanstalk and in December 1955, the Lapidary, Rock & Mineral Society of British Columbia was incorporated to act as a parent organization. At last count over 35 clubs belonged to the society.

The BC Gem Show is held in April each year and many local clubs hold shows throughout the year. Additional information is available at http://www.lapidary.bc.ca/.

I may have mentioned it earlier but I think it bears repeating that BC is a rockhound's paradise; we have so much beautiful rock that a great deal of it had to be put on edge to get it all into one province.

Put on your boots and jeans, grab your rock pick and your lunch, and head for the hills. We may see you there!

Additional Information:

BC Ministry of Energy, Mines and Petroleum Resources
http://www.empr.gov.bc.ca/Mining/Geolsurv/Minfile/products/Jade/default.htm
http://www.empr.gov.bc.ca/mining/titles/Panning/Rec_Panning.htm

British Columbia Lapidary Society
http://www.lapidary.bc.ca/index.html

BC Ministry of Tourism, Sport and the Arts, Archaeology Branch
http://www.tsa.gov.bc.ca/archaeology/

CHAPTER 36

Gems and Minerals

The following is a list of some of the semi-precious gemstones and minerals most likely to be found in the Cariboo region.

Blue agate from Mount Savona, south of Kamloops Lake.

Agate — a form of quartz (chalcedony) with a banded or variegated appearance. Various colours.

Amethyst — a form of crystalline quartz with traces of manganese, which give it a purple colour.

Azurite — a crystalline copper ore, often blue in colour.

Bornite — a bronze coloured copper ore, sometimes called peacock ore.

Carnelian — a red or reddish-brown form of chalcedony.

Chalcedony — a waxy, smooth form of quartz, usually translucent.

Chalcocite — a dark metallic copper ore.

Chalcopyrite — a common copper ore, brassy in colour.

Chert — an impure form of flint (basically quartz).

Cinnabar — a red-coloured mercury ore.

Cuprite — a reddish-brown material formed by the weathering of copper ores.

Epidote — a silicate of calcium and aluminum, which forms slender, dark-coloured crystals.

Flint — a grey, brown, or black quartz, which breaks with a conchodial fracture. Early man used flint for tools.

Galena — a common lead ore, lead sulphide.

Garnet — a silicate mineral, sometimes of gem quality.

Gold — a soft, malleable yellow metal.

Hematite — an important iron ore; can be a dark, shiny mineral.

Jade is valued for its carving qualities as well as for jewelry.

Jade — in British Columbia, nephrite; gem quality jade is usually green in colour, though many other colours have been found.

Jasper — an opaque quartz, usually red, yellow, or brown.

Kyanite — white to blue-grey or black aluminum ore crystals.

Malachite — a copper ore found in various shades of green, which can often be cut and polished.

Molybdenite — a soft, metallic molybdenum ore.

Opal — a non-crystalline form of quartz containing a very small amount of water.

Opal, common — a somewhat translucent opal, milky white, greenish-yellow to red in colour.

Platinum — a heavy silver-white metal.

Prehnite — usually a compact mass of small, light-green crystals.

Pyrite — a crystalline iron-sulphur ore.

Quartz — chemically silica, it is one of the most common minerals in the earth's crust.

Rhodonite — a pink to deep-red manganese ore, sometimes of gem quality.

Scheelite — a glassy, sometimes transparent tungsten ore.

Serpentine — a magnesium silicate, sometimes mistaken for jade.

Tourmaline — an aluminum silicate mostly black in colour. Other colours sometimes make interesting gemstones.

CHAPTER 37

Making Your GPS Work for You! GPS Basics and More

What is GPS?

Pose this question to Google on the Internet, and you'll get more responses than you can possible read. However, the Garmin website has a basic definition that works regardless of the make or model of GPS receiver that you may have or may consider purchasing.

The Global Positioning System (GPS) is a satellite-based navigation system made up of a network of 24 satellites placed into orbit by the U.S. Department of Defense. GPS was originally intended for military applications, but in the 1980s, the government made the system available for civilian use. GPS works in any weather conditions, anywhere in the world, 24 hours a day.

GPS satellites circle the earth twice a day in a very precise orbit and transmit signal information to earth. GPS receivers take this information and use triangulation to calculate the user's exact location. Essentially, the GPS receiver compares the time a signal was transmitted by a satellite with the time it was received. The time difference tells the GPS receiver how far away the satellite is. Now, with distance measurements from a few more satellites, the receiver can determine the user's position and display it on the unit's electronic map.

A Free One-Way System

It is important to note that the GPS network is a one-way system. The two dozen satellites transmit their position and time signals, and your GPS unit receives the signals and processes them with its internal computer to indicate the position of the receiver. Your unit does not transmit any signals to the satellites, nor does it require any subscription codes such as are needed by satellite TV or radio.

It is also important to note that the transmitting satellites are about 19,000 kilometres above the earth and that they transmit a 50-watt signal at 1575.42 MHz. This means that the signal your receiver gets is extremely weak, particularly from satellites near the horizon, and it is subject to line-of-sight interference. It can go through glass or plastic, but mountains, dense timber, or tall buildings can block it.

GPS waypoint data can be entered into your unit directly or via a computer program. It can then be used to confirm your trip routing.

Multi-Channel Receivers

My first GPS, a Garmin 45 purchased in 1995, was the first small one-hand GPS. It had a receiver that stepped through eight channels to track up to eight satellites sequentially. Many of today's units have 12-channel receivers that can monitor a dozen satellites simultaneously. The result is a unit that is much faster to lock on to satellites and much more accurate, particularly in challenging situations.

When hiking, the GPS should be carried as high as possible in order to provide the best satellite coverage.

Accuracy

Prior to May 2000, when the U.S. military turned off the intentional errors they had introduced to civilian GPS signals, variations in horizontal position of +/- 100 metres were common. Altitude variations were easily three times that. Current basic units are usually accurate to within 15 metres, and those with special WAAS (Wide Area Augmentation System) capability are considered accurate to within three metres. Some specialized survey units claim sub-metre and centimetre accuracy.

How Do I Reference the GPS to Maps?

The early GPS receivers certainly weren't capable of survey-quality accuracy, but they could tell you where you were — providing you took the time to learn how to relate the GPS position readings to your maps. Many outdoor enthusiasts gave up after a few tries because of complications, such as relating latitude and longitude readings to map position or correcting for variations in map UTM baseline references.

It took a hike up to a small tarn on July Mountain, near my home, to bring home the reality that the scientific calculations of the shape of the earth had changed with the advent of the GPS. Most of the older 1:50,000 paper maps use the NAD27 datum, based on land surveys in 1927, whereas WGS84 is based on satellite measurements in 1984 and updated as more knowledge is acquired.

The "default" GPS position measurements are based on the WGS84 datum. Not being aware of the finer details, I plugged in the UTM coordinates for the alpine lake based on my Spuzzum 92 H/11E 1:50,000 map and set off to climb the mountain. Noon arrived and the GPS said that we still had a few hundred metres to climb, so we broke for lunch. When we resumed our climb, we discovered that the lake was just out of sight behind a nearby clump of juniper. After a lot of head-scratching and some calculations when I got home, I discovered that the line-of-sight difference between NAD27 and WGS84 in this area was 225 metres. The mixup had placed the lake 200 metres south and 70 metres east of where it really was. While this type of error isn't usually a problem if you are only using the GPS to track where you have been driving or hiking, it can be a problem when you are looking for a road or trail based on its position on a map.

Internal Maps

The extreme miniaturization of computer chips and memory cards has meant that many hand-held and dashboard GPS units now contain their own maps, reducing or eliminating the need to carry paper maps if you have chosen the correct unit for your needs. The "street" units advertised for use in your automobile may contain detailed street and facility data for the larger centres — you can easily map the route to the nearest Tim Hortons coffee shop — but your favourite lake may not be on the internal maps. However, hand-held "trail" units may contain basic maps with the option to upload detailed topographic maps at an extra cost.

My personal "trail" unit is a Garmin GPSMap 76CSx that contains a very basic topographic map and the option to upload proprietary detailed maps to a MicroSD memory chip. The unit will only accept Garmin MapSource digital maps, but with a two-gigabyte memory chip, I can upload the detailed topographic maps for most of western Canada. I can find the alpine tarn on July Mountain, but it won't tell me how to find the Merritt Tim Hortons.

Unfortunately, neither the GPS nor the MapSource program is cheap. Uploadable GPS units are in the $400 to $600 range and the MapSource Topo Canada CD set is in the $150 range. One consolation is that the MapSource data can also be loaded onto your computer for viewing with or without the GPS attached.

External Electronic Maps

There is a third option that is used by many GPS aficionados and that is to connect their GPS units to a laptop and run mapping software on the computer to

Making Your GPS Work for You!

Computer programs such as Memory-Map Navigator and OziExplorer can be used with a laptop or PDA to provide a "moving-map" image while travelling.

create a detailed moving-map image on the PC. One of the best known of these programs is OziExplorer, a program available online for US $95 from www.oziexplorer.com. It has the capability of calibrating and using almost any "bitmap" rasterized image map. In other words, if you have a scanner and an out-of-print or historic map that you want to link to your GPS, with lots of experimentation and patience you can do it.

OziExplorer also works well with "pre-calibrated" digital maps such as the Canadian topographic maps available from Spectrum Digital Imaging at http://www.mapsdigital.com/ or the digital versions of the Mussio Ventures Backroads Mapbook series available from http://www.backroadmapbooks.com/.

Other programs that work with "bitmap" image maps include Memory-Map Navigator available from http://www.memory-map.com/ and Fugawi Global Navigator available from http://www.fugawi.com/.

Satellite Images

However, the ultimate in "mapping" is the new Google Earth service available for those with a high-speed Internet connection. Using a combination of satellite and aerial photography images, the on-line image of the earth can be viewed close-up or tilted to provide a 3D perspective. The free version allows you to look at your world, but for a US $20 per year subscription, you can download data from your GPS and place your tracks and waypoints on the image of the earth. The disadvantage of the Google Earth option is that it requires a connection to the Internet to work. While this might not be a problem in your home or office, it could be a problem on a backroads or hiking trip.

Accessories

So now you are about to buy a GPS unit and are looking closely at digital maps and software. Before you hike down to the store and lay down your plastic, there are a few more items that might not be part of the basic package, but should be in your shopping cart.

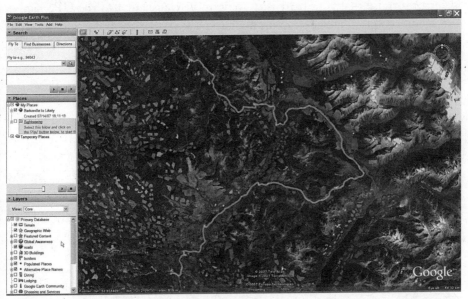

A view of Google Earth on a computer. The track shown is of the backroad between Barkerville and Likely.

Making Your GPS Work for You!

Unless you've got a brother-in-law in the battery business, you'll want a DC adapter to plug into the cigarette lighter jack in your truck. You'll also want a set or two of rechargeable batteries and a charger. The newer nickel metal hydride batteries, although more expensive than the old nickel-cadmium batteries, have enough advantages to make them your first choice. If you do a lot of field work, you'll want a charger that can plug into your cigarette lighter outlet. As this may be hard to find, a good second choice is a DC to AC inverter to power your charger and your laptop computer. A unit in the 200- to 300-watt range should be more than adequate.

You'll also soon discover that an external antenna is a useful piece of hardware — make sure the GPS you purchase can connect to one — particularly if you are using your unit in a camper.

A computer cable is also essential if you are to take advantage of the GPS moving map or download options I've mentioned. Many of the new units use a USB cable and this could be part of the package — if not, it is a $10.00 item from most computer stores. Take along your unit when you go to purchase a cable as connections vary.

Your hand-held unit is likely to come with a belt carrying case, but your belt certainly isn't the best place to carry your GPS. As mentioned previously, the unit needs a clear view of the sky – preferably in all directions. Without being rude, it is fair to surmise that your belly isn't going to be transparent to the GPS signal. I've modified the shoulder strap on my backpack so that the built-in antenna of the GPS sits above shoulder level. While my head may block part of the signal, the unit sees much more of the sky than if it was on my belt.

What Can I Do with a GPS?

So you've blown your budget on a GPS unit and mapping software, and spent a week reading the book, surfing the Net, and walking around the block figuring out how your GPS works. Now what?

To start with, you can track your trips and create waypoints of interest along the way. You can then use this data to return to your starting point or to retrace your steps in the future. If you've set your unit to save your data and you've mastered the computer connections, you can download the data and show it on a map or e-mail it to a friend.

After you've mastered the basics, you can enter or upload waypoints and tracks before you set out on your next adventure and plan your route to your destination.

In the case of an accident or a breakdown, you could use your cellphone (where coverage exists) to notify help of your exact location.

Geo-Reference Your Digital Photos

With appropriate cables and software, you can synchronize your computer clock to the GPS clock, giving you to-the-second accuracy. If you synchronize your digital camera to your computer, you can then use a program such as RoboGEO (http://www.robogeo.com) to geo-reference your photos if you have your GPS tracking while taking the photos.

Geocaching and Letterboxing

The basic idea of geocaching is to have individuals and organizations set up caches all over the world and share the locations of these caches on the Internet. GPS users can then use the location coordinates to find the caches and contribute to them. The basic rules are available at http://www.geocaching.com/. Letterboxing is somewhat similar to geocaching except with an artistic flair and a "passport" component. More information is available at http://www.letterboxing.org/.

What Else Should I Be Aware Of?

Although many GPS units are waterproof and built to withstand some shock, they are electronic units that are not indestructible. Protect them from excessive heat such as near a car window in the summer.

Don't expect GPS units to work when the batteries are extremely cold — particularly rechargeable batteries. Keep your batteries warm. Carry spare batteries and recharge your used batteries. Use the manufacturer's recommendations for batteries and battery settings. Be sure the DC adapter is designed for your unit.

Last, working (or playing) with a GPS can be addictive. While still legal, it can put a strain on your budget and your relationship, and cause your less geeky friends to suffer attention deficit disorder.

Information Sources

100 Mile Nordic Ski Society
PO Box 1888
100 Mile House
BC V0K 2E0
Website: http://www.100milenordics.com

Ace High Resort
Site 2C – C28 RR#1
70 Mile House
BC V0K 2K0
Tel/Fax: (250) 456-7518
E-mail: info@acehighresort.com
or: acehigh@bcinternet.net

Alexander Mackenzie Voyageur Route Association
Website: http://www.amvr.org/

Ashcroft Opera House
401 Brink Street
Ashcroft, BC V0K 1A0
Tel: (250) 453-9009
E-mail: info@ashcroftoperahouse.com
Website: http://www.ashcroftopera
house.com

BC Backcountry Adventures Ltd.
PO Box 1764
Clearwater, BC V0E 1N0
Tel: (250) 674-0200
Toll free: 1-866-CANOE-BC
Fax: (250) 674-0215
E-mail:
info@bcbackcountryadventures.com
Website: http://www.bcbackcountry
adventures.com/

BC Parks General Information
Website: http://www.bcparks.ca
or http://www.env.gov.bc.ca/bcparks

BC Parks Cariboo District Office
281 – 1st Avenue North
Williams Lake, BC V2G 1Y7
Tel: (250) 398-4414
Fax: (250) 398-4686

BC Recreation Sites and Trails
Ministry of Tourism, Sport and the Arts
Website: http://www.tsa.gov.bc.ca/
publicrec

Bella Coola Valley Museum
269 Highway 20
PO Box 726
Bella Coola, BC V0T 1C0
Tel: (250) 799-5767 (June–September)
Tel: (250) 982-2130 (Archives)
E-mail: info@bellacoolamuseum.ca
Website: http://www.bellacoolamuseum.ca

Bella Coola Valley Tourism
Tel: 1-866-799-5202
E-mail: bellacoolavalley
tourism@belco.bc.ca
Website: http://www.bellacoola.ca

Big Bar Guest Ranch
PO Box 27 Jesmond
Clinton, BC V0K 1K0
Tel: (250) 459-2333
Fax: (250) 459-2400
E-mail: info@bigbarranch.com

Bonaparte Bend Winery
2520 Cariboo Highway
PO Box 47
Cache Creek, BC V0K 1H0
Tel: (250) 457-6667
E-mail: info@bbwinery.com
Website: http://www.bbwinery.com

Bonaparte Lake Resort
PO Box 55
Bridge Lake, BC V0K 1E0

Bralorne Gold Mines Ltd.
400 – 455 Granville Street
Vancouver, BC V6C 1T1
Tel: (604) 682-3701
Fax: (604) 682-3600
Website: http://www.bralorne.com

**Bridge River Valley Economic
Development Society**
104 Haylmore Avenue
General Delivery
Gold Bridge, BC V0K 1P0
Tel: (250) 238-2534
E-mail: info@bridgerivervalley.ca
Website: http://www.bridgerivervalley.ca

Bulwer-Lytton Fiction Contest
Department of English
San Jose State University
San Jose, CA 95192-0090
Website: http://www.bulwer-lytton.com

**Cariboo Chilcotin Coast Tourism
Association**
118A North 1st Avenue
Williams Lake, BC V2G 1Y8
Tel: (250) 392-2226
Fax: (250) 392-2838
E-mail: info@landwithoutlimits.com
Website: http://www.landwithoutlimits.com

Chilcotin Holidays Ltd.
Gun Creek Road
Gold Bridge, BC V0K 1P0
Tel: (250) 238-2274
Fax: (250) 238-2241
E-mail: adventures@chilcotinholidays.com
Website: http://www.chilcotin
holidays.com

Circle W Hi Hium Fishing Camp
PO Box 8
Savona, BC V0K 2J0
Tel: (250) 373-2636
Website: http://www.circlew.com

Clearwater Chamber of Commerce
Clearwater Info Centre
425 East Yellowhead Highway,
Box 1988, RR1
Clearwater, BC V0E 1N0
Tel: (250) 674-2646
Fax: (250) 674-3693
E-mail: info@clearwaterbcchamber.com
Website:
http://www.clearwaterbcchamber.com/

Clinton Snow Jockey Club
c/o Robin Fennell
PO Box 25
Clinton, BC V0K 1K0
Tel: (250) 459-2284
E-mail: Robin Fennell
rmbfenn@telus.net

Crooked Lake Resort
PO Box 358
Horsefly, BC V0L 1L0
Toll-free: 1-866-614-1690
E-mail: info@crookedlakeresort.ca
Website: http://www.crookedlakeresort.ca

Echo Valley Ranch & Spa
PO Box 16 Jesmond
Clinton, BC V0K 1K0
Tel: (250) 459-2386
Fax: (250) 459-0086
Reservations: 1-800-253-8831
E-mail: info@evranch.com

Information Sources

Educo Adventure School
PO Box 1978
100 Mile House, BC V0K 2E0
Tel: (250) 395-3388
Fax: (250) 395-2567
E-mail: adventure@educo.ca
Website: http://www.educo.ca

Eureka Peak Lodge and Outfitters
PO Box 1332
100 Mile House, BC V0K 2E0
Tel/Fax: (250) 397-2445
Toll-free: 1-877-538-6566
E-mail: adventure@eurekapeak.com
Website: http://www.eurekapeak.com

Flying U Ranch
PO Box 69
70 Mile House, BC V0K 2K0
Tel: (250) 456-7717
Website: http://www.flyingu.com

Freshwater Fisheries Society of BC
http://www.gofishbc.com

Friends of Nemaiah Valley
1010 Foul Bay Road
Victoria, BC V8S 4J1
Tel/Fax: (250) 592-1088
E-mail: info@fonv.ca
Website: http://www.fonv.ca

Gold Country Communities Society
PO Box 933
Cache Creek, BC V0K 1H0
Tel/Fax: (250) 457-6606
E-mail: info@exploregoldcountry.com

Green Lake Provincial Park
Website: http://www.env.gov.bc.ca/bcparks
/explore/parkpgs/greenlk.html

Hallamore Lake Resort
PO Box 562
Dunn Lake Road
Clearwater, BC V0E 1N0
Tel: (250) 587-6348

Highland Valley Copper
PO Box 1500
Logan Lake, BC V0K 1W0
Tel: (250) 523-3201
Fax: (250) 523-3290
Website: http://www.teckcominco.com/

Hihium Lake Fishing Resort
Loon Lake Rd, RR 1
Cache Creek, BC V0K 1H0
Tel: (250) 459-2306
Website: http://www.hihiumlake.com

Cross-country skiing is considered to be one of the finest ways to get a winter workout.

Historic Hat Creek Ranch
PO Box 878, (junction of Highway 97 and
99, 11 km north of Cache Creek)
Cache Creek, BC V0K 1H0
Tel: (250) 457-9722
Toll-free: 1-800-782-0922
E-mail: hhcr@telus.net
Web: http://www.hatcreekranch.com

**Hope and District Chamber of
Commerce**
347 Raab Street, PO Box 588
Hope, BC V0X 1L0
Tel: (604) 869-3111
Fax: (604) 869-8208
E-mail: chmb@hopechamber.bc.ca
Website: http://www.hopechamber.bc.ca

Hope Visitor Info Centre
919 Water Avenue
PO Box 370
Hope, BC V0X 1L0
Tel: (604) 869-2021
Fax: (604) 869-2160
E-mail: destinationhope@telus.net

Horsting's Farm Market
PO Box 716
Cache Creek, BC V0K 1H0
Tel/Fax: (250) 457-6546
(located 2 km north of Cache Creek)

Interior Whitewater Expeditions
PO Box 393
Clearwater, BC V0E 1N0
Information: 1-800-661-RAFT (7238)
Tel: (250) 674-3727
Fax: (250) 674-3701
E-mail: rafting@interiorwhitewater.bc.ca
Website: http://www.interiorwhite
water.bc.ca

Kumsheen Rafting Resort
Trans-Canada Highway
(6 km east of Lytton)
PO Box 30
Lytton, BC V0K 1Z0
Tel: (250) 455-2296
Fax: (250) 455-2297
Reservations: 1-800-663-6667
E-mail: rafting@kumsheen.com
Website: http://www.kumsheen.com

Lac du Bois Grasslands Park
Website: ttp://www.env.gov.bc.ca/bcparks/
explore/parkpgs/lacduboi.html

Lillooet Tourism Information Centre
Lillooet Museum
Susan Bell, Manager
790 Main Street
PO Box 441
Lillooet, BC V0K 1V0
Tel: (250) 256-4308
Fax: (250) 256-0043
E-mail: lillmuseum@cablelan.net
Website: http://www.lillooetbc.com

Little Horse Lodge
C-1, Site E, RR#1
6143 North Green Lake Road
70 Mile House, BC V0K 2K0
Tel: (250) 456-7524
Fax: (250) 456-7512
E-mail: info@littlehorselodge.com

Lytton Information Centre
PO Box 460
400 Fraser Street
Lytton, BC V0K 1Z0
Tel: (250) 455-2523
Fax: (250) 455-6669
E-mail: lyttoncc@telus.net
Website: http://www.lytton.ca

Information Sources

Lytton Museum
PO Box 640
420 Fraser Street
Lytton BC V0K 1Z0
Tel: (250) 455-2254
Fax: (250) 455-2254
Website: http://www.lytton.ca/

Moose Valley Provincial Park
Website: http://www.env.gov.bc.ca/bcparks
/explore/parkpgs/moose.html

Mount Timothy Ski Society
Box 33, 318 Birch Place
100 Mile House, BC V0K 2E0
Tel/Fax: (250) 395-3772
Snowphone: 1-877-392-1446
Website: http://www.skitimothy.com

Quesnel Visitor Information Centre
703 Carson Avenue
Quesnel, BC V2J 2B6
Tel: (250) 992-8716
Fax: (250) 992-2181
Toll-free: 1-800-992-4922
E-mail: qvisitor@quesnelbc.com

Riverside Adventures
PO Box 2538
Clearwater, BC V0E 1N0
Toll-free: 1-877-674-0001
E-mail: info@riveradventures.ca
Website: http://www.riveradventures.ca

Scout Island Nature Centre
1305A Borland Road
Williams Lake, BC V2G 5K5
Tel: (250) 398-8532

Sky Blue Waters Resort
Pavilion Lake, PO Box 220
Lillooet, BC V0K 1V0
Tel: (250) 256-7663
E-mail: skyblue3@telus.net

South Cariboo Visitor Information Centre
PO Box 340, 422 Hwy 97
100 Mile House, BC V0K 2E0
Toll-free: 1-877-511-5353
Tel: (250) 395-5353
Fax: (250) 395-4085
E-mail: info@southcaribootourism.com
Website: http://www.southcariboo
tourism.com

Spectrum Digital Imaging Ltd.
#3-3990 Marguerite Street
Vancouver, BC V6J 4G1
Tel: (778) 327-9752
Fax: (866) 524-2865
E-mail: spectrumdigital@shaw.ca
Website: http://www.mapsdigital.com

The Cariboo has hundreds of kilometres of hiking trails.

Springhouse Trails Ranch
3067 Dog Creek Road
Williams Lake, BC V2G 4X2
Tel: (250) 392-4780
Fax: (250) 392-4701
E-mail: cariboo@springhousetrails.com

Sundance Guest Ranch
The Rowe Family
PO Box 489
Ashcroft, BC V0K 1A0
Toll-free: 1-800-553-3533
Tel: (250) 453-2422
Tel: (250) 453-2554
Fax: (250) 453-9356
Website: http://www.sundanceguest
ranch.com

Tall Timbers Resort Ltd.
Watch Lake, BC
Tel: (250) 456-7668
Toll-free: 1-888-228-TALL
Off season: (604) 937-3162

**Thompson Okanagan Tourism
Association**
1332 Water Street
Kelowna, BC V1Y 9P4
Tel: (250) 860-5999
Toll-free: 1-800-567-2275
Fax: (250) 860-9993
E-mail: info@totabc.com
Website: http://www.totabc.com/

Thunderbird Lodge
Bonaparte Lake
PO Box 61
Bridge Lake, BC V0K 1E0
Tel: (604) 640-9426

Thuya Lakes Lodge
Neil and Dawn Beeman
General Delivery
James River Bridge, AB, T0M 1C0
Tel: (403) 722-2968 (messages and off-season)
Tel: (250) 372-6867 (resort)
Fax: (403) 722-3634
E-mail: info@thuyalakes.com
Website: http://www.thuyalakes.com

Tourism Kamloops
1290 West Trans-Canada Highway
Kamloops, BC V2C 6R3
Tel: (250) 372-8000
Fax: (250) 372-2121
E-mail: inquiry@tourismkamloops.com
Website: http://www.tourism
kamloops.com

Trails Society of British Columbia
315 – 1367 West Broadway
Vancouver, BC V6H 4A9
Tel: (604) 737-3188
Fax: (604) 738-7175
E-mail: trailsbc@trailsbc.ca
Website: http://www.trailsbc.ca/

Troll Mountain Resort
PO Box 4013
Quesnel, BC V2J 3J1
Tel: (250) 994-3200
Snowphone: (250) 994-3352

Tunkwa Lake Resort
PO Box 196
Tunkwa Lake Resort, BC V0K 1W0
Tel: (250) 523-9697
Website: http://www.tunkwalake
resort.com

Information Sources

Tyax Mountain Lake Resort
Tyaughton Lake Road
Gold Bridge, BC V0K 1P0
Tel: (250) 238-2221
Fax: (250) 238-2528
E-mail: fun@tyax.com
Website: http://www.tyax.com

Vidette Gold Mine Resort
PO Box 329
Savona, BC V0K 2J0
Toll-free: 1 866 843-3883
E-mail: info@videttelake.com
Website: http://www.videttelake.com

Watch Lake Lodge
RR#1, Watch Lake Road
70 Mile House, BC V0K 2K0
Tel: (250) 456-7741
Fax: (250) 456-7492

Wells Gray Provincial Park Information Centre
Website: http://www.env.gov.bc.ca/
bcparks/explore/parkpgs/wells_gry

Wendego Lodge
Norm and Flo Flynn
PO Box 923
Kamloops, BC V2C 5N4
Tel: (250) 819-1713 after 6 p.m. or on weekends
E-mail: info@wendegolodge.com
Website: http://wendegolodge.com

Williams Lake Cross Country Ski Club
PO Box 4026
Williams Lake, BC V2G 2V2
Website: http://www.bullmountain.ca

Williams Lake Stampede Association
PO Box 4076
Williams Lake, BC V2G 2V2
Tel: (250) 392-6585
Toll-free: 1-800-71-RODEO (in BC)
Fax: (250) 398-7701
E-mail: info@williamslakestampede.com
Website: http://www.williamslake
stampede.com

Xats'ull Heritage Village
3405 Mountain House Road
Williams Lake, BC V2G 5L5
Tel On-Site: (250) 297-6502
Tel: (250) 989-2323 - ext115
Fax: (250) 989-2300
Website: http://www.xatsull.com

Rainbow Falls on Angus Horne Creek is easily accessible from the east end of Azure Lake.

About the Author

Murphy Shewchuk has been writing and illustrating articles and books since the mid-1960s. Born in Hamilton, Ontario, he grew up in the British Columbia mining town of Pioneer Gold Mines and developed a triple interest in outdoor exploring, photography, and electronics while still a teenager.

After a stint in the RCAF in eastern Canada and Alberta, he moved back to British Columbia to a job in electronics, with writing and photography as his major interests. In 1971, his "day job" took him to Kamloops, BC, where he began a weekly "Outdoor Scene" column for the *Kamloops Sentinel*. From the column, he moved to "Backroads" features in *BC Outdoors* magazine and many other magazines.

From a base in Merritt, BC, Murphy and his wife, Katharine, have travelled extensively in western Canada, taking copious notes and thousands of photographs in the process. Their backroads exploring has also taken them to the Canadian Arctic, the Maritime Provinces, New Zealand, Costa Rica, Cuba, and Scotland.

More than three hundred of his magazine articles and one thousand of his photographs have appeared in such publications as *Adventure Travel, BC Outdoors, Camping Canada, Canadian Geographic, Field & Stream, MotorHome, Photo Life, Skyword, Western Living,* and *Westworld.*

He has also written 12 other books including: *Exploring Kamloops Country; Fur,*

About the Author

Gold & Opals; Exploring the Nicola Valley; Cariboo; The Craigmont Story; Backroads Explorer Vol 1: Thompson-Cariboo; Backroads Explorer Vol 2: Similkameen & South Okanagan; Okanagan Country: An Outdoor Recreation Guide; Coquihalla Country: A Guide to BC's North Cascade Mountains and Nicola Valley; Okanagan Trips & Trails; and *Coquihalla Trips & Trails.*

In addition to his lifelong interest in photography and exploring the mountains of western Canada, Murphy has been a workshop speaker at writers' conferences across Canada and in the United States. His writing and photography has received awards from the Outdoor Writers of Canada and the MacMillan Bloedel newspaper journalism competitions. Shewchuk is also an active member of the Canadian Authors Association and Trails BC, the organization involved with the Trans Canada Trail in British Columbia.

As this book was going to press, Heritage BC announced that writer, photographer and historian Murphy Shewchuk has been selected by the Honourable Stan Hagen, Minister of Tourism, Sport and the Arts, as the 2008 recipient of the British Columbia Heritage Award.

Akrigg, G.P.V. and Helen B. *1001 British Columbia Place Names* (Vancouver, BC: Discovery Press, 1973).

_____. *British Columbia Chronicle, 1847–1871* (Vancouver, BC: Discovery Press, 1977).

Balf, Mary. *Kamloops: A History of the District up to 1914* (Kamloops, BC: Kamloops Museum, 1969).

Barlee, N.L. *Gold Creeks and Ghost Towns* (Surrey, BC: Hancock House Publishers, 1984).

Bonner, Veera, Irene E. Bliss, Hazel Henry Litterick and Kathleen Telford. *Chilcotin: Preserving Pioneer Memories* (Surrey, BC: Heritage House Publishing, 1995).

Bowering, George. *Bowering's B.C.: A Swashbuckling History* (London: Penguin Books, 1996).

Bulman, T. Alex. *Kamloops Cattlemen* (Sidney, BC: Gray's Publishing, 1972).

Campbell, Colin. *Trails of the Southern Cariboo* (Calgary, AB: Rocky Mountain Books, 1998).

Cheadle, Walter B. *Cheadle's Journal of Trip Across Canada 1862–1863* (Edmonton, AB: M.G. Hurtig, 1971).

de Hullu, Emma. *Bridge River Gold* (Bralorne, BC: Bralorne-Pioneer Community Club,1967, reprinted 1993).

Decker, Frances, Margaret Fougberg and Mary Ronayne. *Pemberton: The History of a Settlement* (Pemberton, BC: Pemberton Pioneer Women, 1977).

Downs, Art. *Paddlewheels on the Frontier* (Surrey, BC: Foremost Publishing, 1971).

Edwards, Ralph and Ed Gould. *Ralph Edwards of Lonesome Lake* (Toronto, ON: Random House, 1957).

Francis, Daniel, ed. *The Encyclopedia of British Columbia* (Madeira Park, BC: Harbour Publishing, 2000).

Elliott, Gordon R. *Barkerville, Quesnel and the Cariboo Gold Rush* (Vancouver, BC: Douglas and McIntyre, 1958).

Foster, Pat. *Historic Ashcroft: For the Strong Eye Only* (Kamloops, BC: Plateau Press, 1999).

Glavin, Terry and the People of Nemiah Valley. *Nemiah: The Unconquered Country.* (Vancouver, BC: New Star Books, 1992). (photographs by Gary Fiegehen, Rick Blacklaws and Vance Hanna

Bibliography

Goward, Trevor and Cathie Hickson. *Nature Wells Gray* (Edmonton, AB: Lone Pine Publishing, 1995).

Green, Lewis. *The Great Years: Gold Mining in the Bridge River Valley* (Vancouver, BC: Tricouni Press, 2000).

Harris, Lorraine. *Barkerville: The Town that Gold Built* (Surrey, BC: Hancock House Publishers, 1984).

_____. *Halfway to the Goldfields: A History of Lillooet* (Vancouver, BC: J.J. Douglas, 1977).

Hill, Beth. *Sappers: The Royal Engineers in British Columbia* (Victoria, BC: Horsdal & Schubart Publishers, 1987)

Hill-Tout, Charles (1858–1944), Ralph Maud, ed. *The Salish People* (Vancouver, BC: Talonbooks, 1978).

Hong, W.M., Gary and Eileen Seale, ed. *And So That's How It Happened:Recollections of Stanley-Barkerville 1900–1975* (Quesnel, BC: W.M. Hong, 1978).

Journals of the Colonial Legislatures. An extensive collection of the Journals is located at the Nicola Valley Museum Archives, Merritt, BC.

Knight, Lyle. *Central BC Rock: The Rockclimbers Guide to Central British Columbia* (Squamish, BC: Merlin Productions, 1996).

Kopas, Cliff. *Bella Coola* (Vancouver, BC: Mitchell Press,1970).

_____. *Packhorses to the Pacific* (Sidney, BC: Gray's Publishing, 1976).

Ludditt, Fred. *Barkerville Days* (Vancouver, BC: Mitchell Press, 1969). Revised edition Mr. Paperback, P.O. Box 3399, Langley, BC, V3A 4R7.

Marriott, Harry. *Cariboo Cowboy* (Sidney, BC: Gray's Publishing, 1966).

Neave, Roland. *Exploring Wells Gray Park* (Kamloops, BC: The Friends of Wells Gray Park, 1988).

Parke, Gordon. *The Parke Ranch - Upper Hat Creek - Four Generations* (Cache Creek, BC).

Patenaude, Branwen C. *Trails to Gold* (Victoria, BC: Horsdal & Schubart Publishers, 1995).

_____. *Golden Nuggets: Roadhouse Portraits along the Cariboo's Gold Rush Trail* (Surrey, BC: Heritage House Publishing, 1998).

Purvis, Ron. *Treasure Hunting in British Columbia* (Toronto: McClelland & Stewart, 1971).

Rothenburger, Mel. *We've Killed Johnny Ussher!* (Vancouver, BC: Mitchell Press, 1973).

Shewchuk, Murphy O. *Backroads Explorer Volume 1: Thompson-Cariboo* (Vancouver, BC: Maclean Hunter, 1985).

_____. *Coquihalla Trips & Trails* (Markham, ON: Fitzhenry & Whiteside, 2007).

_____. *Exploring the Nicola Valley* (Vancouver, BC: Douglas & McIntyre, 1981).

_____. *Fur, Gold and Opals* (Surrey, BC: Hancock House Publishers, 1975).

Smith, Jessie Ann. *Widow Smith of Spence's Bridge* (Merritt, BC: Sonotek Publishing, 1989).

Stangoe, Irene. *Cariboo-Chilcotin: Pioneer People and Places* (Surrey, BC: Heritage House Publishing, 1996).

_____. *Looking Back at the Cariboo-Chilcotin* (Surrey, BC: Heritage House Publishing, 1997).

St. Pierre, Paul. *Breaking Smith's Quarter Horse* (Vancouver, BC: Douglas & McIntyre, 1966).

St. Pierre, Paul. *Chilcotin Holiday* (Vancouver, BC: Douglas & McIntyre, 1984).

Stowe, Leland. *Crusoe of Lonesome Lake* (New York: Random House, 1957).

Turner, Nancy J., Laurence C. Thompson, M. Terry Thompson, and Annie Z. York. *Thompson Ethnobotany: Knowledge and Usage of Plants by the Thompson Indians of British Columbia.* (Victoria, BC: Royal British Columbia Museum, 1990).

Turner, Robert D. *West of Great Divide: An Illustrated History of the Canadian Pacific Railway in British Columbia, 1880–1986* (Victoria, BC: Sono Nis Press, 1987).

Waite, Donald E. *The Cariboo Gold Rush Story* (Surrey, BC: Hancock House Publishers, 1988).

Williams, David R. *"...The Man for a New Country" Sir Matthew Baillie Begbie* (Sidney, BC: Gray's Publishing, 1977).

Wright, Richard Thomas. *Barkerville: A Gold Rush Experience* (Williams Lake, BC: Winter Quarters Press, 1998).

_____. *The Bowron Lakes: A Year-Round Guide* (Vancouver, BC: Maclean Hunter, 1985).

Wright, Richard and Rochelle Wright. *Cariboo Mileposts* (Vancouver, BC: Mitchell Press, 1972).

_____. *Lower Mainland Backroads: Volume 1, Garibaldi to Lillooet* (Sidney, BC: Saltaire Publishing, 1977).

Numbers in italics refer to photographs.

70 Mile House, 146, 189, 195, 197
93 Mile House, 206
99 Mile Ski Trails, 149
100 Mile House, 149, 151, 193
150 Mile House, 153, 239

agate, 337, *382*
Alexandra Bridge, 2, 4, 9–12
Alexandra Bridge Provincial Park, 11
Alice Lake, 50–51, *318*, 341
Alkali Lake Ranch, 51
Anahim Lake, 299
Anderson River, 14
Antler Creek, 244
Arrowstone Protected Area, 123
Ashcroft Manor, *80*, 105
Ashcroft Opera House, 81
Askom Mountain, 34
Azure Lake, 343

back country exploring, 256
Bailey's Chute, 341, *342*
Balancing Rock, 89, 90
Barker, Billy, 164, 246
Barkerville, 140, 171, 246–47
Barkerville Road, 164–73
Barnard Express Stage Coach, *59*, 139, 149
Begbie, Matthew Baillie, 42, 148–49, 151, 168, 171
Bella Coola, 156, 301–302
Big Bar Ferry, *46*, 47, 180–81
Big Bar Guest Ranch, 181, *182*
Big Bark Lake Provincial Park, 48, 184
Big Slide, 24
Blair, Brian, *246*
Blessing, Charles Morgan, 167–68
Bonaparte Bend Winery, 143
Bonaparte Lake, 199, 200, 202
Bonaparte Loop, 195–203
Bonaparte River, 202
Boston Bar, 14, 16
Bowron Lake, 213–14
Bralorne, 271

Bridge Glacier, *258*.
Bridge Lake Provincial Park, 208
Bridge Lake Road (Hwy 24), 204–11
Bridge of the 23 Camels, 24–25
Bridge River, 31, 261–66, *272, 287*
Bridge River Road, 261–77
Bridge River Valley, 258–60
Buck Hill, 347
Bull Canyon Provincial Park, 297–98
Bull Mountain Ski Area, 158
Bullion Pit Mine, 232–33, *238*, 239
Bulwer-Lytton, Edward, 67

Cache Creek, 82, 141, 143
Cameron Ridge Trail, 243
Canadian Pacific Railway (CPR), 3, 21–22, 87
Canoe Creek valley, 49
canoeing, 151, 172, 212–19, *316, 343*
Cariboo Loop,
   East, 220–35
   Southwest, 175–85
Cariboo Trail, 135–40
Cariboo Waggon Road, 66, 72, 135–40, 158, 188–89, 239
Carpenter Lake, 286
Carruthers, A.L., 4
Carson Ranch, 44–45
Carson, Robert, 44–45
Castle Rock Hoodoos Provincial Park, 119
cattle ranches, 293, 373–74
Cedar Point Park, *233*, 241–42
Chasm Provincial Park, 145–46, *147*
Chasm Road, 145–46
Chilcotin, 291–302
Chilcotin Lodge, 304–305
Chilcotin Plateau, 291–93
Chilcotin River, 292
Chilcotin War, 299
Chilko Lake, 309, *312*, 313
Chimney Creek Bridge, *291*
Circle H Mountain Lodge, 47, 178
Circle W Ranch, 118

Clearwater, 335
Clearwater Lake, 320, 342–43
Clearwater River, *352*, 353
Clearwater River Road, 352–58
coal, 108–109
Coast Mountain Circle Tour, 278–90
Clinton, 144–45, 175
Clinton Museum, 144, *145*
Coast Mountains, 33
Coldscaur Lake, *251*, 253
Comet Creek Resort, *246*
Copper Creek, 132
Cornwall Hills Provincial Park, 105
Cottonwood House, 165–66
Cougar Lake, 255
Cougar Point, 177–78
Craigellachie, 3, 21
Crater Lake, *197*, 198
Crooked Lake, 226–27

Deadman Valley, *88*, 113–23
Deadman-Vidette Road, 86, 113–23
Diamond S Ranch, 44–45
Dog Creek, 50
Dome, 303, *304*
Dome Trail, 303–307
Douglas, James, 136, 149
Dowling, "Oregon Jack," 104
Downing Provincial Park, 46, 176
Downs, Art, 16
Downton Lake, 284, *285*
Dragonfly Lake, *325*, 327
Dragon's Tongue, *349*, 351
Duck Ranch, 108
Duffey Lake Provincial Park, 282
Duffey Lake Road, *281*

Earlscourt Farm, 37
Echo Valley Ranch, 178, *180*
Edge Hills Provincial Park, 177
Emerald Bay campground, 191
Emory Creek Provincial Park, 7
Enterprise, 140, 158
Eureka Peak, 216, 217, *227*

Falls Creek, 342
Fandrich, Bernie, 67, 93–94, 96
Farwell Canyon, 292

First Nations peoples,
  history, 17, 19, 62, 236,
    258–59, 292
  protected sites, 375
  Salish, 62, 67, 362–68
  Shuswap, 91
  Skeetchestn First Nation
    Village, 115–16
fishing, 201, 221–23, 265, 268,
  289, 299, 355
Flying U Ranch, 190
Forest Fire Lookout, 148
Fort Alexandria, 160
Fort Langley, 372
Fort St. James, 370, 371
Foster, Pat, 108
Fraser River,
  flooding, 4
  gold rush, 1–2
  Lillooet to Lytton, 28–39
  photographs, 27, 44, 49,
    97, 360
  whitewater rafting, 93–100
Fraser River Trail, Lillooet to
  Williams Lake, 41–53
Fraser, Simon, 1, 67, 160
Frog Rapids, 74, 97
fur trade, 91, 187–88, 369–72

Gang Ranch, 49, 50
geology, 88–89, 359–61
ghost of Walhachin, 82–83
Gladwin Lookout, 72, 73
gold,
  Bridge River, 259–60
  Cariboo gold fields, 171
  Cedar Creek, 232
  Lightning Creek, 167
  Minto, 270–71
  panning, 127, 376, 377
  Quesnel River, 164, 246
  rush, 1–2, 67, 140, 188,
    229, 244
Gold Bridge, 271, 284–85
Gordon Parke Ranch, 107–108
GPS, 384–91
Graymont Limestone Quarry, 58
Green Lake, 197–98
Great Northern Railway, 15
Green Lake Loop, 186–94
Green Lake Provincial Park,
  189, 197
Gun Creek recreation site, 270

Haller, Joseph, 47
Hammer Lake, 200–201
Hanging Tree (Lillooet), 42, 43
Hat Creek, 107, 108
Hat Creek House, 59, 60,
  111, 143
Hat Creek Loop, 101–12
Hat Creek Ranch, 110, 111,
  143, 363
Hell Creek, 266–67
Hawkins Lake, 223
Hell's Gate Airtram, 12, 14
Hell's Gate, 15, 99–100
Hendrix Lake, 224–26
Highway 12, 19–27
Highway 20, 294–302
Highway 24 (Bridge Lake Road),
  149, 204–11
Highway 26, 164–73
Highway 92, 141–63
Highway 99, 54–60, 110, 263
Hihium Fishing Camp, 118
Hill's Bar, 1–2
history,
  cattle ranches, 373–74
  fur, 1, 369–72
  geological, 359–61
  gold, 369–72
  First Nations, 1, 362–68
  railways, 2–3, 374
hoodoos, 88–89, 116, 119
Hope, 5
Horsefly, 229
Horsefly Lake Provincial Park,
  228
Horsefly River, 227–28, 29
Horseshoe Canyon, 265–66
Hurley (Railroad) Pass, 283, 284

Interlakes Corner, 207
Itcha Ilgachuz Park, 293, 300, 359

Jackass Mountain, 2, 17
jade, 376–77, 383
Jesmond, 180

Kamloops, 91, 125
Kamloops Lake, 87, 90, 91
kekuli, 362–63
Kelly Lake Ranch, 47, 177
Kelly Lake, 46, 176
Kettle Rapids, 354
Kirkland Lake, 216

Knight, Lyle, 58
Kumsheen Rafting Resort,
  95, 100

Lac Des Roches, 208, 209
Lac du Bois Grasslands
  Protected Area, 126
Lac La Hache Provincial
  Park, 152
Lake of the Woods, 7
landslide, 74–77
Lemieux Creek Bridge, 210
Lightning Creek, 167, 168–69
Likely 231–32, 240
Lillooet, 26, 27, 29, 42, 136,
  141, 263, 264, 289
Lillooet Museum, 42
Little Fort, 210–11
Little Horse Lodge, 190–91
Lone Butte, 193, 205, 206, 207
Loon Lake, 201
Loring, Greg, 182
Lytton, 17, 19, 21, 38, 66–67
Lytton Ferry, 23, 38

Mahood Lake, 323, 327, 328
Mahood River Trail, 355–57
Mann Creek, 252, 253
Marble Canyon, 54, 58
Marble Canyon Provincial
  Park, 58, 111
Marble Canyon Route, 54–60
Marble Range Provincial
  Park, 179
Marks Lake, 215
Marshall Lake, 268
McAllister, Peter, 107, 109, 111
McLeese Lake, 234
Mile 0, 42, 136, 141, 264
mining, 260
Minto, 270
Moose Valley Canoe Route, 151
Moose Valley Provincial Park,
  151, 212–19
Mount Bowman, 178
Mount Kerr, 178
Mount Tatlow, 310, 311
Mount Timothy Ski Hill, 151–52
Mount Weinhold, 275, 276
Murray, Margaret "Ma," 26,
  29, 30

Newman, Amy Lee, 170, 171

Index

Nicoamen River, 74
Nicola, 116
Noel Lake, *274*
Nu Chugh Beniz Campground, *312*, 313

Onderdonk, Andrew, 3, 16
Oregon Jack Provincial Park, 104

Patenaude, 104, 105, 143
Pavilion-Clinton Road, 55–56
Pavilion Lake, 56–57
Pavilion Mountain, 45, 46, 55
Pemberton, 282
petroglyphs, *302*
PGE Railway, 288
pictographs, 366, *367*
Pinnacles Provincial Park, 160, *161*
Pioneer Flour Mill, 43
Pioneer Mine, 273
Polar Springs, 118
Porter, Roger, *59*, *138*
Pressy Lake, 198–200
Pulpit Rock, 49, *97*, *360*
Puntzi Lake, *297*, *298*
Purvis, Ron, 31
Pyramid Mountain, 319, *320*, 337

Quesnel, 160, 162
Quesnel Forks, *231*, 232, 240–41
Quesnel Museum, *159*, 160

railways,
Canadian Pacific Railway (CPR), 3, 21–22, 62, 64, 87
history, 2–3, 374
PGE Railway, 288
Red Dog Saloon, 47, 183
Red Lake, 131
Red Lake Road, 124–34
Riske Creek, 303–304
River Trail, 158
rock climbing, 58, 90
rocks, 375–83. *See also* geology *and names of individual types.*

salmon, 15, *228*, *288*
sand castles, 119
Savona, 86–87
Schkam Lake (Lake of the Woods), 7

Scout Island Nature Centre, *153*, 155
Seton Lake, 30, *31*
Shewchuk, Katharine, *300*
Simpson, George, 1
Skeetchestn First Nation Village, 115–16
Skihist Provincial Park, 67–72
skiing, 149, 151–52, 158, 168, 184, *347*
Skookum Lake, 119
Sky Blue Waters Resort, 57–58
Smith, Donald, 3
Smith, Jessie Ann, 78–79
Soda Creek, *157*, 158
Spences Bridge, 74–79
Spirit Caves Trail, 7–8
Springhouse, *52*
SS *Marten*, 86
SS *Skuzzy*, 16, 87
St. George's School, 24, 31
St. John the Divine Church, *9*, *137*
Stack Valley Road, 303–305
Stanley Road, 168–69
Steelhead Provincial Park, 87, 90
Stein River, 36, 38
Stein Valley Nlaka'pamux Heritage Provincial Park, 38
Sticta Falls Trail, 349–51

Tatlayoko Lake, *313*, 314
Teegee, Sandra, *371*
Terzaghi Dam, 265, *267*, 268, 287
Texas Creek, *32*
Texas Creek FS Road, 33
Theatre Royal, *170*, 171
Thompson Canyon, *73*
Thompson River, *63*, 93–100
Thompson River Road, 65–92
Thompson River Route, 61–64
Thorsen Creek, 302
Thuya Lakes Lodge, 210
Tranquille Creek recreation site, 178
Tranquille River, 125–29
Tranquille School, 125–26
Trans-Canada Highway, 4, 5–18, 134
Troll Mountain Ski Resort, 168
Trophy Mountain, 346
Trophy Mountain Trail, 335, 345–48

Trutch, Joseph W., 10
Ts'il?os Provincial Park, 308–15
Tyax Mountain Lake Resort, 286–87

Upper Hat Creek Valley, 101, *103*, *106*

Vidette Lake, 120
volcanoes, 319–21, *322*, 347, 355, 359–60

Walhachin, 82–85, 116
Watch Lake, *191*, 192
Watching Creek recreation site, 127–28
waterfalls, 199, 225, 245
Bridge Creek Falls, *150*, 151
Canim Falls, *326*, 328
Dawson Falls, *338*, 339
Deadman Falls, 120–21
Deception Falls, 328, *329*
Helmcken Falls, 333, 339–41
Marshall Creek Falls, 268, *269*, 287
Osprey Falls, *321*
Spahats Falls, *334*, 335
Sticta Falls, *350*, 351
Sylvia Falls, 356, *357*
Third Canyon Creek Falls, *319*, *336*
Tranquille Falls, 128–29
in Wells Gray PP, 317, 319
Wells, 169, 171
Wells Gray Provincial Park, 316–22, 323–31, 332–44, 355
Wells Hotel, *169*
Wendego Lodge, *128*, 129
Whale Lake Trail, 330–31
whitewater rafting, 67, 93–100, *291*, *352*
Williams Lake River Valley Trail, *154*, 155
Williams Lake Stampede, 52, *152*
Williams Lake, 52, 153, 155

Yalakom River, 266
Yale, *7*, 8–9
youth projects, 214–18